Do individual differences in creativity exist?

If so, can such differences be measured reliably enough to make a practical difference?

What, specifically, can management do—beyond selecting creative participants—to foster creativity within and on the part of the organization?

What are the costs of creativity? What must an organization be prepared to give up or tolerate if it wants to increase its creativity?

These were some of the questions posed when the Graduate School of Business of The University of Chicago brought together a group of social scientists, educators, and business executives to present their definitions of creativity and their suggestions for its nurture. The seminar was stimulating, witty, and, of course, highly creative. Participants included Robert Merton, Paul Meehl, Harold Guetzkow, Milton Rokeach, Jerome Bruner, Frank Barron, and Morris Stein, speaking as social scientists; Ralph Tyler, W. Allen Wallis, and Bernard Berelson, speaking as educators; Marvin Bower, B. E. Bensinger, Peter Peterson, and David Ogilvy, speaking as executives; and physicist and Nobel laureate William Shockley and Franz

nalyst, rep-
view.

been as-
orts of the
n, and the
Gary Steiner

his seminar
r the identi-
or the estab-
ization. But
corporations
it take to in-
to the price
The central
Mr. Steiner's
nce between
producing
guaranteed,
und, do not

THE GRADUATE SCHOOL OF BUSINESS
UNIVERSITY OF CHICAGO

FIRST SERIES (1916–1938)
Materials for the Study of Business
Edited by DEAN LEON CARROLL MARSHALL and
DEAN WILLIAM HOMER SPENCER

SECOND SERIES (1938–1956)
Business and Economic Publications
Edited by DEAN WILLIAM HOMER SPENCER

THIRD SERIES (1959–   )
Studies in Business
Edited by DEAN W. ALLEN WALLIS
and DEAN GEORGE P. SHULTZ

The Creative Organization

edited and with an introduction by
Gary A. Steiner

The University of Chicago Press
Chicago & London

Proceedings of a seminar sponsored by
The Graduate School of Business
under a grant from the
McKinsey Foundation for Management Research, Inc.

Standard Book Number: 226–77236–5

THE UNIVERSITY OF CHICAGO PRESS, CHICAGO 60637
THE UNIVERSITY OF CHICAGO PRESS, LTD., LONDON

Foreword

The creation of new knowledge is one of the high purposes of a university. The discovery of new truths is generally the product of long and painstaking thought and inquiry, which universities are uniquely equipped to support. Such discoveries are of vital concern to business as to all of our institutions; and research about problems related to business operations is a major function of the Graduate School of Business of the University of Chicago.

At the School, scholars drawn from a variety of disciplines bring their varied talents and concepts to bear on the problems of business and on the analysis of the business environment. Research covers a wide variety of topics; and results are available to all who have the capacity and the need to employ them.

Beyond the *discovery of knowledge* lies its *dissemination*. To be effective, knowledge and ideas must move outward from the University to the business community. Results of work at the School must be published and made available.

Almost half a century ago the School inaugurated a significant publications program, the present volume its most recent expression.

In *Materials for the Study of Business,* initiated in 1916 under the editorship of Dean Leon Carroll Marshall, and continued by Dean William Homer Spencer, 50 titles were published; many became classics in their fields. In 1938 the series was renamed *Business and Economic Publications;* under the editorship of Dean Spencer, 13 volumes were published. Additionally, in the two decades prior to 1948, the School published some 70 monographs under the general title, *Studies in Business Administration.* The current *Studies in Business* series was initiated under Dean W. Allen Wallis, who edited the first six volumes.

The present volume—ninth in the current series—addresses itself to a host of problems arising from the increasing need for and emphasis on creativity in business operations. These problems are expressed in such questions as: How may creativity be usefully defined? Can creative characteristics be measured? What organization variables under the control of management can foster or retard creativity? These and related questions came under the scrutiny of a distinguished group of scientists, scholars, and businessmen, who considered and commented upon them in a seminar made possible through the generosity of the McKinsey Foundation for Management Research, Inc. This seminar, conducted by the Graduate School of Business and directed by Professor Gary A. Steiner of our faculty, brought to the campus 16 eminent persons whose varying experiences and points of view were directed to consideration of several aspects of this significant topic.

Their papers and comments appear herein—perceptively edited and introduced by Professor Steiner, who undertook the difficult task of identifying the critical issues and integrating the sometimes divergent, if not conflicting, views of the participants.

GEORGE P. SHULTZ, DEAN
GRADUATE SCHOOL OF BUSINESS
UNIVERSITY OF CHICAGO

Contents

Introduction

GARY A. STEINER

On February 1, 2, and 3, 1962, sixteen eminent scientists, scholars, and executives met at a seminar conducted by the Graduate School of Business of the University of Chicago under a grant from the McKinsey Foundation for Management Research, Inc. The topic of the seminar was "The Creative Organization"; its purpose, to explore the factors that foster or impede creativity within and on the part of large organizations.

Participants qualified on one or more of three counts: (*a*) research in the psychology or sociology of creativity, and related organizational matters; (*b*) professional responsibility for educational institutions and programs dedicated to the training of potential creators; (*c*) the actual establishment and nurture of creative organizations.

The list of participants, with their primary titles at the time of the seminar, makes it clear that most fit at least two of the above categories, while some fit all three.

PARTICIPANTS

Franz Alexander (d. 1964), Chief of Staff, Psychiatric Department and Director of the Psychiatric and Psychosomatic Research Institute at Mt. Sinai Hospital, Los Angeles.

Frank Barron, Research Psychologist, Institute of Personality Assessment and Research, University of California.

B. E. Bensinger, Chief Executive Officer, Brunswick Corporation.

Bernard Berelson, Director, Communication Research Program of the Population Council, New York.

Marvin Bower, Managing Director, McKinsey & Company, Inc.

Jerome S. Bruner, Professor of Psychology and Co-Director of the Center for Cognitive Studies at Harvard University.

Harold Guetzkow, Professor of Psychology, Sociology, and Political Science, Northwestern University.

Paul E. Meehl, Professor, Department of Psychology and Neurology, University of Minnesota.

Robert K. Merton, Professor, Department of Sociology, Columbia University.

David M. Ogilvy, Chairman, Ogilvy, Benson & Mather, Inc.

Peter G. Peterson, President, Bell & Howell Company.

Milton Rokeach, Professor, Department of Psychology, Michigan State University.

William Shockley, President, Shockley Transistor Corporation.

Morris I. Stein, Professor of Psychology and Director of the Center for Human Relations, New York University.

Ralph W. Tyler, Director, Center for Advanced Study in the Behavioral Sciences.

W. Allen Wallis, Dean, Graduate School of Business, University of Chicago.

Gary A. Steiner, Seminar Director, Professor of Psychology, Graduate School of Business, University of Chicago.

The following guests also participated in one or more of the sessions: Charles W. Boand, of Wilson & McIlvaine; Fairfax M. Cone, of Foote, Cone & Belding; Thomas H. Coulter, of the Chicago Association of Commerce and Industry; Philip M. Hauser, of the Department of Sociology, University of Chicago; Robert I. Livingston, of Walter E. Heller & Company; Edward C. Logelin, Jr., of United States Steel Corporation; Forrest D. Wallace, of McKinsey & Company, Inc.; and, from the Graduate School of Business, Selwyn W. Becker, Norman M. Bradburn, Robert L. Farwell, John E. Jeuck, James H. Lorie, Manning Nash, and Neele E. Stearns.

The meeting itself was loosely organized around the papers prepared in advance, which, in varying states of revision, form the bulk of this book. The following outline set the boundaries for the papers and discussion at the meeting.

I. The raw material—the individual members of the organization:
   A. Do individual differences in creativity exist?

B. If such differences exist, are they general or specific to particular skills?

C. If such differences exist, and if the differences are large enough to make a difference:

1. Can they be measured in principle?

2. Can they be measured in practice (i.e., reliably and economically enough to be useful in personnel selection), and how?

D. What are the distinguishing characteristics of the creative individual?

E. What are the characteristics of the creative process? What psychological state is optimal for creative production?

II. The organization itself:

A. What organizational variables under the control of management can foster or retard creativity? Is it possible to specify and manage the relevant internal factors?

B. Are these consistent or inconsistent with other organizational objectives; i.e., what are the costs of creativity?

III. The external environment:

A. Consider the organization as a whole, as an organization operating within a larger social and economic environment. What type of environment is most likely to produce a creative organization?

THE PLAN OF THE BOOK

The book contains the sixteen individual presentations and much of the intervening discussion, substantially edited and abbreviated. In this Introduction, I have tried to integrate; to say what it all seems to come to, in answer to the questions that made up the outline. The ground rules for this summary are hard to state, because they were hard to formulate and harder to adhere to. In general, though, here is what I tried to do: (1) put each of the major questions to the transcript and frame an answer that would probably be recognized by most of the participants; (2) maintain some distinction between findings and opinions, however enlightened or stimulating; that is, to separate those questions for which the seminar provided some answers based on research from those treated principally in terms of experience, judgment, and insight; (3) collect the various pieces that bear on any given question and point out consistencies and inconsistencies; and wherever possible, to suggest some resolution for the latter; and (4) do all of this in ordinary English, by skirting or translating the technical jargon, on the one hand, and the management variety on the other.

Beyond that, I have in some instances drawn on research not represented at the seminar, where I happened to know of it and where it seemed particularly germane. But, by and large, this Introduction reports answers only as suggested in the seminar on The Creative Organization. If all that were known about these matters were what was said in our three-day meeting, this is what, to my reading, it would amount to.

DEFINITIONS

First, a few words about what the key terms in this summary mean: "Creativity" has been defined in a number of ways in the psychological literature, in business discussion, in the arts and sciences generally. Within the transcript of this seminar there appear many explicit, and many more implicit, definitions of varying degrees of generality. We make no attempt to frame a master definition at this point. But for purposes of this overview, it is necessary and hopefully sufficient to make this general distinction: *Creativity* has to do with the development, proposal, and implementation of *new* and *better* solutions; *productivity,* with the efficient application of *current* "solutions."

What "better" means, and who is to say, is one of the sticky methodological issues in the field. What it most often means in these pages is better according to professional colleagues or superiors. The meaning of "solution" obviously varies by field; in the following, solutions range from practical answers to specific problems through new concepts in art, music, or architecture to the most general and abstract conceptualizations that characterize a breakthrough in, say, theoretical physics.

Many of the studies we will cite distinguish "high-creative" from "low-" or "average-creative" groups. It should be clear that "high" and "low" are relative, and not absolute, designations. In most of the samples under investigation, both "high" and "low" groups would qualify as highly creative within the population at large and often even within the profession. It would therefore not have been euphemistic—just too clumsy—to use the designations "more highly" and "less highly" creative. Bear in mind, though, that this is what the shorthand distinction between "high" and "low" means.

I. THE RAW MATERIAL: INDIVIDUAL CREATIVITY

Do individual differences in creativity exist? Does it make sense to speak of more and less creative people in some such way as we speak of more and less intelligent, more or less co-ordinated, or more or less musical people? Or is personal creativity, like fathering twins, mostly a matter of being in the right place at the right time?

As important as circumstances are in determining who will create what and when, it seems that there are consistent and persistent differences in individual creativity. Holding conditions constant, some people are likely to be more creative than others; and these differences are likely to show up in other situations and at other times. In fact, in most fields, the distribution of creative contributions is something like the distribution of personal income in the United States: a small percentage of people accounts for a large share of the total. (See Guetzkow, p. 35, and Meehl, pp. 28, 127.)

Are these differences in personal creativity specific to particular areas of endeavor, or is there such a thing as general creativity?

That issue involves the distinction between *capacity* and *performance*. Except for a few outstanding historical examples, the most creative people in one field are not likely at the same time to be the most creative in another. But this may be largely a matter of specialization in training and effort. Is an unusually creative architect likely to be highly creative in chemistry also, assuming equal training and opportunity? And are highly creative architects, or chemists, distinguished only by greater creativity in their respective professions, or can they be distinguished from their less creative colleagues in personal capacities and characteristics beyond differential performance on the job?

The results of various testing programs suggest that the qualities and capacities that distinguish more from less creative practitioners of given fields *do* extend beyond the specific area of professional competence. Creative architects, for instance, differ not only in the way they approach architecture but also in the way they approach any number of situations and tasks, some far removed and apparently unrelated to the specific demands of their profession. (See Barron, p. 125.)

What is more, there seem to be at least some differences that hold across diverse fields; for example, some of the same personality characteristics that distinguish between architects of high and average creativity have been observed in studies of creativity not only in industrial research chemists, but even among high school children differing in general creativity.

Granted that people differ in "creativity," are we really talking about anything more than general intelligence?

Yes. General intelligence seems to bear about the same relationship to on-the-job creativity at the professional level as weight does to ability in football. You have to have a lot of it to be in the game at all; but among those on the team—all of whom have a great deal of weight to begin with—differences in performance are only slightly, if at all, related to weight. In short, in the total population, creativity in most fields is associated with high intelligence, probably more so in some (e.g., physics) than in others (art). But within a given group of practitioners, operating at roughly the same professional level, differences in general intelligence provide no significant prediction of differences in creative performance. (See Barron, p. 124; Rokeach, p. 80; and Stein, p. 160.)

What, then, are the characteristics of the creative individual, especially those that might be subject to measurement before the fact so as to make prediction possible?

Although many characteristics of the creative individual, perhaps some of the most important, undoubtedly vary according to the area of creativity, studies of "highs" and "lows" in various fields are beginning to yield some common denominators. The following list concentrates on those differences that are probably more general. In some cases, this assumption of generality stems only from the fact that it seems reasonable on analysis of the characteristics involved vis-à-vis the general demands of the creative process. In others, the generality of the finding is actually supported by research from independent studies in diverse areas.

INTELLECTUAL CHARACTERISTICS

Although measures of general intelligence fail to predict creativity, highs, as a group, typically outscore lows in tests of the following mental abilities:

Conceptual Fluency. The ability to generate a large number of ideas rapidly: List tools beginning with the letter *t;* novel uses for a brick; possible consequences of a situation; categories into which the names of a thousand great men can be sorted—to name just a few of the tasks that have actually been used. (See Barron, pp. 120–21.)

Conceptual Flexibility. The ability to shift gears, to discard one frame of reference for another; the tendency to change approaches spontaneously. (See Rokeach, p. 77, and Ogilvy, p. 206.)

Originality. The ability and/or tendency to give unusual, atypical (therefore more probably new) answers to questions, responses to situations, interpretations of events.

Highs, for instance, are more apt to give rare—as well as more—uses of bricks; they give fewer "popular" interpretations of what an inkblot looks like; in high school, uncommon vs. common career aspirations (e.g., explorer rather than lawyer). (See Barron, p. 121.)

Preference for Complexity. Highs often exhibit a preference for the complex, and to them intriguing, as against the simple and easily understood.

When confronted with complex inkblots, for instance, they tend to seek a more difficult "whole" interpretation that takes the entire blot into account, rather than to identify detailed aspects that clearly resemble certain things. (See Barron, p. 123, and Stein, p. 162.)

The usual interpretation is that highs take complexity as a challenge; that they enjoy the attempt to integrate and resolve it. (See Stein, p. 163.)

PERSONALITY

Several closely related personality characteristics distinguish highs and lows in a number of studies:

Independence of Judgment. Highs are more apt to stick to their guns when they find themselves in disagreement with others.

In a situation where an artificially induced group consensus contradicts the evidence of their own senses, lows more often yield in their expressed judgment. The same is true when the issue at stake is not a factual one but involves voicing an opinion on an aesthetic, social, or political matter. (See Barron, p. 123.)

Deviance. Highs see themselves as more different from their peers and, in fact, they appear to *be* more different in any number of significant as well as trivial characteristics. (See Steiner, p. 257.)

At the extreme, highs sometimes feel lonely and apart, with a sense of mission that isolates them, in their own minds, from average men with average concerns. (See Guetzkow, p. 41, and Rokeach, p. 81.)

Attitudes toward Authority. A related distinction with far-reaching implications for organizations has to do with the way authority is viewed. The difference between highs and lows is a matter of degree, but to make the point we describe the extremes.

Lows are more apt to view authority as final and absolute; to offer unquestioning obedience, allegiance, or belief (as the case may be), with respect approaching deference; to accept present authority as "given" and more or less permanent. Highs are more likely to think of authority as conventional or arbitrary, contingent on continued and demonstrable superiority; to accept dependence on authority as a matter of expedience rather than personal allegiance or moral obligation; to view present authority as temporary. (See Stein, p. 163.)

Attitudes toward subordinates are related in the appropriate direction; those who pay unquestioned allegiance tend to expect it, and vice versa.

Similarly, and in general, highs are more apt to separate source from content in their evaluation of communications; to judge and reach conclusions on the basis of the information itself. Lows are more prone to accept or reject, believe or disbelieve messages on the basis of their attitudes toward the sender. (See Rokeach, p. 71.)

"Impulse Acceptance." Highs are more willing to entertain and express personal whims and impulses; lows stick closer to "realistic," expected behavior. Highs pay more heed to inner voices, while lows suppress them in favor of external demands. (See Barron, p. 123; Ogilvy, p. 206; and Alexander, p. 237.)

So, for example, highs may introduce humor into situations where it is not called for and bring a better sense of humor to situations where it is. And, in general, highs exhibit a richer and more diverse "fantasy life" on any number of clinical tests. (See Barron, p. 125, and Bruner, p. 210.)

Does the more creative man have more inner impulses or fewer inhibitions, or both, and to what degree? The answer is unknown, but there is at least one intriguing finding that suggests a strange combination of two normally opposing traits:

In the genius and near-genius, a widely used personality test shows "schizoid" tendencies (bizarre, unusual, unrealistic thoughts and urges) *coupled* with great "ego strength" (ability to control, channel, and manipulate reality effectively). (See Barron, p. 125, and Alexander, p. 165.) This line of inquiry begins to speak the cliché that the dividing line between madman and genius is a fine one. According to this finding, the line is fine, but firm. (See Alexander, p. 165.)

In sum, highly creative people are more likely than others to view authority as conventional rather than absolute; to make fewer black-and-white distinctions; to have a less dogmatic and more relativistic view of life; to show more independence of judgment and less conventionality and conformity, both intellectual and social; to be more willing to entertain, and sometimes express, their own "irrational" impulses; to place a greater value on humor and in fact to have a better sense of humor; in short to be somewhat freer and less rigidly—but not less effectively—controlled.

APPROACH TO PROBLEMS

The more detailed aspects of the creative process are taken up in the next section, where we see highs at work. We briefly note three distinctions as personal characteristics of creative problem solvers; all are especially significant in the management of creativity and are elaborated upon later.

Motivation. Highs are more perceptive to, and more motivated by, the interest inherent in the problem and its solution. Accordingly, they get more involved in the task, work harder and longer in the absence of external pressures or incentive, and generally place *relatively* greater value on "job interest" versus such extrinsic rewards as salary or status.

(See Barron, p. 126, and Steiner, p. 257.) There is no evidence, however, that the *absolute* importance of external incentives is any less for highs than for lows.

Orientation. Along somewhat the same lines:

Lows are more likely to see their future largely within the boundaries of one organization, to be concerned chiefly with its problems and with their own rise within it, and to develop extensive ties and associations within the community; in short, to be "local" in their loyalties and aspirations. (See Steiner, p. 104, and Merton, p. 101.)

Highs are more apt to think in terms of a larger community, both residential and professional; to view themselves more as members of the profession (whether management, chemistry, or teaching) than as members of Company X; to take their cues from the larger professional community and attempt to rise within it; to be more mobile, hence less "loyal" to any specific organization; in short, to be cosmopolitan in orientation and aspiration. (See Stein, p. 162.)

Hence, the local is more willing to change assignments, even professions (for example, from chemistry or engineering to administration), in the interests of the organization and his own career within it. The cosmopolitan is more likely to change organizations to pursue *his* interests and career within the larger profession. In short, highs change jobs to pursue their interests, not their interests to pursue their jobs. (See Steiner, p. 260.)

Pace. Highs often spend more time in the initial stages of problem formulation, in broad scanning of alternatives. Lows are more apt to "get on with it."

For example, in problems divisible into analytic and synthetic stages, highs spend more time on the former, in absolute as well as relative terms. As a result, they often leave lows behind in the later stages of the solution process, having disposed of more blind alleys and being able to make more comprehensive integrations as a result of more thorough analysis. (See Stein, p. 162.)

One interpretation is that highs have less anxiety to produce, that they are confident enough of their eventual success to be able to step back and take a broad look before making commitments. (See Stein, p. 162, and Steiner, p. 258.)

Can such differences be measured reliably enough to be of use in selection programs?

Many of these qualities can be measured, at least in part, by simple paper-and-pencil tests or other controlled observations. But the instruments are far from perfect and, perhaps more seriously, the correlation between each of these distinguishing characteristics and on-the-job creativity is limited. The characteristics "distinguish" highs from lows only in the sense that highs, on the average, have more of, or more often exhibit, the particular quality. And that is far from saying that all highs have more of each than all lows.[1]

As a result, as with all actuarial predictions of this sort, the procedure becomes more useful as the number of cases to be predicted increases. If many people are to be selected and it is important that some of them will turn out to be highs, a testing program can improve the odds. This would apply, for instance, in the selection of college or graduate students, Air Force Research and Development Officers, or chemists in a major industrial laboratory.

But if few people are being selected and it is important that almost all of them turn out to be highly creative (the chiefs of staff; the top management team; or the scientists to head a project), it is doubtful that, at present, a testing program will improve the odds beyond those of careful personal appraisal and judgment. (See Meehl, p. 25, and Steiner, pp. 129, 256.)

In this connection, there is the interesting suggestion (not documented) that highs may themselves be better judges of creativity in others; that it "takes one to tell one." (See Peterson, p. 93, and Barron, p. 120.)

As the examples suggest, testing to predict creativity is perhaps least effective where needed most: where the importance of the individual cases is the greatest.

What are the observable characteristics of the creative process; how does it look to an outsider while it is going on?

The appearance of the creative process, especially in its early stages, poses a problem to administrators. Up to a point, it may be hard to distinguish from totally non-productive behavior: undisciplined dis-

---

[1]In general, validity coefficients for specific tests at best attain values around .60, which means that they predict about 36 per cent of the variation in observed creativity. (See Barron, p. 125.)

order, aimless rambling, even total inactivity. (See Steiner, p. 258.)

Irregular Progress. Creativity is rarely a matter of gradual, step-by-step progress; it is more often a pattern of large and largely unpredictable leaps after relatively long periods of no apparent progress. (See Stein, p. 162; Ogilvy, p. 207; and Alexander, p. 238.)

The extreme example is the sudden insight that occurs after a difficult problem is put aside, and at a time of no conscious concern with the matter. Many anecdotes support the film cliché where the great man cries "Eureka!" in the middle of the night or while shaving—or, as in this famous case, while getting on a bus:

Just at this time I left Caen, where I was then living, to go on a geological excursion under the auspices of the school of mines. The changes of travel made me forget my mathematical work. Having reached Coutances, we entered an omnibus to some place or other. At the moment when I put my foot on the step the idea came to me, without anything in my former thoughts seeming to have paved the way for it, that the transformations I had used to define the Fuchsian functions were identical with those of non-Euclidean geometry. I did not verify the idea; I should not have had time, as, upon taking my seat in the omnibus, I went on with a conversation already commenced, but I felt a perfect certainty. On my return to Caen, for conscience' sake I verified the result at my leisure.—POINCARÉ

At a level of more immediate concern to most administrators, since few have the problem or the prowess of a Poincaré, the same sort of progress pattern distinguishes creative from merely productive work, and more from less creative activity, in the kind of problem-solving that characterizes the day-to-day activities of the organization. (See Alexander, p. 238, and Steiner, p. 258.)

Suspended Judgment. The creative process often requires and exhibits suspended judgment. The dangers of early commitment—sometimes to "incorrigible strategies"—are apparent at various levels. In the perceptual laboratory, for example, people who make an early, incorrect interpretation of a picture in an "ambiguitor" (a device that gradually brings a blurred picture into focus), will tend to retain the wrong perception—actually fail to "see"—even when the picture has been fully and clearly exposed. (See Bruner, p. 113.)

Similarly, in the type of small-group problem-solving or decision-making so typical of the modern organization, people will "stick to their guns" to support a position they have taken publicly, beyond its apparent validity and usefulness.

Finally, at the level of the organization itself, financial, technical, or corporate commitments to products, techniques, physical facilities, affiliations, and the like, often stand in the way of change even when it is recognized as necessary and inevitable. (See Peterson, pp. 191, 193; Bruner, p. 196; and Merton, p. 194.)

"Undisciplined" Exploration. Again, many creators stress the importance of undisciplined thinking, especially in the initial stages, probably because it serves to expand the range of consideration and raw material from which the new solution will emerge.

In this connection, we hear of the use of artificial disorganizers and "boundary expanders," such as alcohol, brain-storming sessions, sometimes even narcotics; and, frequently, the observation that inspiration cannot be willed or worked on, that pressure and preoccupation with the problem are least likely to produce insight—though they may indeed sustain effort in other phases of the process. (See Ogilvy, pp. 203–4, 207, and Barron, p. 166.)

The administrative enigma, then, is to distinguish, before the fact, incubation from laziness; suspended judgment from indecision, "boundary expansion" from simple drinking; undisciplined thinking as a deliberate exploratory step from undisciplined thinking as a permanent characteristic; brain-storming from gibberish by committee. In short, how can one tell the temporarily fallow mind—open and receptive, working subconsciously, and just on the threshold of the brilliant flash—from the permanently idle one? There may, of course, not be an answer. In time, outward predictors and distinguishing characteristics (beyond the individual's past history) may emerge. But for the moment, tolerance for high-risk gambles on creativity is probably one of the prerequisites or costs of playing for the higher stakes creativity provides when it does pay off.

What are the characteristics of the psychological state optimal for creative production?

Motivation. How much should be at stake; how hard should a man be trying, in order to maximize his chances of being creative? There is an apparent paradox:

First, we often hear that the creative process is characterized by a tremendous sense of commitment, a feeling of urgency, even of mission, that results in enormous preoccupation with the problem and perseverance. (See Rokeach, p. 81, and Meehl, p. 27.)

On the other hand, there is evidence that extremely high motivation narrows the focus and produces rigidity, perseveration rather than perseverance, which not only precludes creativity but reduces productivity (freezing up in the clutch). Some go so far as to say that the absence of pressure is a common denominator in situations conducive to creativity. (See Alexander, p. 238.)

There are two suggested resolutions: One is that the relationship is curvilinear; that creativity first rises, then falls, with motivation—you need enough to maintain effort at high levels but not so much as to produce panic attempts at immediate solution (jumping out of the window instead of looking for the fire escape). And there is, in fact, good evidence of such a relationship in laboratory studies of human and even animal problem-solving.

The other possible resolution involves a distinction in quality of motivation—between "inner" and "outer," "involvement" and "pressure," "drive" and "stress"—related to the earlier observation that highs are more driven by interest and involvement in the task itself than by external incentives. Perhaps external pressure impedes creativity, while inner drive and task-involvement are prerequisites. (See Rokeach, pp. 79, 81.)

In short, it may very well be that "Genius is 90 per cent hard work" but that inducing hard work is unlikely to produce genius.

The two resolutions are not mutually exclusive. Motivation of both kinds may have a breaking point, a level where they do more harm than good; although it seems reasonable to suppose that higher levels of "intrinsic" than of "extrinsic" motivation are compatible with creativity.

At any rate, other things being equal, interest in, and commitment to, the problem for its own sake should point to a creative outcome more often than sustained effort purchased by some externally attached reward, simply because the former is more apt to channel energy in the relevant directions.

Open-Mindedness versus Conviction. What intellectual attitude toward one's ideas and suggestions is optimal: how much conviction versus continual reappraisal; self-involvement versus objective detachment? Again, both tendencies appear, and in the extreme.

On the one hand, creativity is characterized by a willingness to seek and accept relevant information from any and all sources, to suspend judgment, defer commitment, remain aloof in the face of pressures to take a stand. (See Alexander, p. 239, and Barron, p. 127.) On the other hand, creators in the process of creating are often described as having conviction approaching zeal. (See Shockley, p. 137.)

There may in fact be a sort of simultaneous "antimony" or inter-action between "passion and decorum," "commitment and detach-ment," domination *by* a problem and yet a view of it as objective and external. (See Steiner, p. 257, and Bruner, p. 115.) The process may involve the continual and conflicting presence of both compo-nents. (See Peterson, p. 208.) Or it may be a matter of stages. Perhaps the creative process is characterized by open-mindedness in the early, idea-getting phases; then by a bull-headed conviction at the point of dissemination and execution.

There could be at least two reasons. A more open mind, that initially examines more alternatives, is more likely to be convinced of the one it finally selects. An early commitment to a less carefully analyzed ap-proach may be more vulnerable in the face of attack; beliefs developed through more painful and agonizing appraisal are more apt to stand the test of time. (See Bruner, p. 116.)

In addition, creators almost always find themselves on the defensive in the period after the idea has been developed but before it has been "sold." There is an inevitable stepping on toes, effrontery to the status quo and those responsible for it, that usually leads to some re-jection of the maverick, especially if the innovation is not immediately, demonstrably superior. And people on the defensive are apt to over-state their case. In short, open-minded probers may become fervent proselytizers.

As a working summary hypothesis:

In the exploratory, idea-getting stages, there is great interest in the problem; perhaps commitment to its eventual solution but certainly not to any particular approach; an open-minded willingness to pursue leads in any direction; a relaxed and perhaps playful attitude that allows a disorganized, undisciplined approach, to the point of putting the problem aside entirely. But at the point of development and execu-tion, where the selected alternative is pursued, tested, and applied, there is great conviction, dogged perseverance, perhaps strong per-sonal involvement, and dogmatic support of the new way.

II. THE ORGANIZATION ITSELF

What does all this have to do with organization? What are the characteristics of the creative organization; and what are the implications of individual creativity, if any?

There are various ways to approach this question.

One is to reason, deductively, *from* the characteristics of creators and the creative process *to* the kind of environment that ought to be congenial to them and conducive to creative activity. What does the nature of individual creativity imply about the environmental factors that foster or impede it? For the most part, this is the way we proceed in what follows.

Another approach is to treat the organization, as a whole, as the creative unit. Perhaps some of the characteristics that distinguish "high" and "low" individuals also apply to high and low organizations as such.

The characteristics of creative individuals suggest a number of rather direct translations or counterparts at the organizational level; and many of the characteristics independently attributed to creative organizations seem to match items in our description of individual highs.

Here is a brief summary:

The Creative Individual	*The Creative Organization*
Conceptual fluency . . . is able to produce a large number of ideas quickly	Has idea men (see Guetzkow, p. 40.)
	Open channels of communication (see Guetzkow, p. 40.)
	Ad hoc devices:
	Suggestion systems (see Guetzkow, p. 42.)
	Brain-storming (see Guetzkow, p. 42.)
	Idea units absolved of other responsibilities (see Guetzkow, p. 43.)
	Encourages contact with outside sources (see Guetzkow, p. 40.)

Originality . . . generates unusual ideas

Heterogenous personnel policy (see Merton, p. 62.)
Includes marginal, unusual types (see Guetzkow, p. 43.)
Assigns non-specialists to problems (see Guetzkow, p. 43.)
Allows eccentricity (see Guetzkow, p. 43.)

Separates source from content in evaluating information . . . is motivated by interest in problem . . . follows wherever it leads

Has an objective, fact-founded approach (see Bower, p. 174.)
Ideas evaluated on their merits, not status of originator (see Bower, p. 170.)
Ad hoc approaches:
  Anonymous communications
  Blind votes
Selects and promotes on merit only

Suspends judgment . . . avoids early commitment . . . spends more time in analysis, exploration

Lack of financial, material commitment to products, policies (see Peterson, p. 190.)
Invests in basic research; flexible, long-range planning (see Alexander, p. 47.)
Experiments with new ideas rather than prejudging on "rational" grounds; everything gets a chance (see Alexander, p. 46.)

Less authoritarian . . . has relativistic view of life

More decentralized; diversified (see Guetzkow, pp. 37–38.)
Administrative slack; time and resources to absorb errors (see Guetzkow, p. 39.)
Risk-taking ethos . . . tolerates and expects taking chances (see Guetzkow, p. 39.)

Accepts own impulses ... playful, undisciplined exploration	Not run as "tight ship" (see Guetzkow, p. 39, and Meehl, p. 27.) Employees have fun (see Bruner, p. 210.) Allows freedom to choose and pursue problems (see Guetzkow, p. 65) Freedom to discuss ideas (see Guetzkow, p. 40.)
Independence of judgment, less conformity Deviant, sees self as different	Organizationally autonomous (see Guetzkow, p. 67) Original and different objectives, not trying to be another "X"
Rich, "bizarre" fantasy life *and* superior reality orientation; controls	Security of routine ... *allows* innovation (see Guetzkow, p. 42, and Merton, p. 63.) ..., "philistines" provide stable, secure environment that allows "creators" to roam (see Merton, p. 63.) Has separate units or occasions for generating vs. evaluating ideas (see Guetzkow, pp. 43–44.) ... separates creative from productive functions (see Guetzkow, p. 43.)

This analogizing has serious limitations and it may be misleading. (See Guetzkow and Merton, p. 263.) But the table does serve as an organized index to some of the major characteristics attributed to creative organizations, and it is interesting that so many of them sound like the distinguishing characteristics of individual highs.

Finally, there is direct, empirical study of actual creative organizations. This may well turn out to be the most fruitful approach, but it was not the major focus of the seminar. In part, this reflects the state of knowledge; systematic studies of creative organizations, as such, simply do not exist as yet. In part, the composition of the symposium is responsible. A meeting with six psychologists and one psychoanalyst, against three sociologists, inevitably speaks mostly in psychological terms.

At any rate, we make no attempt to represent, let alone do justice to, the sociological investigation and analysis of organizational factors that relate to creativity. In what follows, we reason and abstract mostly from the nature of individual creativity, partly from rather informal observations of actual organizations.

What, specifically, can management do—beyond selecting creative participants—to foster creativity within and on the part of the organization?

Values and Rewards. What explicit and implicit goals and values characterize the creative organization? What system of rewards and incentives maximizes creativity?

First the creative organization in fact prizes and rewards creativity. A management philosophy that stresses creativity as an organizational goal, that encourages and expects it at all levels, will increase the chances of its occurrence. (See Guetzkow, pp. 43–44.)

But it is one thing to call for creativity, another to mean it, and still another to reward it adequately and consistently when it occurs. More specifically, creativity as a value should find expression in the following:

Compensation. In most areas of day-to-day functioning, productivity rather than creativity is and should be the principal objective; thus, general reward policies tend to measure and stress regular output. But even where creativity is truly desired and encouraged in good faith, activities that are potentially more creative may be subordinated to those more visibly and closely tied to reward policies. (A familiar academic illustration is the "pressure to publish," which may lead to a plethora of relatively insignificant formula-projects that minimize chances of failure—non-publication—but also of creativity.) (See Berelson, p. 103.)

In the business enterprise, a similar grievance centers on discrepancies in reward between the sowing and reaping aspects of the operation; with the greater rewards for work that shows immediate, measurable results (e.g., sales) as against that which may pay off in the longer run (such as basic research).

It may be inevitable that work closer to the balance sheet will be more swiftly and fully compensated than efforts that have tenuous, uncertain, and in any case long-range effects on corporate profits. But creativity and guaranteed, immediate results do not go together; not between, nor within, assignments. If creativity is to be fostered, not impeded, by material incentives, they will have to be applied by a different yardstick. (See Stein, pp. 94–95; Shockley, pp. 96–97; Alexander, pp. 98–99; and Ogilvy, p. 212.)

It is probably this simple: Where creativity and not productivity is in fact the goal, then creativity and not productivity should in fact be measured and rewarded. And if creativity is harder to measure and takes longer periods to assess, then this probably requires some speculative investment on the part of the firm that wants to keep and nurture the few men and the few activities that will eventually be worth it.[2]

Channels for Advancement. Where concern is with creativity in a professional unit or other specialized function operating within the larger organization, there is this related implication: To the extent possible, there should be formal channels for advancement and status within the area of creativity. (See Shockley, p. 97.)

Where it is impossible to promote a creative chemist without taking him out of chemistry, he faces a choice between money and position on the one hand, and chemistry on the other. The company is likely to lose his services as chemist in either case: to administration within its own walls or to another organization where a chemist as such can get ahead. (This is one of the chief organizational advantages and attractions of the major university for the research scientist or scholar: parallel channels for advancement, of at least equal status, exist outside of administration.) (See Alexander, p. 99.)

To some extent this is a matter of size; it is hard to provide for advancement within a department of one or two persons. But size alone is not enough. The nature and number of status levels established, their labels, and especially their actual value within the firm and the larger community, will determine their worth to individuals who hold them. (See Shockley, p. 101.)

"Freedom." Within rather broad limits, creativity is increased by giving creators freedom in choice of problem and method of pursuit. In line with the high's greater interest and involvement in his work,

---

[2]High potential pay-off and low risk are, unfortunately, incompatible—just as they are in the stock market and at the gambling tables.

greater freedom is necessary, to maximize those satisfactions that are important to him and that channel his efforts into avenues most likely to prove creative. (See Alexander, p. 239.) Whether and where there is an upper limit is a point of much contention and no evidence. (See Steiner, p. 260.)

But such freedom often puts the appropriate objectives of the organization at odds with the demands of maximum creativity. The symposium itself produced two striking examples.

In one instance, a participant "distracted" himself and the group by working out and presenting an elegant general solution to a mathematical problem that had been mentioned only in passing, as a task assigned to subjects in a creativity experiment. From the point of view of the seminar, he was out of bounds. By following his own interests, he was creative. (Would he have arrived at an equally elegant *psychological* insight had he been constrained to the issue as externally defined?) (See Shockley, pp. 88–89, and Steiner, p. 260.)

More dramatically, after the first few hours of the meeting had been spent in rather academic and abstract discussion, one participant reminded us that the purpose of the meeting was to develop useful and understandable guidelines for management and that we had better get on with it. This precipitated a short but heartfelt donnybrook between the advocates of "No nonsense! Keep your eye on the target," and "Take it easy; it's interesting; let's see where it leads"; between "What good is it if you can't tell us what it means for management?" and "Our job is to create, yours to apply."

Both approaches are valid but as means to different ends. Those responsible for a meeting are rightfully concerned with maximizing its output. By the same token, creative individuals who attend it are not so concerned with the product of the particular conference as with the pursuit of interesting lines of inquiry, whether or not they happen to reach fruition during the session. And curtailing and channeling discussion into areas known to be productive obviously limits the chances of coming up with something outside the range of the ordinary.

This, then, is probably one of the principal costs in the nurture of creativity: Except in the rare and fortunate case where a creative individual's interests exactly match the day-to-day operating objectives of his organization, and continue to do so over time, the organization pays a price, at least in the short run, for giving him his head.

What he returns to the organization may or may not compensate it many-fold.

Communication. Many observations point to the importance of free and open channels of communication, both vertical and horizontal. (See Guetzkow, p. 40, and Bower, pp. 169–70.)

On the one hand, potential creators need and seek relevant information whatever its source, within or without the organization; on the other hand, they are stimulated by diverse and complex input.

Equally important, ideas wither for lack of a grapevine. A possible approach, a feasible but half-baked notion, or even a well worked-out solution must be communicated to those with the power to evaluate, authorize, and implement. (See Guetzkow, p. 40, and Bower, p. 177.)

The presence of formal channels is not enough. People must feel free to use them, and channels must not be clogged by routine paperflow that ties up time with "programmed trivia," and creates an air of apathy and neglect toward incoming messages because it is so unlikely that they will contain anything of value. (See Guetzkow, p. 41.)

Since highs tend toward cosmopolitan, professional orientation, the organization must at least provide for and perhaps encourage contact and communication with colleagues and associations on the outside. (See Merton, p. 101, and Shockley, pp. 138–39.)

As a special case, there is the matter of scientific and professional publication in the appropriate journals, which is often of great personal importance to creators.

There may be problems of security and the natural jealousy of corporate secrets and employee loyalties. But in many cases, these are unrealistic or exaggerated, given the high rate of horizontal mobility, the discretion of the professional, and the fact that most "secrets" are not. At any rate, there may be no reason to think that the balance of payments will be "out"; there should be at least as much information gained as given away in most external contacts. And in many cases, and within broad limits, the net gain in satisfaction, creativity, and perhaps tenure of highs will probably offset the time and trade secrets lost to the outside.

What, specifically, are the costs of creativity? What must an organization be prepared to give up or tolerate if it wants to increase its creativity?

Answers were scattered throughout the preceding, but it may help to pull them together.

First, creativity, by definition, is a high-risk enterprise, not for society or industry, at large, but for any given unit that attempts it. The greater the departure from present practice, the less likelihood that the innovation will work; the greater the potential payoff, the less the odds of its occurring. Conversely, the larger the number of workers or units independently pursuing any problem, the better the chances that one or more of them will succeed. (See Merton, pp. 59–62.)

In the abstract, then, decisions as to whether and where to attempt creativity, and how much to try for, are much like decisions concerning what to insure, and for how much—although the hopes and fears are reversed. (See Peterson, p. 198.)

Second, within the unit under consideration, fostering creativity assesses costs in assured productivity. To the extent that energy is consumed in investigation and exploration, it does not go into work known to be productive. (See Bensinger, p. 153, and Bower, p. 182.)

Finally, depending on the personal tastes and preferences of management, there may or may not be costs in "security," "comfort," and "congeniality" of the environment: (*a*) Highs are not as deferent, obedient, flattering, easy to control, flexible to *external* demands and changes, conventional, predictable, and so on, through a long list of desiderata in "good" employees. (*b*) In addition, highs are more mobile, less "loyal"—harder to hold by ordinary extrinsic rewards—but easier to acquire by the offer of interesting opportunities. At any rate, they make for a less stable and secure, more challenging but perhaps more disturbing environment. (*c*) A creative organization itself is more committed to change; operates on a faster track; has a less certain or predictable future than the efficient, me-too operation. (See Steiner, p. 259.)

In short, maximizing creativity is not the principal objective of any organization at all times, or even of all organizations at some times. When it is, there are some rough guidelines to how it may be fostered—but not, it is suggested, at no cost.

Consider the organization as a whole, operating within a larger social and economic environment. What type of situation is most likely to produce a creative organization?

The seminar produced little agreement, let alone evidence, on this matter. There was some discussion about the effects of competitive position, size, age, and general success of an organization as they affect its need and chances for creativity. (See Steiner, p. 262.) But nothing approaching a conclusion is visible.

One of the more interesting recurrent debates centered on the relative merits of firmly led, "one-man" organizations versus decentralized corporate entities; on charismatic, inspired leadership by a "great man" versus the greater democracy of the professionally managed organization. (See Hauser, p. 195.) This debate was not resolved, but it does call attention to some distinctions that may be important.

Some Final Distinctions. Last, we take note of some distinctions that may be helpful, suggested simply by the experience of trying to discuss "the creative organization." For instance, the preceding debate may reflect a failure to distinguish between a creative organization and one that produces for a creator.

An organization can be an efficient instrument for the execution of externally created ideas and yet not be in itself creative: for instance, a smooth military unit under a great strategist, a top-notch symphony orchestra, or, in the same terms, a business that hums to the tune of a creative president. These may all implement creativity and yield a product appropriately called creative, but they are not, *ipso facto,* creative organizations. And the characteristics that make for creativity within and on the part of an organization as a whole may in fact be quite different from those that make it the efficient tool of a creative master. (See Alexander, pp. 179, 242.)

Along the same lines, it may be helpful to distinguish between getting people to be more creative and getting creative people to be more productive. The conditions that induce a Frank Lloyd Wright, an Ogilvy, or a Shockley to turn out more of the same—to repeat or elaborate earlier innovations—may be quite different from those that produce the original and subsequent departures.

In short, organizations, like people, may increase their net yield of creative *products* either by the terms that go into their conception or those that enter into their output. And while the net effects may often be the same, the means are probably not.

For the eventual understanding of "the creative organization," it may be important to learn the difference between creating productivity and producing creativity.

I

The Creative Individual:
Why It Is Hard To Identify Him

PAUL E. MEEHL

The psychology of creativity is not my field of research competence; however, as a former department head, I have had to face the problem in personnel selection and assignments. Also, the creative process seems closely akin to some processes which occur during psychotherapy, about which I do know a little something. Then, too, the psychometric methodology of assessment has been one of my professional research areas.

Thus far, we cannot claim that psychological tests and other traditional techniques for assessment have demonstrated high power in identifying those persons who will subsequently produce creatively. I shall attempt a largely armchair analysis of why this might be expected to be so. At the risk of sounding pessimistic, I shall suggest some possibly permanent limitations on the psychologist's ability to devise measuring instruments for this purpose. If these limitations turn out to be really permanent, what practical alternatives exist for maximizing the odds of selecting creative individuals by an institutionally oriented decision policy? I shall consider only the problem of identification and shall not treat the subsequent influences of the institutional context after the individual has been selected, although the context of selection itself (i.e., the impact of the assessment procedure upon samples of behavior obtained) will be briefly examined, since it has direct relevance to the validity of these procedures.

Identifying the highly creative person in advance of his creative production is a special case of the always difficult problem of *forecasting a rare event.*

I shall accept the distinction between psychological test responses as "signs" versus "samples." That is, if the psychometric procedure is one which duplicates, in all qualitative essentials, the situation and response variables of primary interest, it is a "sample." Its validity in forecasting then depends solely on two factors: (1) temporal stability of the individual with respect to the dispositions sampled; and (2) adequacy of the behavior sample in the purely statistical sense of its *size*. (An example would be the measurement of spelling ability by dictating words chosen randomly from a dictionary.)

By contrast, some psychometric procedures involve presentation of stimuli (including instructions and physical materials) which are not, at least apparently, very close, "qualitatively," to the stimulus inputs which will be present on those future occasions we desire to forecast; and the nature of the response dimensions we score is not superficially similar to the response aspects of predictive interest. In such cases, the test-elicited behavior is treated as a "sign" rather than as a "sample"—an indirect indicator, analogous to a medical symptom or a Freudian slip, of some latent internal variable which we believe to be capable of qualitatively diverse expressions. The validity here depends upon adequacy of sample size, closeness of the causal nexus between the postulated latent variable and the indicator, and contribution of the latent variable to the behavior being forecast. In the use of tests as "signs," we are commonly presented with a situation in which the kind of behavior to be forecast is complexly determined by a *group* of latent variables, variously related to one another. The prediction problem then requires an additional step beyond that of the "sample" situation; namely, choice of an optimal mathematical function for combining the estimated latent values to yield a composite score.

In the application of these assessment principles to the prediction of individual creativity, we confront certain psychological difficulties.

The first is the specificity bugaboo. When almost any domain of behavior is explored carefully, it turns out that people's dispositions are a good deal more "specific" than might be expected from our use of ordinary language. Thus when we alter slightly the qualitative character of a psychometric task, its statistical relations with superficially "similar" tasks undergo sizable changes. In the present case, we cannot be sure in advance that "creativity," as a single *word* used, actually denotes a sufficiently homogeneous or psychologically uniform dimension to make prediction possible. This is particularly likely because the psychological unity of most highly predictable behaviors is associated with a similarity of behavior *content;* whereas the very concept "creativity" is "content-free," being instead a kind of *formal* category referring to the *heightened probability that novel behavior of a statistically infrequent kind will occur.*

Furthermore, there are peculiarities of the "creative state" which contribute to difficulty in psychometric assessment. Introspection by highly creative producers, as well as a good deal of the research on problem-solving and on psychometric assessment, agree on the whole in the picture they give of the psychological state optimal for creative production. Normally we would expect that such agreement as to the nature of a state would lead to efficient selection techniques, but here the intrinsic properties of the state suffice to explain why psychometric forecasting is so difficult in practice. (It is *not* always true that the-oretical-causal understanding of a process facilitates accurate pre-diction of the individual events—it may instead lead to the causal understanding of why such forecasting is unfeasible.)

The state of creativity occurs rarely, even in creative individuals. Typically, they report that they can identify it rather clearly when it happens, and they try to arrange their life circumstances so that such opportunities can be grasped by putting all other tasks and interpersonal involvements utterly aside.

The subjective experience tends to be one of *intense* yet somehow *relaxed* involvement. The state combines active and passive elements in a special way, such that although the individual is "doing some-thing," he feels somehow as if the "something" were being done in or through him. The urgency to "get it out" and to "keep cooking" has at times an almost mystical necessity of expression, which is very different from the anxiety-toned, task-ridden urgency produced by an external demand or a moral commitment.

Like the mystical experience, the creative state is remarkably spon-taneous, even capricious, and cannot be forced or artificially induced. It is apparently true that one can *lower* the probability of its occur-rence by certain adverse circumstances, but avoidance of these cir-cumstances will not guarantee its presence.

During the experience, attention is entirely upon the subject matter, rather than upon oneself ("How am I doing?") or upon remote consequences of successful creation ("This will go over big!"—"Will other people believe me?"—"This should get me promoted to full professor.").

Criticality is largely suspended; it takes over when the heightened phase has begun to pass. It seems universally agreed that the inability of many otherwise able persons to create significantly is partly due to neurotic or situational constraints that prevent this free-wheeling suspension of critical judgment in the formative, synthetic stage of a creative process.

We can see that limitations of psychometric assessment arise from these characteristics of the creative state. Thus, the examinee is highly unlikely to be "in state" when tested, purely for *statistical* reasons; we pick a restricted time interval, and the "state" intervals in a life history are (*a*) rare and (*b*) short. The psychological set induced by a test situation runs counter to the creative state in factors such as (1) examination anxiety, even in relatively secure individuals; (2) "extrinsic" task motivation rather than "intrinsic" fascination; (3) possible resentment—especially in very able, previously creative persons—arising from the seeming irrelevancy or artificiality of what they are being "judged" by; (4) anxiety aside, the realistic situational factor that poor guesses waste limited time, tending to raise the criticality attitude and shift the set toward relatively "safe" or "sure-fire" approaches—better to be *sound* than *daring*.

We also can see certain statistical difficulties, mostly mirroring the psychological difficulties discussed above. E. L. Thorndike said, "If a thing exists, it exists in some amount; and if it exists in some amount, it can be measured." Does Thorndike's dictum apply *in practice* to the prediction of rare events? Not so easily.

Consider individuals as urns filled with marbles. Each urn contains varying proportions of black marbles ("uncreative ideas") to white marbles ("creative ideas"). Treating the test as a sample, in effect we draw a small number of marbles from each urn and count the proportion of white ones. Our hope is to arrange the urns in order of their true white-marble composition on the basis of these samples. But even the most creative individuals have only a very small proportion of white marbles available. Hence the true (unknown, parametric) proportions of white marbles has only a small variance over the urn population. We may therefore be discriminating among urns more on the basis of sampling error than on the basis of the inter-urn variation in true white-marble proportions. Another way of looking at this is that, given a small sample of marbles, both the high- and low-creative person will tend overwhelmingly to give us only black marbles.

A second statistical difficulty involves non-monotonic and configural functions when tests are used as signs rather than samples. There is some evidence that the latent variables involved in creativity determine the latter in complex ways. For instance, take the problem of "optimal ranges." It has long been known in industrial psychology that an output variable may not be a monotonically increasing function of a certain personality variable used as a predictor. Certain semi-routine factory jobs, for example, are best performed by workers with IQ's in a certain range, and scores either above or below this optimal intelligence range are predictive of poor performance. It seems likely that this may be especially true of creativity. Here are some examples of latent variables which theory suggests might pass through a maximum.

Idiosyncratic, free-spirit, non-conforming attitudes: The future creator is often hard to distinguish from the grandiose beatnik.

Endocathection: intense involvement with ideational and aesthetic events going on inside.

Pertinacity, persistence, "stick-to-it-iveness" in the face of obstacles and repeated failures: This is a touchy one, since it is somehow related to a kind of obsessional tendency which can operate against creativeness in the form of rigidity.

Cognitive readiness to perceive subtle, analogical, or remote relations (as by Rorschach Z and Miller Analogies Tests): This one produces the paradox of a schizoid Newton, and a state hospital schizophrenic with cosmological delusions, being distinguished not chiefly by their difference in mental health but by the objective success of their respective cognitive products.

Available knowledge which (*a*) minimizes false starts in previously tried directions and (*b*) maximizes richness of available content: However, *too much* knowledge often reflects a pedantic tendency adverse to originality. Some of the most creative psychologists I know have a studied policy of avoiding reading other people's contributions to a given domain while they themselves are actively involved with it.

Energy level (drive, "push," enthusiasm, stamina): One study of highly successful executives showed an almost uniform history of going without sleep during productive periods. But we cannot use a crude "sleep" measure, since, for every such sleep-neglected producer, there will be a score or more of neurotic insomniacs who may describe themselves as "going without sleep to work" but in reality were mostly just worrying and engaged in low-efficiency waste motion. *Why* you are not sleeping, and *how you feel during it,* are the crucial questions psychologically. "Energy level" may be a non-monotonic affair; we all know men whom we suspect *could* be creative if only they would stop acting once in a while and give the engine a chance to idle for a change.

As for configural effects, the extreme rarity of creative outputs suggests that the combination of latent variables is not additive but multiplicative. This means that a powerful predictive function of test scores used as signs must involve non-linear relations, particularly those in which the predictive impact of a given variable is potentiated by values of other variables. Such systems are troublesome in practice for the following reasons: (1) Lacking a rational curve-type derived from theory, we face a wide choice of functional relations as candidates. (2) Even given a selected function form, fitting parameters into highly configural functions greatly increases the danger of capitalizing upon sampling errors. (3) This in turn necessitates a very large sample, which is hard to obtain when the incidence of really high-creative persons is so rare.

How about psychometric assessment as an exclusion procedure? We know more about factors which impede creative states than we do about factors that raise their probability. Among anticreative factors susceptible to measurement are (1) extremes of psychopathology (too anxious, too low self-esteem, too schizoid, too compulsive, too much intrusion of fantasy material, preoccupation with personal problems, etc.); (2) deficiency in relevant capacity variables (insufficient abstract intelligence; specific disabilities); and (3) strongly competing interests, such that very little investment in the domain is psychologically possible on an *intrinsic* basis. (For example, Robert Thorndike showed that a very strong interest in helping other people directly through personal contact—"social worker syndrome," "uplift pattern"—was a highly *negative* predictor of scientific productiveness. One is reminded here of Freud's reference to *furor therapeuticus* as being harmful to the psychoanalyst's creative powers as he listens to the patient's material. It is well known that many of the greatest creative contributors to human welfare were only mildly interested in "helping mankind," especially during the actual creative process.)

Whether the joint use of several psychometric hurdles to screen out low-creative persons is pragmatically justified depends on many extrascientific questions, such as size of the labor market, ethical policies, costs of screening, effects upon morale, etc. If used, the screening system should presumably be based on a "successive hurdles" model rather than on a "compensatory" (regression-type) model.

As an alternative to psychometric methods, let me conclude with a few remarks on the life history as a behavior sample. One principle which works in several domains of behavior prediction (e.g., criminal recidivism, academic success, chronicity of mental illness, marital success, salesmanship) is simple: "The best way to predict a person's behavior is to examine the net outcome of his behavior in the past." This method bypasses the psychometric problem of signs and samples, and it has the advantage of being applicable prior to the development of a powerful theory or *causal* understanding of creativity, in terms of the inner events involved. It also escapes the statistical dilemma of the urn model, because it makes use of a much larger behavior sample, which is the person's life up to the date of prediction. The disadvantage, of course, is that we usually have no great problem in identifying successful creators at a late stage in their careers. The locus of our decision problem is the "fresh young aspirant," and he is often still only a "potential creator" when we get him.

Even so, two factors still work in our favor:

1. The *most* creative products—even if few in absolute number—that a person has emitted in his life are likely to be closer to his "top" than is likely to be true of a psychometric sample, since they will presumably be examples of what he can do *when* he is in a spontaneously occurring "real life" creative state.

2. Even behavioral signs—not samples—that reveal a creative potential, via less high-level creative outputs (e.g., catching the drift of a complex idea quickly in casual conversation), will have been noted by others. Hence, ratings by peers and superiors can be a sub-

stitute for highly creative products early in a man's career. However, it is probably desirable to rely upon ratings by individuals who are *themselves* known (by longer output samples) to be highly creative. My impression has been very strong that in order to judge the creative potential of others (short of their having already produced a dramatic and clearcut major creation, plain to any unbiased observer), you must be batting in the big leagues yourself. Uncreative persons usually tend

——not to *perceive* the creativeness; or

——to be threatened by it if they do; or

——to confuse genuine creativeness with other things, such as the pseudocreativeness of mere non-conformers and rebels or of scattered, hyperactive, work-driven persons; or

——to be taken in by superficially brilliant conversationalists.

As things stand, I would personally trust the considered judgment of one or two carefully chosen peers or superiors of high creativity more than I would any psychological assessment procedure available today.

Discussion

Bower

I think that industry would subscribe, in general, to the theory that you can best judge people by what they have done, including creativity. So I wonder what the psychologists have done to identify the correlation between early behavior and creativity? Is there, for example, a rough index of creativity that can be used with some success in industry? For example, if you find a person who has, in high school and college, engaged in dramatics, music, and writing on the newspaper, you may have a fairly reliable index of a generally creative person. Have psychologists identified early behavior of that kind as an indication of creativity?

Shockley

With regard to measurement of creativity in people who are being interviewed as candidates, I would like to refer to the procedure at Bell Telephone Laboratories—which is certainly a creative organization—and I think almost exactly the same procedures would apply for RCA and General Electric. Almost no psychometric tests are used. The technique of finding individuals generally is this: Technically competent people go to the universities, give some lectures, and hope this will provoke some discussion. They interview candidates, ask the professors how good they are, and use very simple, low-brow methods, such as looking at their grades. It is my impression that this is generally the way it goes.

I did a study in about 1953, at which time I was concerned at Bell Telephone Laboratories with whether or not we were making good enough offers to attract people.

First, I got the interview records of a large group of candidates over a period of about two years. Then I had these interview records graded by several technical people. In some cases there were very clear indications, such as: "X came into our laboratory; we started to show him our apparatus, and he exhibited very little interest. Did not inquire about how it worked, etc."; or "When we showed Y the apparatus, he at once made the suggestion that it might be improved in some way, which was incorrect. But as soon as we pointed this out, he grasped the idea and proposed that something else be done instead, something we had not thought of, which was a good idea."

It was practical to group these candidates into four categories, A, B, C, and D, on the basis of the interview records. It turned out, as I recall, that we had hired almost none of the straight A people. We missed practically all the ones who looked best on these records. But we had hired some that did not look quite so good and some who looked very much less good. These employees had been there for several years at the time I did this test, so what I did was to look up their payroll records.

They had come in over a rather narrow range, at nearly the same salaries. I then plotted the rate at which their salaries had gone up against the scores of the interview records. There was a very high correlation. The ones who had made an excellent impression in the interview had continued to make an excellent impression, which had been recognized by their being advanced faster in salary. I don't know of another study of this sort.

Peterson

Tell me, would you guess that the kind of person that can pick *good* men in industry is also the kind of person that could pick *creative* men? Is there a relationship between sensing creativity and *general* empathy with other people, or do you feel that sensing creativity is something really unique? If we could identify good "sensers," perhaps we should hire such people and have them talk to everybody.

Shockley

Well, I know that I can't pick very well and I don't trust anybody who says he can. As time goes on, I have less confidence in what I do. I feel I do better, but I am less confident.

Steiner

Problems of this complexity are best approached by making them still a little more complicated. Can you identify them in advance, how do you put creative people together, and what does that have to do with their creativity?

2

The Creative Person in Organizations

HAROLD GUETZKOW

My task is to speculate about the way organizations influence creativity. It is important to remember that people in government and industry are imbedded, always, in their organizations. How do characteristics of these organizations influence the creativity of their members? If we take literally Paul Meehl's remarks about the "creator extraordinary," we argue that the organizational situation has no relevance. All is determined by the creative processes within the individual. The organizational context would not interfere with the creator; vice versa, one could not enhance creativity by changing the organizational environment.

But many of us—and we are psychologists, too—are concerned with more than just the top one-tenth of one per cent of individuals who produce effective originalities, who exhibit newness in their solutions, and who penetrate deeply in the development of innovations. There is reason to believe that creativity is distributed among humans as are most other personal characteristics—many are modestly endowed; some are either generously or miserly gifted; there are a few at the extraordinary extremes. For the large group of mortals, the social context may make some difference in the way their creative talents can be elicited in ongoing social situations. But Paul Meehl's paper also included the notion that one can remove impediments to creativity. It is here that he and I can perhaps find common ground, if we allow that suitable organizational conditions may permit further expression of creativity. But then one no longer focuses on the "creator extraordinary"; rather, one is concerned with increasing in organizations the occasional innovation of individuals who possess considerable or moderate talents.

As was suggested, let me approach a complex problem by being complex. There are two kinds of organizational processes, (1) those which hinder the development of innovative behavior and (2) those which enhance the creativity of the members of the organization. (It may be that these two sets of processes are simply the inverse of each other, but, because this area of inquiry is quite "data-free," I really do not know.) As individuals engage interdependently in complex undertakings, their organizations provide a way of specializing, as the work is divided among them. The specialization becomes more intense as the members lose face-to-face contact with each other and depend upon third parties for their communications—somehow the participants must co-ordinate their efforts. But, as Max Weber pointed out, one then seeks to regularize the behavior of members of the organization so that their activities may be more easily meshed and controlled. Such development of routines is prized in organizations. In the very heart of the organization, then, are important built-in forces for regularizing—for conformity. One then manages organizations by reducing the uncertainties, by discouraging originalities, by ridding the organization of the unexpected. In the very process of becoming a surviving, thriving organization, the creative innovations of the members are inhibited.

The environments of organizations, however, are not stable. Soon, the very stabilities in behavior which proved so useful at one time become burdensome and inappropriate. Countervailing pressures develop for change—for innovation. Such pressures come not only from external environment; inside the organization itself there are demands for innovation. As the size of the organization increases, as the division of labor shifts, new patterns of communication and supervision are needed. These constitute sources of demand for creative acts, and they allow scope for the creative individual.

In summary: *Organizations exhibit simultaneous demands for routinization and for innovation. The balance of these countervailing pressures determines the organization's climate for the creative member.*

Within the framework just presented, I shall submit six additional variables. It may be that the following three organizational processes, with three features of organization structure, are of consequence in building environments which stimulate the ordinary, as well as the extraordinary, members of an organization to further creativity.

ORGANIZATIONAL PROCESSES RELATED TO PROPENSITY FOR INNOVATION

Three factors in organizational functioning which may be of central importance in determining whether an organizational environment is provocative of creativity are (1) the way the organization handles its distribution of authority, (2) how the organization's slack is used for error absorption, and (3) the manner in which the organization's communication facilities serve the diffusion of innovative ideas. Let us examine each of these facets of organizational process separately.

THE CENTRALIZATION AND DECENTRALIZATION OF AUTHORITY

The authority system provides premises for decision within the hierarchy of the organization. The commands of a superior are taken as "givens," thus decidedly limiting the freedom for decision of the subordinates. When there is centralization within an organization, many decisions are taken at the top of the authority structure, so that decisional latitude is narrower for those in intermediate and lower positions, thereby restricting opportunities for non-conforming, creative decisions. A decentralized decisional structure provides scope for innovative behavior through its emphasis upon the development of solutions appropriate to the different environments encountered in the various extensions of the organization. When authority is delegated, full advantage can be taken of broad latitude by those able to develop creative responses to an ever-changing environment in which their organization functions.

Yet decentralized organizations need to possess feedback systems which allow the executives at their top to assess the performance of the quasi-autonomous parts. These may take two forms: (1) There are those feedbacks which monitor the outputs of the decentralized unit, such as financial reports. (2) Then there are those feedbacks which monitor the means used by the decentralized units for achievement of goals, such as "progress" reports which describe the techniques and approaches employed.

When it is possible to evaluate the accomplishment of tasks within a company, the former method is often used, allowing the decentralized decision-makers greater latitude in the means they employ. When it is difficult to co-ordinate operation with goals, there is a tendency in organizations to appraise the unit's performance in terms of the extent to which headquarters' prescriptions of means have been heeded. In either case, when the top executive group finds itself dissatisfied, intervention in the affairs of the decentralized operation occurs, thereby reducing opportunity for innovation. Thus, the requirement that the creative decision be simultaneously practical and innovative imposes a countervailing tendency within the organization to restrict decision latitude. This tendency is less strong when achievement of the company's goals can be easily appraised with some objectivity.

The successful functioning of a decentralized authority structure influences the expression of creativity within the higher levels of management. Because top management's decision-making now is limited within its own organization—inasmuch as many of the internal decisions have been delegated successfully to others—these executives turn outward for opportunities to exercise their creative talents. Thus, much energy is focused upon innovation in the acquisition of new organizational components, as through mergers, or by extensions of the company's capital resources. At times service in community organizations—such as the Chamber of Commerce—is exploited by top management as an occasion for creative self-fulfilment, when the scope of decision-making within the company is restricted because of decentralization.

Within those organizations in which there is much technical specialization and within those exhibiting much diversification, one would predict the tendency to intervention by top management in day-to-day operations to be less. In such situations—regardless of formal administrative policy on the distribution of authority—it would be likely that occasions for innovation by lower management would be greater. Such circumstances induce a *de facto* decentralization of decision-making, inasmuch as members of the upper echelons of management do not possess the technical competence required to assert premises for decisions by those working in constituent units of the firm.

Thus one speculates: *A dispersed distribution of authority within a firm provides more occasions for innovation, creative decision-making, especially when the decentralized unit exists within a diversi-*

fied firm and possesses relatively objective criteria in terms of which its output may be appraised.

ORGANIZATIONAL SLACK AND INNOVATION

Creativity pushes thought into unexplored areas, and thus is fraught with potential for error. Because new ideas, by their very definition, have not been tried before, the chances that they are impractical are great. Yet it is difficult to know whether innovations are contributions or sports, until they have been winnowed by further research and development; but to avoid premature judgment, one needs time and resources. Does the organization have sufficient slack to absorb the costs involved in innovative errors?

When an organization has little slack—when the ship is tightly run—the climate is unfavorable for innovation. Immediate assessment must be made of the short-run payoff of new ideas, for the organization is not able to survive, in the long run, if it fails to eliminate its short-run errors. Managers are forced to introduce impediments to creativity, as described by Meehl: The individual becomes anxious, he restricts the depth of his exploration of new paths, he centers his attention upon items closely related to the company's immediate output. If there is little organizational capacity to absorb the consequences of errors, one bets only on sure things. I wonder whether the increased pace in innovations of American industry has not come from the displacement of the smaller organization, fashioned around one or two potential inventions of the creator-enterpriser, by the larger organization, quite able to absorb unproductive, bizarre ideas.

Coupled with organizational slack, one finds an ethos within the organization that is conducive to change. Risk-taking is legitimate, and expected. The norms within the organization are so set that one may properly talk about one's failures as well as one's successes in innovation. In fact, managers within such enterprises internalize the query: "Come now, how can this be done better, were we to take a fresh look at the whole problem?"

One speculates then: *The greater the organizational slack, with its increased capability of absorbing errors and ethos for risk-taking, the greater the propensity for innovation.*

Inasmuch as organizations must survive in the short run in order to be permitted to benefit from creativity in the long run, pressures often develop to remove organizational slack when the organization encounters immediate rough going in an adverse environment. Yet, it is then that innovation is needed. Thus, again, a paradox obtains: During times of stress, just when creativity is needed, some of the slack conducive to innovation is taken up. One way out of the dilemma is proposed below, in the utilization of special *ad hoc* group structures for innovation, such as the task force. Thus, although organizational slack is reduced in general, special innovative groups may be able to handle the immediate crises confronting the organization.

COMMUNICATIONS AS CATALYSTS FOR INNOVATION

The creative individual has contact with his organizational environment by means of its communication system. The employee talks with others; he reads and writes messages. The very problems he tackles often are called to his attention by the communication system —and unless they are the more fundamental ones confronting the organization, the individual's creativity is brought to bear upon trivia. In some companies, an attempt is made to alert upper management to occasions for innovation by communicating directly when programmed routines seem inadequate. If the communication system filters out the unpleasant and distorts the realities so as to present, by and large, images of integrated, successful operations, managers throughout the communication net will not have the disjunctive components with which to create new solutions; they will be lulled into acceptance of things as they are.

To increase the relevance of the creativity of the individual, the communication system must work well in both the vertical and the horizontal dimension. Each person in the organization must be heard as well as talked to, and the communication net must not be so overloaded as to drive out the half-formed thought which needs sharing, so that only the hard-sell, well-formulated notion survives. The need is not merely to increase the flow of ideas upward; equally important is the need to share ideas sideways and downward.

An executive situated at a peculiarly fruitful junction within the communication system may bubble with "half-baked" ideas. He must be able to relay these ideas to associates, both peers and subordinates, for further creative development. The functional specialties like sales and engineering must have an adequate language for communication of their problems to each other, so that the bonds of assumed constraint may be broken and innovations achieved. When there is geographical dispersion, counterpart persons in different sites need opportunities to spark each other's ideas, so that adaptations of solutions to similar problems may be creatively molded to fit widely different regions—a need of special relevance, for instance, to those involved in international operations.

To this point, emphasis has been placed on communication processes within the organization which might enhance creative work by its members. But communication systems can also inhibit innovation, especially by overlooking the communication burdens of participants in the system. When the channels are crowded with routine paper flows —when there is emphasis upon the emptly "In" basket—then not only will there be less time for innovation, but creative ideas will be drowned in the seas of programmed trivia. As is so often the case in the operation of organizations, the communication process must be balanced and timed, so that one does not make "too much out of a good thing," thereby defeating the original purposes.

It seems clear from studies that individual creativity is often a "lonely" process, with the innovator at times needing isolation and seclusion. Just as it is quite legitimate in business practice to hold telephone calls because an executive is "in conference," some day it should become as acceptable to block communications because a man is "in creative thought."

Thus one may speculate: *The communication system of an organization may be tuned so as to provide materials for creative activities without depriving members of the organization of time for creative work.*

In this discussion of the organizational processes related to propensity for innovation, only three processes were treated: authority, slack, and communications. This means that such important components as the organization's status system, its recruitment and internal promotion procedures, and its purposes and goals were neglected. Yet these latter factors are worthy of exploration, too.

ORGANIZATIONAL STRUCTURES AS VEHICLES FOR INNOVATION

It is useful to consider a more static way of inducing innovation, by rearranging the division of activity among the participants in an organization, either temporarily or permanently. Three such structural arrangements will be discussed: (1) *ad hoc* devices, which provide for rearrangements on short-time bases, (2) role differentiations, and (3) subgroup specializations, of which the two latter arrangements establish divisions of labor with respect to the creative function in organization for longer periods of time.

My earlier analytic distinctions between process and structural ways of increasing innovation in organizations are arbitrary, for the effectiveness with which the structural devices operate will depend importantly upon the organizational processes which exist within these various structures. As one cannot consider all factors simultaneously, distortion of reality can be avoided if we bear in mind the intimate interrelations which hold between process and structure.

AD HOC DEVICES

It is feasible at times to establish special devices on an *ad hoc* basis to tap the innovation reservoirs of the organization. For many years now, suggestion systems have been signals for the flow of ideas from all members of the organization, even those involved in the most routine work. Based on the premise that each individual in the organization is potentially able to develop innovations for the improvement of the organization, the suggestion systems provide special occasions on which creativity is expected from all, with opportunity for special rewards. In one company, special creativity training has been found most useful in raising the productivity of the suggestion system, demonstrating that more innovations and innovations of higher quality emanate from this attempt to capture the creative impulse of all members of the organization by providing a special structural device to elicit and screen suggestions for improvement. Or, in communications terminology, increasing the quality of input in this fashion improves the quality of output.

More elaborate, perhaps, in the way of providing for *ad hoc* techniques to elicit innovation is the special conference called to solve particularly difficult problems—the "brain-storming" group. By attempting to separate evaluative activities from those fluency processes needed for the production of fresh ideas, the "brainstorm" session provides a seedbed for potential innovations. This device may be invoked at any time by any individual or co-operative set-grouping within the company. For the hour or two of its existence, it provides a structure within which there is opportunity for innovation. Grotesque and outlandish ideas are legitimized, even though, under ordinary conditions, such ideas would be ruled out of bounds.

Sometimes the *ad hoc* group is placed upon more permanent footing, as when junior members of management are constituted into a "shadow board," convening regularly just before each company board meeting on an identical agenda. Such "junior boards" have proved productive of innovations, often outside the ken of seasoned directors, whose long years of experience limit the founts of their creativity. Or, within the heart of the company, two or three persons may be freed for a month or two from regular duties to constitute a "task force" for the development of special insights on particularly vexing problems. These teams may be of special usefulness in spanning existing departmental structures in which rigid boundaries restrain the innovations of solutions which cut across previously established borders. The "task force" has been used constructively in the innovation of solutions in government, as witnessed in the work of the two (Hoover) Commissions on the Reorganization of the Federal Government.

CREATIVE ROLES

The society in which organizations are imbedded often provides norms prescribing special roles to the creative individual: He is given a tolerance and at times even a license to which more ordinary souls dare not presume. Sometimes the productive person gains such freedom by merely being different. These role prerogatives for the artist and "mad scientist" exist within the industrial and governmental organization, as well as within the society at large.

Most organizations have their "geniuses." These "oddballs" are allowed, even expected, to "get away" with much, as their transgressions are overlooked. They serve as gadflies, asking impertinent questions. Wise management cherishes men who plug unusual solutions into ongoing routines. Although I have never heard of a company that formally prescribed positions for the "Vice-President of the Offbeat," much can be done informally to take full advantage of rare creative talents.

The authority patterns may be so arranged as to legitimize such creative roles; in fact, I know of one company which requires that the vice-president of each division periodically identify its "idea men," so they may be placed in work positions possessing slack and located at frequently used communication junctures within the organization. Should the creative individual tend to isolate himself, efforts can be made to place him at points of access, so that the organization as a whole can tap his inventiveness. In fact, it is possible that the sheer fact of identifying the innovator will accentuate his propensity for creativeness—because roles usually involve reciprocated expectations.

GROUP SPECIALIZATION

Within organizations, one may establish on a more or less permanent basis groups of varying size whose central function is innovation.

These are small teams, such as a research group, which may be attached to a product division of a larger company. Its focus may be narrow, attention being given only to product improvement. Or the team may be attached to upper management, as in the case of an operations research unit, with authority to tackle the entire range of management problems, from accounting to maintenance.

There are larger groups, too. A whole division of a company might be devoted to "Research and Development." Or a special pilot plant may be constructed for purposes of innovation. Planning departments attempt to look ahead, and then to devise creative adaptations to predicted changes in the company's environment.

But, be the unit small or large, it must have adequate authority for its operation—it must be given slack—and it must communicate its output to other parts of the organization. Specialized groups for creative work within organizations are beset by many of the same organizational problems as are more routine operations. In fact, the organization as a whole will often attempt to encyst the disturbing, innovating unit within its midst.

This description of the way organizational processes capture the innovating groups is familiar to us all: Too many ideas are produced for development, so one must sit in judgment on which ideas will be allowed to move forward. Then, resource allocations must be made. And soon one has a decision apparatus of some magnitude for processing (in a somewhat orderly, bureaucratic way) the fruits of innovation.

Consider the problem of organizational slack: At first, there is ample free time, and the innovators roam far and wide. But only those ideas which are practical tend to be rewarded. As time goes on, the innovators identify more and more closely with the organization's goals. They then prohibit themselves from tackling problems with solutions that are remote, since the risks now seem hardly justified. In one "think company," the creative scientists have become too involved in their pressing tasks even to take vacations—and now the company purchases slack for its own employees by paying bonuses to those who are willing to take vacations, thus attempting to maintain their readiness for innovation year after year.

So one may speculate: Ad hoc *and permanent rearrangements of the group structures of organizations may be used to induce increased propensity for innovation.*

Just as each process may be used to enhance creativity—be it the way authority is exercised, the way organizational slack is utilized, or how the communication system functions—so both structure and process changes may serve as vehicles by which innovations are suppressed and reduced. As my remarks have indicated, the development of organizations to provide seedbeds for innovative activity by ordinary and extraordinary members, is a thoroughly complicated process—and I am sure that my speculations constitute but a bare beginning toward improved understanding of these fascinating problems in the organization of human behavior for creativity.

Discussion

"SLACK" AND "FREEDOM" FOR CREATORS VERSUS
ORGANIZATION, DISCIPLINE

Guetzkow

In terms of the "slack" notion: Sometimes one of the ways you try to motivate individuals in your research and development organization is by giving them free time as a bonus. They can have more free time for carrying out their own ideas. But if they are very good, they become identified with the organization and pretty soon they begin taking all of their slack time, which was supposed to be devoted to nondirected activities.

Ogilvy

How many institutions do you see around the country which encourage or even allow free-wheeling, irresponsible creators?

Guetzkow

I have not made a survey in this area, but there are not so many. This is the exception.

Alexander

Irving Langmuir (I think he was with General Electric) some years ago gave a radio talk in which he emphasized that the company gave him complete freedom: It did not tell him what to discover, but simply let him play. And he said that, according to his belief, that is the only source of real creativity—to let a man play around and not ask whether what he plans is useful or not. Assume that we had taken this experimental idea to the pharmaceutical industry some years ago, before the antibiotics had been discovered. If one company had had the idea, let us say, to engage a few ingenious bacteriologists then, they might have engaged Fleming to play around with whatever he wanted. (Only accidentally did he come across penicillin, and then it was not developed, because there was no apparent immediate use for it and costs were an impediment.)

Now, one can cite many such accidental discoveries, which later proved to be very useful, made in a playful experimental way. Would it not be a very lucrative and practical investment to select these potential creators in industrial organizations and pay them not to discover useful things, but to play around?

"USEFULNESS" AS A BARRIER

Originally, nothing is useful. The airplane was not discovered for passenger traffic, or for throwing bombs, but only to go up in the air—no other purpose. Nobody foresaw the practical potentialities. All great discoveries were made in this way: the calculus with which today bridges and skyscrapers are built was discovered without any practical purpose. So my question to you is: After it has been so clearly demonstrated that the creative process is not goal-directed but comes about by free, experimental, playful activity, why not simply select the right individuals and pay them to play, in their own fields with their own ideas, and hope that in ten or twenty years what they find will become practically important?

Peterson

Let me then, as an organization man, argue that I will have to have some devices by which these products of play are transformed into practice. It may be that there are hundreds of inventions, of creative acts, which have never been isolated, because no one has been able to translate them into anything "effective."

Meehl

Also, the number of men who would probably be available to "play around" is vastly in excess of the proportion who, if they were so permitted to play, would come up with something.

Alexander

We are counting on you to show us how to select them.

Berelson

Let me ask Mr. Guetzkow a question, but first let me say that it arises from a worry of mine about what he said about organizing for creativity. It sounds so much like what we academics think is the best of all possible worlds—namely, our own, the universities. According to Guetzkow's analysis, the universities should be the most creative institutions in the world, because they have everything he mentioned and all the criteria he set forth.

Relative to some other organizations, they have decentralization: Nobody can tell a department what to do; nobody can even tell a full professor what to do.

And they have slack built in. As soon as you have tenure, you have all the slack in the world to work with.

They have communication built in from the students, and you are supposed to spend a third of your time reading what other people have said.

The question is: Is there any real evidence that decentralization and slack do lead to creativity among the *ordinarily* creative people, as against the relatively rare, *extraordinarily* creative ones? I have the impression, for example, that the International Geophysical Year was a very successful year for science. That was a highly organized affair, if I read it correctly. How do I know that such a method is not just as creative as the other, if not more so?

Bower

I think there is evidence that playing around in industry is not generally productive. In the du Pont Company, where they study creativity from all angles, one of their psychiatrists who had conferences with their most productive people found that when they were put into a rigid pattern and told what to go after they produced more than if they were just playing around, hoping to stumble onto something.

Alexander

But that is productivity, not creativity.

Bower

Productivity of creative ideas.

Ogilvy

The same thing is true in art. Great creative work in art, I believe, has almost never been created by rich artists who were free to play around. It has been created by very poor artists who had to create something very good in a hurry to eat. Handel wrote *The Messiah* because he was broke.

Alexander

I would not accept that as cause and effect.

Ogilvy

Well, I do. I've been thinking about this for years, and I say the greatest discipline of all is the discipline of breadwinning upon the creator.

Barron

I suggest a distinction between behavior and inner experience as relevant here. Frequently, the actual work is done not at the time you are making the marks on the paper, or doing the things that eventuate palpably in a product; the work is done at other times, when the mind is genuinely at play. This playing time cannot be put down into this or that period of the day or under specific conditions when you are paid to play. Play is a general condition favoring fruitful combinations.

URGENCY

Peterson

I am surprised that you do not take into account the factor of urgency. It has been my observation in advertising that people often work on something for years and then some urgent situation comes up—for example, the night before the presentation for the client—and it suddenly comes through. Now, in our case, we had an 8-millimeter electric-eye movie camera in development, and we anticipated that it would take about three years to complete. Then one day, the marketing vice-president decided to try a different technique. He took something down to the engineers and said, "I just got an announcement that our competitors have an 8-millimeter electric-eye camera!" Within twenty-four hours, they had a completely different approach. I wonder just what is the role of urgency?

3

The Environment of the Innovating Organization: Some Conjectures and Proposals

(EDITED COMMENTS)

ROBERT K. MERTON

In asking me to reflect on the connections between the innovative organization and its environment, Gary Steiner managed to be both perceptive and sadistic: perceptive, in identifying an important focus for inquiry into innovation which is ordinarily lost to sight; sadistic, in knowing that even on the most latitudinarian view, there has been precious little investigation of the subject. In effect, he is asking me to look at the environment of the innovating organization and to report what I see through the dense sociological clouds, all the while keeping my feet firmly planted in the thin air of sociological speculation. This is a foolhardy enterprise at best. To make it just a little less hazardous, I'll limit myself to some scattered remarks.

THE SUCCESSIVE CONTEXTS OF INNOVATION

I shall begin by trying to locate the subject within the conceptual structure of this seminar. It is situated at the outermost limits of a series of successive contexts, at the center of which is the *act* of innovation. By this I understand a socially valued departure from past practice or thought. For certain purposes, innovative acts can be treated as though they were self-contained units of behavior, with their own phenomenology, psychology, and sociology. Inquiry on this plane calls for intensive descriptions of innovative behavior, together with analytical reconstructions of the psychological processes and the social interactions giving rise to it.

The immediate context of the innovative act is provided by the notion of the creative *man,* to which Paul Meehl addressed himself. This type of man is usually identified empirically by sampling his behavior. Formal testing or less controlled observation finds that he innovates more than the run of others with whom he is being compared. The core problem is therefore to devise ways of identifying potentials for creative work. A particular act of innovation will be differently interpreted when it is a lone specimen and when it is only one of a series of innovations by the same man. From the standpoint of concentric contexts, then, the innovative man provides a context for the innovative act.

The next context, which Harold Guetzkow examined, is the *milieu* of the innovative man. This is made up of the people with whom an innovative man is in direct contact and of the patterns of interaction among them. The core problem here is to specify the attributes of milieus that affect the rate and kinds of innovation by men with comparable potentials for creative work. Harriet Zuckerman at Columbia is now engaged in a study of all Nobel Prize winners in the sciences now living in the United States, in order to identify the patterns of collaboration which they have found particularly fruitful. The studies of differing styles of research supervision belong to this same tradition of examining the effects of differing milieus upon innovation in science Among other things, these inquiries hang a question mark on the tacit assumption that creative potential and creative realization are pretty much the same.

Beyond this context is that of the *organization,* which is made up of many milieus. For most people in organizations, most of the time, the organization *is* their own milieu. This is part of their direct, day-by-day experience of the organization. Nevertheless, we know that organizations differ in the kinds of local milieus they generate. Some are evocative, providing a system of direct and unplanned rewards for significant ideas, facilitating their effective transmission, and so generating further ideas. Other organizations provide a lethal environment for new ideas, which are regarded as disruptive.

As a final context for the innovative act is the subject assigned me: *the environment of the organization.* Pursuing the logic of successive contexts, we recognize that just as human beings have their distinctive environments, so in turn do organizations. But the theory of organizations developed in the last generation or so has largely neglected the interchanges between organizations and their environment. It has focused instead on the internal structure and operation of organizations. In this respect, the developing sociological theory of organizations differs greatly from economic theory which, from its beginnings, centered on the environment of individual firms by dealing with price systems, markets, and mechanisms of allocation. (It might be argued by some that the theory of social systems developed chiefly by Talcott Parsons and his associates deals with the environments of social subsystems. But the Parsonian scheme of analysis has not been brought to the point where its beneficiaries can apply it to the subject in hand, the environment of innovating organizations.)

The notion of successive contexts makes it clear that the concept of the innovative act or the innovative man is a very high abstraction from concrete reality. It abstracts from the milieu, the organization, and the organizational environment. It treats the innovative man as though he were entirely exempt from the social and interpersonal conditions under which he lives and works and so expresses his capacities no matter how much these conditions vary. The abstraction is of course justified if it is deliberately and temporarily instituted. But it should be recognized as an assumption, not taken as a fact. It is by no means self-evident that Newton, Darwin, or Kelvin would have made significant scientific contributions had they lived in *any* kind of social environment. Had they been born into Bantu culture, they might still have been innovative but the character of their innovations would surely have been different.

Once we consider such a limiting case in the range of variation of environments, we are forced to recognize the high abstractions employed when we pretend for a while that individual men of genius will express themselves in much the same way under any conditions. We see that the Robinson Crusoe of innovation is as much a fiction as the Robinson Crusoe of old-fashioned economics.

The same act of innovation, then, can be interpreted within the successive contexts of the man, the milieu, the organization, and the environment of the organization. The creative man may feel himself at home in his milieu or be at odds with it; the milieu may accord or conflict with the environing organization; the organization may have any of various kinds of environments, ranging from those made up of many organizations of the same type, through progressively limited numbers to the case of duopoly (where each of the two organizations provides the major environment for the other), to the limiting case of monopoly.

THE INTERCHANGE OF ORGANIZATION AND ENVIRONMENT

Among the processes that connect organizations and their environments, the most conspicuous is the interchange of personnel. The mobility of men represents both input and output of organizations, and this gives rise to interesting questions.

The first question involves the possibility of a growing gap between available trained talent and the accelerating demand for such talent that results from the increased organizational complexity of society. Suppose we start with the premise (actually, it is a mere extrapolation) that so long as mankind manages not to eliminate itself altogether, populations will continue to grow.

Now, so far as the scattered evidence permits us to say, the *proportion* of a population with creative potential does not greatly change, so that the absolute number of potentially creative men grows at about the same pace as the population itself. At the same time, accumulated knowledge seems to grow exponentially (see the work of Gerald Holton, Derek Price, and others). This suggests that the demand for trained talent tends to outrun the increase in supply, giving rise to greater competition for such talent among enlarged numbers of enlarged organizations. This pits a premium on devising means both for recruiting talent and for increasing the extent to which innovative potential can be realized.

The gap may help to account for the phenomenon that organizations of every kind try to modify their internal environment, in order to induce talented persons to join them and convert more of their potential into actuality. (For example, scan the advertisements for engineers, scientists, and mathematicians in the columns of the *Scientific American,* and note how industrial organizations set out their claims to provide ever more benign environments for intellectual work.) That organizations should energetically compete for men of high talent seems self-evident; each organization stands to gain by doing so. But what is far from evident, and even paradoxical, is that the same pattern of lively competition is found in the free professions (which are largely staffed by independent practitioners rather than organized firms). By examining the pressure for recruiting top talent in the free professions, we can better see that it involves more than an effort to improve one's own competitive position.

RECRUITMENT OF TALENT TO THE FREE PROFESSIONS

At first glance, it seems evident that "every profession should try to attract men and women of the greatest potentiality for good work." Yet the value attached to the objective tends to conceal an underlying paradox; for when individual practitioners advocate this objective, as they commonly do, they are in effect calling for more severe competition for themselves. The more capable the new recruits, the more disadvantaged is each practitioner in the competition for clients. By way of comparison, it might seem a bit odd, in a system of competitive business enterprise, for each firm to do all it could to induce men of talent to set up rival firms in their own field. Were individual professionals geared exclusively to rational self-seeking, they would try to halt the flow of highly qualified recruits into their profession, so that their own trained capacities would yield them greater returns.

The paradox remains, of course, only so long as it is assumed that the professions consist of practitioners each trying exclusively to improve his own economic prospects. The essential point is that the professions are not so constituted. Practitioners do want to advance their economic interests, and sometimes they are better at it than their brethren in business; but they are also members of a professional collectivity, with which they identify themselves. They want to have the knowledge on which the profession rests advanced as rapidly as possible; they want long-standing problems of practice solved. Their short-run personal interest may not be served by the great emphasis on recruiting new personnel of the highest available capacities, but their collective purposes are. Only if this is recognized, can we resolve the paradox of men avidly seeking to improve the quality of their potential competitors.

This also helps us understand the almost universal complaint of the professions that they do not get enough recruits of high caliber. That this complaint is widespread can be documented to the point of acute boredom. A spokesman for American medicine in 1946 referred to the "clear evidence of the need for more superior students in medical schools." A decade later, a conference of physicians claimed that the condition had grown steadily worse and that "perhaps what is happening is that others get in there and get the students away by either earlier attention to their needs or by glamor. Perhaps we have to go out and glamorize medicine a little more for the A student."

The complaint of the physicians is echoed by the lawyers. Not enough men and women of real capacity are entering the law. As a result, it is said, resources of the profession are misspent in trying to train students without the needed potential for excellence. The lament of the physicians and the lawyers finds its counterpart among the social scientists. It is reported, with implications apparently so clear that they need no statement, that "even in the graduate schools, nearly one-half of the social science majors come from the lower two-thirds of their undergraduate classes." Plainly, the social scientists too are deprived of their due share of talent.

What begins as a concert of complaints *within* each profession ends in a cacophony of complaints as all the other professions join in the same dirge, but in different key. Engineers, social workers, dentists, architects, chemists, librarians, nurses, pharmacists, and veterinarians, all persuaded that the needs of their profession for personnel of high quality are not being met, add their voices of disillusionment and despair to those of the physicians, lawyers, and social scientists.

So long as the complaint of each profession is considered without reference to the other professions, it seems to have some basis in fact. When we find all of the professions arguing that they are not getting their appropriate share from the reservoir of talent, however, an interesting question arises: Where are all these talented people going? It may be, of course, that they are entering the non-professional occupations. But this does not seem to stand up under inspection, for we find representatives of business firms and of government engaging in the same complaints. In fact, they hold that too much available talent is being siphoned off by the professions.

The fact that all the professions complain about the caliber of their recruits, that all maintain they are not getting *enough* of the highest quality, suggests in part that there may not be enough talent to go around. If talent is generally in short supply, then each profession will have a hard time trying to recruit a sufficiency of talent. This is one possible aspect of the problem: Growing requirements outrun available talent. But, at most, it is only one aspect, for the spokesmen for the various professions do not suggest that we are a nation of mediocrities and that that is why each profession is understaffed in point of quality. Rather, each emphasizes the thesis that they are not getting *enough* of the supply of talent assumed to be available.

The puzzle can be resolved by putting the question a little more definitely and then examining its implications. How many talented recruits to a profession will be judged, by members of the profession, as "enough"? Whatever the measures of talent—intelligence tests or demonstrated aptitude, grades in school or class standing—the question remains: "How many is enough?" Should medicine or law or engineering be recruiting *only* students of "A" grade? Or would 90 per cent of A students be enough? Or 80, or 50, or 10 per cent? To raise the question is to glimpse a fact that helps explain the chorus of complaints about an insufficiency of talented recruits to any profession: *There are not and cannot easily be commonly accepted standards of the* appropriate *distribution of talent among the professions.* Almost any proportion of talent in a profession, short of full saturation, will be conceived as "not enough."

There can be no settled frame of reference for assessing, with genuine agreement among the professions, the proportion of talented recruits judged "appropriate" for each profession. One set of criteria for "sufficient" supply of talent for a profession might seem to be a higher caliber of recruits today than in the past; but this is plainly unstable. For example, in 1955, physicians deplored the decline in the proportion of A students entering medicine, from 40 per cent in 1950 to 16 per cent in 1955. Yet back in 1950, they were still complaining that this was patently not enough. And we can hazard the guess that if the proportion of able students should return to the previous high level, it would not result in the leaders of the profession claiming that, finally, enough talent was being recruited. What holds for medicine holds in its way for the other professions; comparison of present and past situations does not provide a stable basis for judging the "adequacy" of supply.

Another possible frame of reference might be provided by comparisons with other professions. It might be supposed that the professions with the highest proportions of talented recruits would come to believe that they had enough. But this, too, turns out to be a deceptively stable basis for judgment. Among the professions, medicine has long had the highest known proportion of talented recruits; yet this has not quieted the complaints. Why should it not have even more? How much higher a proportion of A students should be recruited by medicine or law or physics than by engineering or architecture or sociology? And are the architects, engineers, or social scientists expected to concur in the judgment that medicine should receive the lion's share of talent? If, in each age, professions were to accept their relative standing as the appropriate one, then physicians and surgeons would scarcely have advanced from the low status assigned them in centuries past. Each profession aspires to improve its collective capacities for solving the problems which are in its province, and each profession aspires to enlarge the social recognition of its accomplishments. Professions will therefore not readily accept the current distribution of talent as the appropriate one.

The fact is that no profession will remain content with the caliber of its personnel or with its current accomplishments. This is not because professionals are by nature discontented people; nor because they are individually driven by ambition; nor is it a result of the personal proclivities of those in the profession; it is a result of the commitments of the profession itself.

The people manning each profession are culturally committed to advance the knowledge, work, and standard of practice in the profession, and to do this *without assignable limit*. There are no fixed aspirations which can be met, once and for all. The aspirations incorporated in the professional ethos are insatiable. There can never be "enough" talent, therefore, to satisfy these ever advancing aspirations. In effect, the professions are committed to unending discontent with what they have collectively done and with what they are prepared to do. To declare that they do not have their "fair share" of talented recruits is only to reaffirm this commitment. That is why the question "How much talent in a profession is enough?" is a symbolic question, deceptively meaningful in syntactical form but without a determinate answer. The allocation of talent among the professions is the resultant of imperfectly identified forces of competition. My welfare-economist friends tell me, moreover, that it is not all clear just what would be an optimum allocation judged from the standpoint of advancing the public welfare.

For individual organizations, the recruitment of men of talent and the rate of innovation tend to be mutually reinforcing. The innovative organization recruits men of creative potential and helps them convert that potential into productive innovation by providing them with an effective environment *within* the organization. As the flow of innovation becomes visible to others in the environment *of* the organization, it facilitates the recruitment of new men of talent. The cycle is renewed and amplified in magnitude. You then get the phenomenon of the leading organization: the leading business firm, the leading university, the leading research laboratory. In the jargon of our trade, these organizations become role-models and reference groups for individuals and other organizations in the environment.

The nineteenth-century French sociologist, Le Play, once remarked that the most important product to come out of the mine was the miner. Adapting this remark, we might say that the most important product of the innovative organization is the men that it produces. At least, this seems to be the import of the well-known fact that the leading organization in a particular field is particularly subject to the attempted raiding of personnel by rival organizations. Such attempted raids are a collective tribute to the innovative organization.

Even when successful, they are not disadvantageous to that organization. There is nothing quite like losing a few topflight men to other organizations to stimulate a thoroughgoing examination of the organization that could not hold them. Moreover, it is not at all clear that an innovative organization thrives best in an environment where its outstanding position remains unchallenged. Occasional losses of key personnel or superior innovations by competing organizations provide the stimulus to improve the internal environment (*milieu intérieur,* in the words of Claude Bernard) in an effort to cope with the challenge of the external environment (*milieu extérieur*). From the standpoint of the larger social system, there can be an excessive concentration of talent in particular organizations. Their wider dispersion presumably tends to result in a greater amount of effective innovation (and its practical utilization) within the system as a whole. A particular case in point will illustrate this line of analysis.

THE FUNCTIONS OF REDUNDANCY IN SCIENTIFIC DISCOVERY

We hear a good deal of talk nowadays about the dangers of "wasteful duplication" in scientific investigation. So much is this the case that the two words have almost been cast into a single idea: duplication of scientific research is itself evidence of "waste." I would like to challenge this idea, as I have been doing for some time. I propose that a certain, though still an indeterminate, amount of redundancy in scientific research advances effective innovation in science.

The history of science is peppered with unnumbered cases of the same discovery having been made by two or more men working independently. (In a sample of 264 of these, Dr. Elinor Barber and I found that most of them—179—were doublets; 51, triplets; 17, quadruplets; 6, quintuplets; 8, sextuplets. We also found one septuplet and two nonaries, in which most of the nine independent co-discoverers presumably were willing to entertain the hypothesis that if any one of them had not arrived at the discovery, it would have been made in any case.)

Now, this sort of thing has usually led to the conclusion that these multiple discoveries were "inevitable," in the sense that if one scientist had not made the discovery, another would have (as we know from the fact that he did). But this "inevitability" holds only under certain, still poorly identified, conditions. In cases of multiples, we ordinarily know only of the several scientists who actually made the same discovery. We usually do *not* know how many others worked on the same problem without solving it. In other words, we really do not know how many scientists, of what degrees of competence, are required to work on a particular problem in order to provide a high probability that it will be solved in a given span of time. We do not know how much redundant effort is needed to achieve the result. If the number of scientists working on a problem is progressively reduced, through what may at first seem to be a rational policy of allocating support to only one research group, or to only a few, then the solution may become anything but inevitable, at least during a specified interval.

That replication of scientific effort is wasteful may be true when the problems in hand are fairly routine and bound to yield to a solution once a scientist elects to work seriously on them. But these are, of course, the small change of science. When it comes to basic problems, which are far from routine and, once solved, have far-reaching implications, duplication, triplication, or a higher multiplication of effort may be anything but wasteful.

Nor do we know that the *same number* of scientists of given competence will produce the same results when they are all in one organization working together on the problem and when they are distributed in several research groups within several organizations. We still have a good deal to learn about the optimum distribution of scientific research.

It would be ironic if current planned efforts to achieve efficiency in creative scientific work were self-defeating. In the past, when the support of science was slight and thinly dispersed, the efficiency-of-the-seemingly-inefficient pattern resulted in many multiple discoveries partly because a fair number of scientists, often not knowing that this was so, elected to work on the same problems. A superficial notion of "wasteful duplication" might result in a pattern of the inefficiency-of-the-seemingly-efficient, by so allocating funds for research as drastically to restrict the range of scientists at work on the same problem, thus reducing the probability not only of multiple independent solutions but of any solution whatsoever at the time.

The fallacy of assuming that all replicative effort in science is wasteful is much like the fallacy that has long afflicted the interpretation of multiple discoveries in science. This fallacy made use of an old-fashioned concept of redundancy—strictly old-fashioned, for it has been going the rounds of philosophers, historians, and sociologists for a couple of hundred years. The argument goes as follows: The occurrence of a multiple discovery is proof in itself that all but one of the actual discoverers were redundant (i.e., superfluous). For if all the other co-discoverers had not made the discovery, it would have been made in any case. Ergo, the fact of multiple discovery attests their superfluity.

Now, this old notion of redundancy merged two distinct meanings. For one thing, it meant abundant, copious, plentiful—in the special sense of having more resources than are abstractly required to achieve a particular purpose. For another, it meant superfluous in the special sense of that which can be *safely* done away with.

The merger of these two meanings smuggled in an extravagant

fallacy. This was the absolutist fallacy of assuming that something was either redundant or not, once and for all, and irrespective of the situations in which it is found. The newer, more differentiated concept of redundancy is relative and statistical. It recognizes that efficiency increases the prospect of error, that redundancy (or reduced efficiency) makes for safety from error. It leads us to think of and then, in certain cases, to measure a functionally optimum amount of redundancy under specified conditions: that amount which will approximate a maximum probability of achieving the wanted outcome but not so great an amount that the last increment will fail appreciably to enlarge that probability.

Multiple discoveries in science constitute a particular kind of redundancy that can be thought of in terms of the new, fruitful concept which opens our eyes to what was presumably there all along, but which went unnoticed. There is safety as well as truth in numbers of similar independent discoveries.

This concept also enables us to see the fallacy of the apparently cogent thesis that, in multiple discoveries, all but one are superfluous. This can now be seen as logically airtight and sociologically false. For we have now to ask: superfluous for what? For the discovery to have been made? That can hardly be questioned, since others did in fact make the same discovery.

But science, as an ongoing institution, is more than the finding of new knowledge by this or that person. Science is a *shared* body of knowledge. The older view assumes what remains to be demonstrated. It assumes that a discovery has only to be made in order for it to enter the public domain of science.

But these—the discovery by an individual and its acceptance by other scientists—are not identical, as the history of science attests. Often, a new idea or a new empirical finding has been achieved *and* published, only to go unnoticed by others, until it is later uncovered or independently rediscovered, and only then is it incorporated into the science. After all, that is what we mean by rediscovery: The signals provided by a discovery are lost in the noise of the great information system that constitutes science, and so must be issued anew. With the great increase in the bulk of publications, there may be greater danger that the originally published contribution will be overlooked for a time. (The young Nobel laureate, Mossbauer, reports that this was at first the case with the contribution which is now described as his own.)

But multiple discoveries—that is, redundant ones—have a greater chance of being perceived by others in the social system of science and so, then and there, of affecting its immediate further development. From this standpoint, multiple discoveries are redundant, but not necessarily superfluous. When the all-but-one versions of the same discovery are described as superfluous, this refers only to the personal experience of the discoverer: He has indeed made the discovery; it is a genuine psychological experience. But such a description neglects the sociological components of discovery which deal not only with the probability of the discovery having been made in the first place but, once made, of its being assimilated as a functional part of the science.[1]

PHILISTINES AND CREATIVE MEN IN ORGANIZATIONS

Hal Guetzkow pointed out that a wise management in any organization will provide a place for creative men, for men with ideas that might pan out. Put in this way, this sounds at first like a prime candidate for a commonplace: In the abstract, who will admit to a policy of squelching creative men? But organizational behavior is not a matter only of abstract policies. Administrators do not ordinarily see themselves as blocking "the creative man"; once they have fixed this tag on a man, they are in effect announcing that they will give him a good deal of leeway. Instead, they will see themselves only as making certain that a man does his job as he should, that he not be allowed to upset the applecart by ignoring rules of the organization, that he not get too far out of line. After all, it is no fun to put up with the deviant, who seems to take a perverse pleasure in doing things his own way rather than in the way established by administrative wisdom.

But it is just at this point that we come to the question of the possible functions of the Philistine for the creative man in an organiza-

---

[1] Since reporting these ideas on the functions of redundancy in science to this seminar, I have incorporated them in a paper, "Resistance to the systematic study of multiple discoveries in science," *Archives Européennes de Sociologie* (1963), IV, 237–82, at 245–48.

tion. The usual assumption (as persuasively argued by William Whyte, for example) maintains it as practically self-evident that the two types of men—the Philistine and the creative man—will necessarily clash. The first are the routinists who put a premium on the stability and predictability of the organizational environment; the second are the deviants, who aim for new ways of achieving old objectives and for creating new aims altogether.

But, as Dorothy Emmet has implied in her important book *Function, Purpose and Powers,* certain types of men who manage organizations, though themselves anything but creative, provide the kind of organizational framework in which creative men flourish. The general idea holds that creative men are not at their best unless they are working within a social framework which they can take for granted while getting on with their own activity. The routine observance of norms in the organization by most people most of the time provides such a framework. Within it, the ordinary and the extraordinary members of an organization become necessary to one another, rather than being inevitably opposed. The more stable and secure the organization, the greater the possibility of allowing for exceptional ability to go its way. Within such an organization, conflicting types of personality can become mutually supporting. Each meets different functional requirements of the organization—order and change, stability and innovation, organizationally patterned behavior and departures from these patterns. Administrative men can provide the stable environment in which difficult but creative men can best realize their potential.

Discussion

Bruner

I would like to add one conjecture: I am struck, now that we have taken Francis Bacon as one of our culture heroes, by his remark to the effect that "neither hands nor mind nor heart increases the power of intellect in any major degree but, rather, what is needed is the means, the instruments, the techniques."

With respect to the problem of creative technique, let me turn to the question of parallel discovery. If you take a good, close look, you find that one of the things that makes parallel discovery possible is a prior discovery; something that has now become part of a tradition of technique. In the field of formal logic, for the eight or ten years following the development of the notion of truth tables, you will find all kinds of very, very handsome discoveries about various techniques of proof, methods of formalization, and the rest of it—parallels such that the race for publication in the philosophical journals was thick and fast.

To take a current example: We can be sure that in the next ten years a great deal will be done by way of controlling the spread of pests in various areas of the world, because somebody has worked up the bright idea of irradiating female insects who can go into the situation and essentially divert the male from his proper function—or irradiating males and making them sterile. This is going to lead to a whole new technology, full of technological innovation.

With respect to talent, it is quite clear that before Leibnitz and Newton, talent could only go so far without the calculus. But if you put that technique into society prior to the performance of a creative act, you find that a great many people can ride along on the shoulders of a Leibnitz or a Newton. So that even though you may say—by the current social standards at a given time—that the proportion of talent is not increasing, the fact of the matter is that *what we call the proportion of talent has not much relation to the number of people who are capable of wielding the powerful techniques that make subsequent discoveries possible.*

So, then, to your list of "act, man, milieu, organization, and society," I would like to put in one that is prior to the creative act and speak of a "fruitful technique," defining "technique" very broadly to include instrumental ideas.

Merton

The best testimony to our agreement is that the portion of the remarks I suppressed all have to do with "cultural accumulation," which I think is essentially what Jerry Bruner refers to. In every case of multiple, independent discovery I have examined, we find a prior state of the art reaching a level such that the next step becomes simultaneously evident to a number of people. In terms of our subject here, the question is one of the time at which these next developments become known outside a particular organization. You see, your observation about the new technique presupposes something, namely, general knowledge of the technique. In some fields, that happens at once; in others, it is restricted and delayed. You get a certain "lead time" which gives a higher rate of innovation within a particular organization, until the technique becomes more generally known.

Steiner

I am impressed with the basic similarity between Paul Meehl's criterion of creativity and Bob Merton's; in both cases, we have a social and, therefore, in some sense, objective criterion for the creative act. Merton said that "raiding" constitutes, in a sense, the ultimate criterion applied to an organization. When other organizations think they are creative enough, they try to steal those people away and that means we have creativity. In Paul Meehl's usage, the social criterion applies within the firm. When peers feel that an individual is creative, then he is.

All of this is certainly objective and a way out of the criterion problem. But it seems in some sense paradoxical, because it means that when people who have a stake in the status quo believe something to be creative, it really is—and this runs counter to at least some notions of a more subjective psychological definition. One could suppose it is precisely when those people with an investment in the status quo think something is *not,* in effect, creative, that it is likely to be so.

4

In Pursuit of the Creative Process

MILTON ROKEACH

Our collective strivings to understand the nature of the creative process and the conditions which foster it bring to mind the image of a toddler chasing after a beautiful butterfly. At the last moment, the butterfly always manages to elude its pursuer, and then the chase begins all over again. So it is with the creative process. If we say it represents the ability to think original thoughts; that is, thoughts not thought by most people; someone is bound to ask whether a psychotic, thinking original thoughts, is by that token creative. If we then add that creativity also involves the emergence of something valuable, someone is bound to ask: Valuable for whom?

CREATIVE THINKING AND THINKING IN GENERAL

Because the creative process is so difficult to conceptualize, explain, predict, or measure, we pursue it in various ways in the hope of getting a bit closer to it. A favorite place to start is to look eagerly at the introspections of mathematicians, scientists, artists, and poets in the hope that they will tell us how they go about creating, inventing, or discovering. For example, Hadamard, in his interesting book, *The Psychology of Invention in the Mathematical Field*,[1] tells us that what he has to say is based only on reports from men who have made significant discoveries. But the processes he describes often turn out to be the well-known stages characteristic of all thinking (preparation, incubation, illumination, etc.) rather than the stages of uniquely

---

[1] New York: Dover Press, 1945.

66

creative thinking—a confusion between the specific and the generic. Similarly, Einstein writes, "I lived in solitude in the country and noticed how the monotony of a quiet life stimulates the creative mind."[2] We know from recent work on sensory deprivation[3] that solitude and monotony can stimulate all minds, creative or not.

PROCESS AND PRODUCT

In one of the most illuminating and comprehensive reviews[4] of various approaches to the study of thinking and creativity to appear to date, we hear the opinion expressed that the identification of the creative process is not probable. "I think it unlikely," Taylor writes, "that we shall ever be able to differentiate sharply between creative and uncreative processes, between those processes that occur in thinking resulting in novel and worthwhile ideas and those that occur in thinking that fails to produce such results (p. 115)." It it thus no wonder that Taylor and many others who are empirically oriented take the position that creative thinking is "best defined not in terms of process but in terms of product. Examination of a variety of proposed definitions of creativity indicates that although there is disagreement, common to most of them are the ideas of novelty and worth. Novelty or originality is ordinarily regarded as a necessary but not a sufficient condition; if what is new is to be regarded as creative, it must also be of value by some criterion. Creativity may best be defined as that thinking which results in the production of ideas (or other products) that are both novel and worthwhile (p. 108)."

The arguments over the relative merits of the *process* and *product* approaches are too well known to require restatement here. These arguments come up time and again in discussions on creativity. See, for example, the report of a recent symposium.[5] But I think it is fair to say that to approach creativity by defining product rather than

[2]A. Einstein, *Out of My Later Years* (New York: Philosophical Library, 1950).
[3]*Sensory Deprivation*, ed. P. Solomon, *et al.* (Cambridge, Mass.: Harvard University Press, 1961).
[4]D. W. Taylor, "Thinking and Creativity," *Annals of the New York Academy of Sciences*, LXV (1960), 108–27.
[5]*Creativity and Its Cultivation*, ed. H. H. Anderson (New York: Harper & Row, 1959).

process is generally favored by those actively engaged in empirical research on creativity, with the possible exception of Guilford[6] who uses a factor analytic approach.

The most favored approach is first to isolate people who are reliably known to have produced ideas and products regarded as novel and worth while and then proceed to study background variables, personality traits, and personality organization in the hope of finding differences which distinguish those who produce valuable innovations from those who do not. Because the creative process is so elusive, the emphasis shifts away from a concern with the creative process as such to personality processes that are in general thought to differentiate creative from less creative people; that is, the emphasis shifts away from the necessary and sufficient conditions involved in the creative process to a more general description of personality patterns associated with creativity.

The "Inside-Outside" Problem

The theoretical difficulty inherent in the objective study of the creative process is not a unique one; it is one we have encountered before. It is a difficulty which Floyd Allport[7] has diagnosed as the "inside-outside" problem, and it also comes up in discussions of the nature of normality, mental health, and conformity. Here, too, one can discern "process" approaches and "product" approaches. And, here too, depending upon which approach one takes, one comes up with sometimes conflicting notions about the nature and scope of the phenomenon, the conditions which give rise to it, how to bring it out or modify it, and how to measure it.

The need for an "outside" approach to the "inside"

My own feeling about process versus product approaches, or about whether to approach creativity from the "inside" or "outside," is that neither approach is satisfying if we value theoretical understanding as well as empirical prediction. In the one case, there is a

---

[6]J. P. Guilford, "Structure of Intellect," *Psychology Bulletin*, LIII (1956), 267–93; "Basic Conceptual Problems in Psychology of Thinking," *Annals of New York Academy of Sciences*, XCI (1960), 6–21.

[7]F. H. Allport, *Theories of Perception and the Concept of Structure* (New York: Alexander Wiley & Sons, 1955).

gain in intuitive richness at the expense of objectivity; in the other case, objectivity at the expense of richness. What seems to be required, ideally, is a way of thinking about creativity which permits an objective "outside" view of the subjective "inside," so that neither richness nor objectivity is lost. In Brunswik's terms, the ideal to strive for is a "tough-minded" approach to a "tender-minded" problem.

I will try here to formulate the problem of creativity in a way which, hopefully, will permit us a somewhat closer "outside" view of the "inside." What must happen in the mind of a person in order that his responses, the products of his thought, will be regarded as novel and/or worth while? And how would such processes be distinguishable from other thought processes leading to responses or products that would not be so regarded? What operational procedures —tests or tasks—must be followed in order that the various attributes of creative thinking may be revealed to the extent they are there and fail to be revealed to the extent they are not there?

I will try to address myself to those questions from a standpoint presented elsewhere[8] on the organization of belief systems, the theory and measurement of belief systems along a continuum from open to closed, and the study of individual differences in the cognitive functioning of persons characterized as having relatively open and closed belief systems. While this work was not specifically directed to the problem of creativity, I believe that what we have learned from it is directly relevant to the understanding of the creative process, in that, on the one hand, it deals with differences in the thought processes of open- and close-minded persons in problem-solving situations, and, on the other, it throws light on the thought processes of conformity and independence.

CONFORMITY, INDEPENDENCE, AND CREATIVITY

What have conformity and independence got to do with it? I have often noted that, in discussions on creativity, the term which is most frequently used to refer to its opposite is *conformity*. This strikes me first as strange and second as theoretically interesting, because the opposite of conformity is not creativity but independence. For ex-

---

[8]M. Rokeach, *The Open and Closed Mind: Investigations into the Nature of Belief Systems and Personality Systems* (New York: Basic Books, 1960).

ample, those subjects in Asch's[9] experiments who were able to resist the group pressure to yield can readily be called independent but by no stretch of the imagination can they be called creative. I mention this peculiar imbalance among the three concepts not because I think they ought not to be linked in this way but, quite the contrary, because the imbalance points to the possibility that the process of conformity is indeed an "opposite" of creativity, and the process of independence is indeed an "opposite" of conformity. This statement will make better sense if we conceive of the processes of conformity, independence, and creativity as representing a single dimension from lower-order to higher-order mental activity.

There are several implications which seem to follow if this view of the unidimensional character of conformity-independence-creativity is a valid one: (1) An adequate description of the process of conformity will describe those processes which do not occur in creative thinking and thus at least say what the creative process is not. (2) An adequate description of what it means to be independent will represent a part-theory of the creative process to the extent that independence is a necessary condition of creative thinking. (3) An adequate description of the creative process will also contain within it a description of independence and conformity processes.

What I am suggesting, then, is that we follow a heuristic strategy in which, instead of starting with the baffling problem of what goes on in the creative process, we start with processes somewhat better understood[10] and which are believed to be intrinsically related to it.

FROM CONFORMITY TO INDEPENDENCE

THE ABILITY TO DISTINGUISH INFORMATION FROM SOURCE

It has been proposed elsewhere[11] that persons characterized as having relatively open and closed belief systems differ fundamentally in terms of a single cognitive process; namely, the ability to dis-

---

[9]S. E. Asch, *Social Psychology* (New York: Prentice-Hall, 1952). "Studies of Independence and Conformity: I. Minority of One against Unanimous Majority," *Psychological Monographs,* LXX, No. 416 (1956).

[10]M. Rokeach, "Authority, Authoritarianism, and Conformity," in *Conformity and Deviation,* ed. E. A. Berg and B. M. Bass (New York: Harper & Row, 1961).

[11]M. Rokeach and F. Restle, "Fundamental Distinction between Open and Closed Systems," in Rokeach, *Open and Closed Mind.*

criminate between message and source and to evaluate and to act on the information received *from* the source and information *about* the source on their own intrinsic merits. With this basic definition as a point of departure, it is possible to generate or derive a number of other cognitive variables as defining characteristics of open and closed belief systems, and from these derivations further to generate many attitudinal items to make up a scale—the Dogmatism Scale— which reliably measures individual differences in the extent to which belief systems are open or closed.

There are many differences in the cognitive functioning of relatively open and closed persons,[12] which can be interpreted in terms of this ability to discriminate information from source, but direct evidence regarding such cognitive differences has not been available until recently. Vidulich and Kaiman[13] have shown that, in the autokinetic experiment, closed-minded subjects agreed significantly more with high-status confederates and significantly less with low-status confederates.

By contrast, the judgments of autokinetic movement made by open-minded subjects were independent of the prior judgments made by high- or low-status confederates. More decisive is a recent study by Powell,[14] who was able to measure directly a person's ability to discriminate information from source by means of Osgood's semantic differential technique.[15] Powell's open-minded and closed-minded subjects rated Kennedy and Nixon and three sets of statements made by Kennedy and Nixon during the 1960 presidential campaign. By measuring the distance in the semantic space between ratings of message and ratings of source, Powell found that open- and closed-minded persons differed consistently, sharply, and significantly in their ability to discriminate messages from sources.

This fundamental difference in the cognitive functioning of relatively open- and closed-minded persons is further revealed in certain

---

[12]Rokeach, *Open and Closed Mind.*

[13]R. N. Vidulich and I. P. Kaiman, "Effects of Information Source Status and Dogmatism upon Conformity Behavior," *Journal of Abnormal and Social Psychology,* LXIII (1961), 639–42.

[14]F. A. Powell, *Open- and Closed-Mindedness and Ability to Differentiate Message from Source,* unpublished Master's thesis, Michigan State University, 1961.

[15]C. E. Osgood, G. J. Suci, and P. H. Tannenbaum, *The Measurement of Meaning* (Urbana: University of Illinois Press, 1957).

problem-solving tasks. Suppose we ask a subject to approximate the answers to the following questions without benefit of paper and pencil: (*a*) multiply 13.2 by 14.1; (*b*) divide the answer by 11.9; (*c*) multiply the answer by 9.8. Each time the subject responds, the experimenter *arbitrarily* says "too high" or "too low." In such an experimental situation, the subject is able to draw on two sources of information in arriving at his answer: one source being his own past experience, the other being the experimenter or authority. Allard[16] found that in such an experimental setup, closed-minded subjects were more influenced than open-minded persons by the arbitrary pronouncements of authority, despite the fact that the nature of the task was such that they could assess for themselves how well they were performing.

Consider, finally, another study by Restle, Andrews, and Rokeach,[17] in which open- and closed-minded subjects were compared with respect to their ability to learn simple discrimination, reversal discrimination, and oddity problems. Open- and closed-minded groups did not differ with respect to their performance on discrimination and reversal learning problems. But, on the oddity problems, the closed-minded group made significantly more errors than the open-minded group. A major source of this greater difficulty of the closed group was readily apparent: Following authority, they responded to the oddity problem with the same stimulus reinforced by authority in the immediately preceding trial.

To these findings, let me add additional findings. Plant and Telford[18] report that open-minded junior college students demonstrate significantly more achievement via independence as measured by Gough's California Personality Inventory than do the closed-minded students. Rubenowitz[19] in Sweden finds that the more open-minded the person, the earlier the age at which he earned his first money. When

---

16Marvel Allard, *Study of Relations between Orientation toward Authority and Susceptibility to Influence,* unpublished Master's thesis, Michigan State University, 1960.

17F. Restle, Martha Andrews, and M. Rokeach, "Differences between Open- and Closed-Minded Subjects on Learning-Set and Oddity Problems," *Journal of Abnormal and Social Psychology,* LXVIII, No. 6 (1964), 648–54.

18W. T. Plant and C. W. Telford, "Contrasts between Groups High and Low in Measured Dogmatism," paper read at annual meeting of California Psychological Association, 1961.

19S. Rubenowitz, *Swedish Version of Rokeach's Dogmatism Scale,* unpublished manuscript, 1961.

all these findings are taken together, they point to the same pervasive, fundamental difference in the cognitive processes of open- and closed-minded persons. They all suggest that closed-mindedness is a state of mind which leads to conformity to arbitrary authority because of cognitive inability to discriminate information from sources; conversely, open-mindedness is a state of mind which frees the person from dependence on arbitrary authority by virtue of the cognitive ability to make such discriminations.

THE PSYCHOLOGICAL FORMULATION OF NOVELTY

True independence goes much deeper than the mere capacity to distinguish information from source. True independence from authority—which is not to be confused with rebelliousness, a process more akin to conformity—implies a psychological freedom from authority which permits one to entertain or to be receptive to new ideas or beliefs and to combine them into new systems of ideas or beliefs.

One reason why the creative process remains so elusive is that it is difficult to define the concept of novelty in purely psychological terms and, at the same time, to assess it in purely objective terms. How can we conceptually represent whether an idea or system of ideas is really psychologically new or not new for the person holding it? We have tried to deal with this problem in our studies of the differences in the cognitive functioning of relatively open- and closed-minded persons by defining new in the following way: A belief or a belief system is psychologically new to the person holding it if, and only if, he holds and gives up an older belief or system of beliefs contradictory to it.

An illustration might be helpful here. Consider, for example, a belief we all share, a belief which is known to be present in most people's belief system: We all believe that if you cut an object, say of paper, all the way through with a pair of scissors until you can cut no more, you always end up with two pieces. Consider now a Moebius strip.[20] If you cut it all along its length until you can cut no more, how many pieces will you end up with? The vast majority of people we have asked will say two and will express amazement and disbelief when this is demonstrated not to be so; in fact, you end up with a single object twice as long. Often they will suspect a

---

[20]To make a Moebius strip, take a long strip of paper, twist it once, then tape the ends together.

trick and will go to the trouble of making their own Moebius strip to repeat the experiment. This sort of behavior seems to be a function of the fact that people have difficulty in accepting the new belief; namely, that when you cut something all the way through, you always end up with two pieces.

Consider now a somewhat more complicated problem which is relatively difficult to solve, because its solution hinges partly on the requirement that the thinker entertain the new belief that when you cut something you can end up with three pieces. Imagine a man who needs to put up at a hotel for seven days but is flat broke. He asks the manager whether he would be willing to accept, in lieu of the seven days' rent, a rather expensively embroidered, gold-braided chain made of seven interlocking links. The manager agrees but refuses to accept payment in advance or to extend credit. He stipulates that he will accept payment only for each day separately, one link for every day. Since the chain is a family heirloom which he hopes someday to retrieve, our guest is reluctant to make any more cuts in it than absolutely necessary. Problem: What is the minimum number of cuts our guest has to make and why?

As I have already indicated, one of the reasons this problem is difficult to solve is that the thinker must be able to entertain the novel idea that when you cut something through you can end up with three pieces, a belief which violates an older belief known to exist in many adult persons.

The seven-link problem is germane to my discussion here for another reason: It illustrates the further notion that in creative thinking, especially in creative system-building, it is often the case that there are two or more novel ideas which must first emerge separately and then be synthesized to form a novel system of ideas; that is, a system which violates the beliefs of one's previously held system. In the seven-link problem, the second novel idea is that you can *make change* with objects of value even if they are not money. Note that even though I have stated the two novel ideas inherent in the seven-link problem, the solution is not yet apparent. This is because what is next needed is a further thought process, *synthesis,* which will probably take time beyond the time taken to get rid of two old ideas and replace them with two new ones.[21]

---

[21]The solution to the seven-link problem: one cut, third link.

In our research on the nature of the differences in cognitive processes between persons with relatively open and closed belief systems, we have not as yet employed the seven-link problem, but we did employ another problem—the Doodlebug Problem—which appears to have exactly the same properties. This problem involves the behavior of a hypothetical bug living in a hypothetical world wherein the rules governing its behavior are not only different from but also contradictory to the rules we live by in our everyday world.

To solve the problem within the framework of this novel system of rules, it is necessary for the thinker first to get rid of three old ideas, A, B, and C, and replace them with three new ones, X, Y, and Z. This is the process of analysis. Then comes the process of synthesis, which involves the simultaneous integration of X, Y, and Z into a new system: X Y Z. With our procedures, it is possible to isolate and to measure separately the analytical phase of thinking and the synthetic phase of thinking.

The results of these studies have been described in detail elsewhere[22] and need not be reviewed here. But two points are worth making. First, we have found many reliable relationships between personality and cognitive behavior which are consistent with our theoretical notions about the nature of belief systems and with notions regarding differences in the receptivity to new idea systems among persons differing in open-closed mindedness. And, second, these conceptualizations and findings are relevant to the present inquiry, because receptivity to novel ideas and to novel systems of ideas, crucial variables in the study of the creative process, is objectively defined. We require the thinker to replace an old idea or system of ideas, which we objectively know he entertains, with new ones contradicting them, which we objectively know he did not previously entertain.[23] And in the same way that we have learned how to objectively

---

[22]Rokeach, *Open and Closed Mind*. S. Fillenbaum and A. Jackman, "Dogmatism and Anxiety in Relation to Problem Solving," *Journal of Abnormal and Social Psychology*, LXIII (1961), 212–14. R. Vidulich, *A Re-examination of the Distinction between Dogmatic and Rigid Thinking*, unpublished manuscript, 1961.

[23]"Kepler's life work was possible only once he succeeded in freeing himself to a great extent of the intellectual traditions into which he was born. This meant not merely the religious tradition, based on the authority of the Church, but general concepts on the nature and limitations of action within the universe and the human sphere, as well as notions of the relative importance of thought and experience in science." In Einstein, *Out of My Later Years*, p. 226.

define novelty in purely psychological terms with respect to the formation of new conceptual systems, we have also learned to define novelty in studies involving the formation of new perceptual systems[24] and the enjoyment of new musical systems.[25]

The hypothesis that relatively open belief systems represent a more receptive state of mind than relatively closed belief systems has recently been extended in two different kinds of studies. Ehrlich[26] gave the same sociology test to students in sociology on four separate occasions: at the beginning of the quarter (Time 1), at the end of the quarter (Time 2), five months later (Time 3), and five years later (Time 4). He reports the following correlations between scores on the Dogmatism Scale and sociology scores obtained at Times 1, 2, 3, and 4: −.30, −.52, −.54, and −.43. These correlations decrease negligibly when intelligence is held constant, and the Dogmatism Scale is a uniformly better predictor of performance on the sociology test at any time from 1 to 4 than is the score of an intelligence test. The generally greater receptivity of open-minded subjects is further indicated by the fact that, compared with closed-minded subjects, they "entered the sociology classroom with a higher level of learning, learned more as a result of classroom exposure, and retained this information to a significantly greater degree."[27]

In an altogether different setting, a counseling situation, Kemp[28] found that closed-minded students had more personal problems than open-minded ones, and that the former were less receptive to new information gained in the counseling situation, as indicated by the fact that they did not improve significantly while open-minded students did improve significantly as a result of equal numbers of counseling sessions.

From Independence to Creativity

It is reasonable to assume that creative people will be more open-

[24]J. M. Levy and M. Rokeach, "The Formation of New Perceptual Systems," in Rokeach, *Open and Closed Mind.*
[25]B. Mikol, "The Enjoyment of New Musical Systems," *ibid.*
[26]H. J. Ehrlich, "Dogmatism and Learning," *Journal of Abnormal and Social Psychology,* LXII (1961), 148–49; "Dogmatism and Learning: A Five-Year Follow-up," *Psychological Reports,* IX (1961b), 283–86.
[27]"Dogmatism and Learning: A Five-Year Follow-up," p. 283.
[28]C. G. Kemp, "Influence of Dogmatism on Counseling," paper read at annual meeting of American Personnel and Guidance Association, 1960.

minded than uncreative people, and Cohen[29] found that this is indeed the case when art students judged by their teachers to be creative were compared with art students not so judged. It is very tempting, in view of the elusiveness of the creative process, to conclude from this finding, as well as from other data cited before (concerning the relative ability of open-minded and closed-minded persons with respect to the discrimination of message from source and with respect to differences in receptivity to novelty), that the Dogmatism Scale measures the creative process and that the reason why it does so is to be found in the theory of the organization of belief systems which guided its construction.

However, it is clear that creativity involves something more than open-mindedness. An open belief system, however open, is not necessarily a belief system which will generate novel and worthwhile products. Representing as it does a discriminating and receptive state of mind, it is in a good position to recognize the creative productions of others as creative but is not necessarily itself creative. We have thus far merely described some necessary but insufficient conditions characterizing the creative process. What additional attributes must be present in an open belief system, over and above the fact that it represents an independent, discriminating, and receptive state of mind, in order for it to be also a belief system in a position to create?

THE PSYCHOLOGICAL SIGNIFICANCE OF FORMULATION

Where do we look for this something "over and above" which uniquely characterizes the creative process and no other thought process? It is fruitless to seek an answer from empirical research on problem-solving or thinking or research on the computer simulation of thinking,[30] because all such research contains a basic methodological flaw with respect to the study of the creative process. Such research always requires the subject (or the computer) to produce an answer but not a question. There is a division of labor: The researcher provides the question, the subject provides the answer. The researcher sometimes studies the subject to ascertain the process by which he arrives at the answer. A full and complete description of this process,

---

[29]I. H. Cohen, *Adaptive Regression, Dogmatism, and Creativity,* unpublished doctoral dissertation, Michigan State University, 1960.

[30]A. Newell, J. C. Shaw, and H. A. Simon, "Elements of a Theory of Human Problem-Solving," *Psychological Reviews,* LXV (1958), 151–66.

even if it were forthcoming, can never be a full and complete description of the creative process; because all creative work begins with a formulation, a question the creator necessarily puts to himself.

I think it was Einstein who once said that to ask a question is to answer it. In a recent article in *Life* magazine (September 1, 1961, p. 75), Leo Szilard was quoted as saying, "The most important step in getting a job done is the recognition of a problem. Once I recognize a problem, I usually can think of someone who can work it out better than I could." Hilgard[31] says that "detecting the problem is as important as finding the answer." And Hadamard[32] says, "Before trying to discover anything or to solve a determinant problem, there arises the question: What shall we try to discover? What problems shall we try to solve (p. 124)?"

It is not quite accurate to say that the creative process begins with the formulation of a question. If this were so, probably everyone under the sun would qualify as creative, and the concept of creativity would become so broad that it would also become meaningless. A more precise way of putting it is that the creative process begins with a *significant* formulation.

In Newton's case, one can certainly see, from the beginning, a continuous course of thought constantly directed toward its goal. But this process was started by the initial recognition that the subject was worthy of this continuity of attention—Hadamard, p. 44.

Then, how are we to select subject of research? This delicate choice is one of the most important things in research; according to it we form, generally in a reliable manner, our judgment of the value of a scientist. Upon it we base our judgment of research students. Students have often consulted me for subjects of research; when asked for such guidance, I have given it willingly, but I must confess that—provisionally, of course—I have been inclined to classify the man as second rate. In a different field, such was the opinion of our great Indianist, Sylfain Levi, who told me that, on being asked such a question, he was tempted to reply: Now, my young friend, you have attended our courses for, say, three or four years and you have never perceived that there is something wanting further investigation?—Hadamard, p. 126.

[31]E. R. Hilgard, "Creativity and Problem-Solving," in *Creativity and Its Cultivation*, p. 71.
[32]*Psychology of Invention in Mathematical Field*, 1945.

Significant to whom? Society? The individual? In what way significant? Once again we are entangled within the web of the "inside-outside" problem. I say "once again," because once before it was the notion of novelty that was causing the difficulty.

THE PSYCHOLOGICAL FORMULATION OF SIGNIFICANCE

I would suggest that we try to resolve the difficult conceptual problem of defining significance or worth in the same way we tried earlier to resolve the definition of novelty; namely, by representing it in purely psychological terms, as some sort of process going on in the creative mind and not going on in the uncreative mind. The next question is how.

Some clues are provided once again by Hadamard: "The sense of beauty can inform us and I cannot see anything else allowing us to foresee (p. 127)." He states further that it is a sense of scientific beauty and a special aesthetic sensibility which guides us in our drive for discovery. Hadamard adds that Renan also calls this scientific taste or literary taste or artistic taste. Of course, Hadamard is not the only one who has drawn our attention to these matters. Beauty as well as elegance, parsimony, and comprehensiveness are values recognized and appreciated by all men of culture and science.

The aim of creative work, whether through the rigorous procedures of mathematics or science or through the intuitive procedures of the artist, is not knowledge or expression but significant, fundamental, beautiful knowledge or expression. This aim can be conceived as having its cognitive counterpart and representation in the form of certain beliefs existing in the central regions of a belief system regarding what is and what is not significant. The person capable of engaging in the creative process has certain beliefs (some psychologists will want to call these values) in what is significant which involve criteria different in degree or kind from beliefs about significance entertained by less creative persons. These beliefs about significance guide the formulation of questions and enable the creative person to discriminate between relatively significant and relatively trivial questions, something the less creative person cannot do.

This does not mean that thought processes in uncreative work are not guided by beliefs regarding what is and is not significant. It means only that such thought processes are guided by beliefs involving other criteria of worth, such as money, status, power, the crudest kind of practicality, and so on. I once knew a man who believed that facts were terribly important, all facts, because you never knew when they might come in handy. His intellectual aim in life seemed to be to learn as many facts as possible. At the end of each year, he would await eagerly the new edition to the *World Almanac,* so that he could study it to ascertain which facts were different from the facts of the previous year. "Did you know," he once told me, apropos of nothing we were talking about, but with enthusiasm in his voice and facial expression, "that the population of Montana has decreased (or did he say increased?) by so-and-so much per cent in the last year?"

This is, of course, an extreme instance and is mentioned here only to stress the point that men differ in their beliefs about what is and is not significant. To some, a significant problem means that it has implications, ramifications, and consequences which can be specified; to others (e.g., our man who pores over his *World Almanac*), significance is defined in terms of some other criterion, not that what he is doing has specifiable ramifications but that some day his knowing a fact may turn out to be useful. Creative work, starting with the search for a formulation and ending with a solution, is guided by beliefs, often implicit, unverbalized and unverbalizable, that what one is doing is significant because one is extending, relating, interrelating, unifying, simplifying, making more elegant, more beautiful, reaching out to the genotypic reality behind the phenotypic appearance, groping for the structure, the form, the process, the function behind the content. "Invention," Hadamard tells us, "is discernment, choice (p. 30)."

Let us imagine a man, X, living thousands of years ago, who constructed a truly novel object, a wheel, but used it only as something to roll down an incline for his own amusement. Imagine also that one day Y noticed this object and, seeing its implications, used it to transport heavy loads. Who created the wheel? In my view it was Y, because he *saw* both its novelty and its implications.

Not everybody defines significance in this way. For one thing, such beliefs probably require a high order of intelligence, but not everybody who is intelligent necessarily holds such beliefs. Roe[33] reports that highly creative people are uniformly intelligent, but not

[33]Anne Roe, *The Making of a Scientist* (New York: Dodd, Mead & Co., 1953).

all intelligent people are creative. No doubt, too, personality structure, temperature, innate talent, and environmental influences also play a role. The conditions leading to differing beliefs regarding significance and the criteria for judging significance seem quite obscure.

THE LONELINESS OF CREATIVITY

Rogers[34] has observed and Roe has found that the creative process is a lonely one and that creative people have a feeling of apartness. Why should this be so? I would suggest that this is so because the creative process is also, paradoxically, a social process. In creative work, unlike any other work, there is really no one to rely on but oneself; hence the loneliness. At the same time, the point of departure is always the state of knowledge, belief, or expression developed by other men to whom the creative person eventually has to re-address himself, whether to discredit prevailing views, extend them, or re-arrange them. Creative work is lonely work, not only because one is strictly on one's own, but also because one often cognitively anticipates a day of reckoning, when the fruits of one's labor will be evaluated socially by others, often by one's authorities, the very ones who have investments in prevailing beliefs and belief systems.

HARD WORK AND THE SENSE OF DESTINY

So creativity is a lonely process, although there are no Robinson Crusoes. Anne Roe has pointed out that the eminent scientists she has studied have in common the fact that they work very hard and have an intense devotion to their work. And Hilgard cites prominently Gough's finding of a sense of destiny in creative people.

Again, I will ask: Why should this be so? I would hypothesize that given two scientists of equal intelligence, one perceiving the significance of his work in terms of implications and the other not, the first one would have a greater sense of mission and work harder. Asking the right questions carries a motivational bonus; it provides one with just the right amount of extra motivation needed to see one's work through, even though the cost is great. Asking a significant question gives rise to a tension state so intense, possibly so unbearable

---

[34]C. R. Rogers, "Toward a Theory of Creativity," in *Creativity and Its Cultivation.*

that the only way to reduce it is to single-mindedly work through all the implications to a satisfactory conclusion, the tension state itself providing the extra fuel needed to carry the creative act to completion. Thus, the reason why creative people work so hard, and seem "driven," is because they are literally driven along by the tension arising from the significant questions they ask themselves.

Definition of the Creative Process

To summarize all the preceding material is really to define the creative process so that (1) it is distinguishable from thinking in general and from uncreative thinking in particular; (2) it is placed squarely in relation to the processes of conformity and independence; (3) the social character of the creative process is revealed no less than its private character; and (4) it is compatible with a definition of creativity from the standpoint of product: The creative process is that sequence of thinking leading to ideas or products which, sooner or later, will be regarded as novel and worthwhile because (*a*) it is an activity characterized by the capacity to distinguish, cognitively, information from source and to evaluate them separately on their own merits which, in turn, (*b*) frees the person to be receptive to, acquire, integrate, and transform new beliefs into new belief systems which violate previously held beliefs and belief systems, (*c*) all such activity being driven and guided from beginning to end by tension states arising from significant questions put to oneself, significance being cognized as that which has implications or consequences for the ideas, products, feelings, and welfare of other human beings.

Training for Independence and Creativity

I would like to conclude with some remarks designed to point out some implications concerning training for independence and creativity which seem to be suggested by the analysis of the creative process just presented.

Are Children Creative?

The assumption that most children are creative while most adults are not seems to be held by many psychologists. A corollary of this view seems to be that adults are uncreative because they have lost whatever it is children have that makes children creative.

I cannot share this view, because I do not think that most children are creative, and it is moreover my opinion that such a view leads us into a theoretical blind alley; it would be disastrous to build a theory of the creative process in adults with the child as a model. Children are indeed more spontaneous, more playful, fresher in perception, and more innocent in outlook, and I would not dream of taking these qualities away from them. But I would not call children creative precisely for these reasons. There is nothing to stand in the way of children who reach out in all directions. To call children creative because they are playful, for example, would require us to call kittens creative because they too are playful. Before socialization there are no traditions, taboos, or prevailing ideas to be got rid of. Children do indeed learn new things all the time, but I would not for this reason want to say that they have novel ideas, at least not if we conceive of novelty in the psychological terms discussed earlier. An adult who is said to have a novel idea is not going through the same thought process as the child who is learning something for the first time. The adult has first to unlearn what he has learned and then to replace it with something else.

Similarly, I would not want to call the spontaneous child creative, because the second criterion of creativity—worth—is also missing. Beliefs about worth, particularly the kinds of beliefs about worth discussed earlier, such as beliefs about beauty and unity, probably develop relatively late in the growth process.

A final point to be made in this connection is that if we insist on viewing children as creative because they are still free of social inhibitions and prohibitions, we are really viewing creativity as an asocial-psychological process or, at least, as anything but a social-psychological process.

FOSTERING CREATIVITY IN CHILDREN

There are many who would maintain that we can best foster creativity in children by keeping our restraining hands off them, by encouraging and rewarding their spontaneity, by being loving and permissive, by respecting them as individuals, and so on. If only we can keep children as fresh as they are as they grow into adulthood, so this view goes, creativity will take care of itself.

My own reaction to this view is that while it is hardly possible to disagree with it, it is too vaguely put to constitute a program which can be translated into concrete operations. In line with the analysis of the creative process which I have presented, I would suggest instead that, if we wish to foster creativity in children, we must find ways to train them, or condition them, along other than present lines. There is nothing self-contradictory, for example, in the notion of *training for independence* or *training for creativity*. If conformity can be trained, why not also independence and creativity?

It is beyond the scope of this paper to enter into a detailed analysis of what training for independence and creativity might look like concretely. But perhaps it is possible to spell out here the broadest outlines of an educational philosophy designed to foster independence and creativity. Before doing so, however, two reservations should be noted.

First, there are often deep-lying personality factors, such as those considered in *The Authoritarian Personality*,[35] and in *The Open and Closed Mind* which predispose one to a conforming, rather than an independent or creative, state of mind.

Second, it should be recognized that, at best, we might be able to train children generally for independence, but not generally for creativity. Creativity is often specific to a person's talent, interest, temperament, and motivation. A person may, for example, be specifically creative in art but be generally independent. Creativity often requires a profound knowledge of a specific area in order to provide a background against which implications may be seen.

TRAINING FOR THE ABILITY COGNITIVELY TO DISCRIMINATE INFORMATION FROM SOURCE

The first place to focus attention is on training for independence, a general state of mind, as I have tried to show, which is intermediate between the conforming and creative states of mind. Because the infant is both dependent and ignorant as he starts out in life, it is no accident that he develops a belief that his parents know everything and a faith that if he does not know something he has only to ask them. A child will often say this quite explicitly: "My Mommy knows everything." "Santa Claus is true because my Daddy says so." As the child comes of school age, he will often attribute this omniscience to the teacher also.

---

[35]T. W. Adorno, Else Frenkel-Brunswik, D. F. Levinson, and R. N. Sanford, *The Authoritarian Personality* (New York: Harper & Brothers, 1950).

Many parents and teachers probably never go to the trouble of deliberately disabusing the child of this pervasive belief about the nature of authority, deliberately conditioning the child not to be conditioned. Often they will punish the child who shows signs of believing otherwise. As a result, the child will develop a secret theory about the nature of authority, to the effect that authority is absolute and the most that the child can ever accomplish is to know as much as authority but no more. Such a child may never find out that his parents and teachers did not know everything, because parents and teachers often need to pretend they know even if they don't.[36]

I am sure that many children, because they have powerful needs to know as well as powerful needs not to know,[37] eventually learn to cognitively discriminate information from its source, at least to some extent, despite the best efforts to the contrary of adult referents. But what I am suggesting specifically is an institutionalized program of training in a new kind of curriculum which cuts structurally across all other curricula, having as its main focus the deliberate and systematic training of the cognitive ability to discriminate information from source and the independent evaluation of each. This is really tantamount to a curriculum designed to teach children a certain kind of theory about the nature of authority, a theory about how to go about relying on authority in such a way as to make the child free and independent of authority, and in order to make the child realize early that it is within his potential to know things his parents and teachers do not know, and some day perhaps to rise above them in wisdom and understanding.

These are the sorts of things a child should be taught explicitly early in life, rather than left to find out haphazardly. As Bruner[38] points out, "Any subject can be taught effectively in some intellectually honest way to any child at any stage of development." He also says a good deal about "the teaching and learning structure" and, while Bruner is not using the concept of structure in quite the same way as

---

[36]Patrick Suppes has made the interesting observation that one of the byproducts of teaching set theory to grade-school children is the child's discovery that his parents do not know everything. Roe writes, "The discovery that it is possible to find things out for oneself is not a natural part of growing up for every child in our culture" (p. 238).

[37]Rokeach, *Open and Closed Mind.* A. H. Maslow, "The Need to Know and the Fear of Knowing," *Journal of General Psychology,* LXVIII (1963), 111–25.

[38]J. S. Bruner, *The Process of Education* (Cambridge, Mass.: Harvard University Press, 1960), p. 33.

it is implied here, the kind of systematic training for independence discussed here can be thought of as training in the development of certain structures within belief systems and not other structures.

TRAINING IN THE RECOGNITION OF NOVELTY

Let me first distinguish the production of novelty from the recognition of novelty. It is reasonable to assume that a person who is unable to recognize (which means also to appreciate) another's novelty when he sees it will be unable to produce novel ideas and/or products himself. I would therefore suggest that the teaching of receptivity to novelty begin with cross-curricular training specifically oriented to teach children to recognize and discriminate between the novel and non-novel productions of others. Surely, there are many examples of novel concepts in the history of human thought present in many curricula taught at various stages in the child's educational career which could be pulled out for use as instructional material.

Whatever educational emphasis there may presently be on new concepts in science, art, and literature is an emphasis on the concept rather than its novelty. Without in any way minimizing the importance of the former, I think that it would take but little extra effort to stress also the latter. This could be done by making more explicit the drama and excitement of innovation, how and why in the history of man new concepts and theories arose, within a broader social context of issues, controversies, and unresolved problems, ultimately leading to the dethronement of prevailing views and their replacement by new ones.

Finally, it should be made far more explicit to the child that the story does not end with the coronation of the new idea, that the new ideas of today may become the old ideas of tomorrow, leading to new unresolved problems, new issues, and controversies in a spiral of advancing knowledge which never ends. Would not such training stimulate the child to become aware early of the possibility that perhaps he too can one day take his place among contributors to culture and knowledge?

TRAINING IN THE RECOGNITION OF SIGNIFICANCE

First, there should be a reversal of the emphasis in education from answering questions to asking them. And, second, there should be training in the criteria for asking significant questions. There are several social contexts in which questions and answers are particularly important. In the classroom (or lecture hall), the teacher asks a question and no matter how good or bad the question, the child tries to answer it. Less often, the child asks the teacher a question and, again, the teacher tries to answer it no matter how good or bad the question. There seems to be a pervasive norm (a belief about how people ought to behave, shared by many) in our present educational system, from grade to graduate school, that the quality is to be sought in the answer rather than in the question. This norm is so pervasive that it would be considered boorish if, say, a lecturer were to complain about the quality of a question put to him. The rule seems to be that if a lecturer agrees to answer questions, he must answer all questions put to him without regard to quality. This is understandable, perhaps as an instance of the "democratization" of ideas or perhaps as an illustration of the fact that we do not like to hurt people's feelings. Whatever the reason, though, this norm defeats the educational goal of training for independence and creativity.

A similar point can be made about the role played by question and answers in about context: examinations. Would not an examination that tests the student's ability to ask questions, significant questions, accomplish its goal better than present examinations, since to formulate a significant question implies, first, that one already has the background knowledge and, second, that one is probing beyond?

I have already discussed some of the criteria for asking significant questions. The only point that needs to be added here is that these criteria, too, can be explicitly made the focus of attention, discussion, illustration, and elaboration in the various curricula in order to develop in the child beliefs about the nature of worth and unworth.

A host of other questions come to mind as deserving consideration. Is the present analysis of the creative process as applicable to art as to science? Can computers be programmed to simulate the creative process as here described? What is the difference between ingenuity and creativity? Is a person creative in our sense of the term if he is able, as Guilford claims, to think up clever plot titles or manifold uses of brick, or give rare word associations? To what extent do Maslow's concept of self-actualization and Rogers' concept of growth overlap with the present view of the creative process? What personal and social determinants facilitate and hinder the creative process considered as a whole and the subprocesses discussed earlier considered separately? And, finally, how would one go about measuring the various facets of the creative process here described?

These are questions which require further study and much empirical research. But the question I ask myself is whether I have at all succeeded in my pursuit of the creative process. The answer is clear: Like the toddler chasing his butterfly, I was sure I would catch it while pursuing it. But now that I have arrived at the end, I see that it has got away again.

Discussion

SHOCKLEY DISCUSSES THE "LINK PROBLEM" . . . THE CREATIVE
MAN FOLLOWS HIS INTERESTS

Shockley

> I think that a number of the things that Dr. Rokeach mentioned hit very close to home, and I intend to say something about my own role in transistor inventing later on. But right now, I'd like to ask something about his "link" problem (see p. 74). I do not know whether he has this happen with his subjects, but I got caught up in the following situation: The next natural number of links in the chain is 63, and the next natural number of links in the chain is 2,047. For the 63, you make three cuts and for the 2,047, seven cuts. Is this a familiar result?

Rokeach

> I have never extended it that way, but I think it could be; it sounds right.

Shockley

> Well, the point is, you see, you ask yourself the question—and I am posing it, as a living demonstration of some of the comments you made. Seven is obvious, and this is a binary system of numbers.

Rokeach

> It has not been obvious to the people we have tried it on.

Shockley

Well, once you look at it, it is obvious that this is a binary system of getting numbers, 1, 2, 3. What is the next step in this binary system? This is where you would have three cuts; you will have one, two, and three—three cuts—and then what is left, to go on with the four pieces that fit beyond the three cuts? Two cuts does not fit in a natural way, because you can make one and two with the individual cuts; this does not fit sensibly into the binary scheme, I ask myself the significant question in this regard: What two cuts you need one more, so you can get up to three. This means that you might as well have three cuts in the first place. If you have three cuts in the first place, that leads you to 64 minus 1.

But the point I am making here is that in order to fit into your scheme, I ask myself the significant question in this regard: What is the logical extension of this seven? At that point, you lost half or two-thirds of my attention for the rest of your talk, until I got the formula for this. I am fitting into your framework there myself, you see.

Rokeach

It all goes to show that one of the difficulties with illustrations is that we get so interested in the illustration that we forget what it was we were trying to illustrate. Actually, I was only trying to illustrate the psychological difficulty that the thinker has to overcome before he can go to work on this problem.

Shockley

I agree with your point completely, but I am saying, "I am one of those people who gets caught up in a question." At this point, I got caught up with a question, and I would not have been happy if I had not got the answer by this time.

Wallis

I think Bill is illustrating the point that one caveman will roll the wheel down for amusement, and somebody else will try to determine all of its applications.

CONCLUSION: "USEFULNESS" VERSUS "ACADEMIA"

Merton

The traditional way of formulating the issue that Mr. Bower raised is to say that there are academic men who have no concern with what is often called practical use, who talk only to one another, and consequently do not address themselves to others in the social system. This argues that the problem can be solved —if it is to be solved at all—by academic men learning how to translate what they are saying in such a way that it can be utilized by practical men. I take issue with that view.

Steiner

It was certainly our belief, in organizing this seminar, that the academic men would be of great value to the men of affairs. But it was also our belief that the men of affairs would be of great value to the academic men.

The conception of this seminar was that it would provide a forum for the confrontation of the two points of view, not for one to instruct the other, either in abstruse language *or* in simple terms. We all agree that the objective is to arrive at some workable guidelines or, at least, some awareness as to where workable guidelines cannot be drawn. But in order to do that in the course of this session, I think it is crucial that the men of affairs in the room attempt to make precisely the kind of translations you suggest. Or, if they cannot do so, to say why, on the basis of their practical experience and present problems, these things seem to them to be untranslatable.

In listening to Mr. Rokeach's paper, for example, I was struck with this kind of question, which I would like to hear the men of affairs speak to: Is his model only for individual creativity or are aspects of it applicable to organizations? For example, if individuals are more likely to create if they can distinguish information from source, does that translate itself at all into organizational lines? Does the creative organization, for example, divorce information from source? Are memos signed or unsigned? What is the relative importance that the organization places on from *whom* a message comes as against *what* it says? That is just one simple kind of illustration.

Now, can we make that kind of translation? Does it make sense at all and, if so, what kind of questions does it raise?

Bower

One of the notions that I think has great practical value will illustrate my response to your question. Mr. Rokeach says independence is a necessary condition of creativity.

Now, one of the problems of an organization is to create a sufficient degree of independence so that people will be more creative. I have observed that and I will comment on it in my paper. How do we get independence? How important is it? What is the judgment of this distinguished group on that point?

I think we only have to get about a dozen judgments to make this a valuable and worthwhile exercise. I do not think that it has to be too well documented, nor do I think that we have to tell people how to do anything. I think we have to raise questions or suggest principles, and in such a way that people can take a book and read it. That is as clearly as I can express it in terms of this paper, which I think is an excellent paper and can be applied. That is why I do not accept the thesis that we have to talk in two different worlds. I think they can be brought together.

Alexander

We do not need to talk in two different worlds. There is a problem of the meeting of minds, obviously, because the academician has an emphasis which is different from that of the man of affairs. But I think it is a two-way street. Maybe I misunderstood, but I think your expectation is that the academicians should do both: They should be the oracle—"What is creativity?"—and then also translate it into what is useful for you.

I think Mr. Rokeach gave a classical example: the man who discovers the principle of the wheel and the man who uses it for a wagon. These are two different things and usually two different kinds of persons do them. The businessman's, or the man of affairs', job is a much more active job than simply to listen to the oracle and then ask both questions of the academician: "Please explain to me what creativity is and then help me apply it to my business." I think the creative businessmen will listen to the oracle and will be the wagon-maker, leaving the scientists to be the discoverers of the principle of the wheel.

TIME LAG IN EVALUATING CREATIVITY

Shockley

There was one very specific suggestion for action here which, it seems to me, has sort of slipped away. The business of trying to evaluate the people who can select employees for creativity is a pretty high order of activity, and it has a damned long time lag. I know that if I hired a man, or if Bell Labs hired a man, you might not know for a year whether you were right or not, and sometimes the decision would be made two years later.

Bensinger

That is the point, I think, on which businessmen split a bit: this time lag, this desire to have an aura of loneliness, to let the deep-dreamer thinkers go off with no pressures on them. All this I think we are fully alive to. But then we have to be a little bit practical, and that is one of the problems *we* face; we have budgets and certain objectives to attain. I think any of us would be hard put to let this time lag extend two, three, or four years. We cannot set aside funds out of current earnings and just hide them away somewhere, not reporting them. As a public corporation, we have to make reports. There are shareholders. So an immediate conflict comes to my mind about the practicability aspects and the desired theoretical points.

EVALUATING EVALUATORS

Shockley

Let me suggest something specific that could be done. There are "body-snatching" firms in the country. They go around and produce candidates with various degrees of recommendation. A study that might be useful would be to try to gain access and co-operation from these people. Look at what they put down in evaluations of people; then go to the company and check on how these people actually work out.

Peterson

In other words, it is just as likely that you could pick out a sample of people who have demonstrated that they are good evaluators, and try to figure out what it is about them that makes them that good, as that you could study all the characteristics that Paul Meehl so eloquently explained are so difficult to measure. I think any businessman does the same thing, whether he does it with an employment firm or someone within the company. He does not do it systematically, and he should. He keeps a kind of running batting average, and pretty soon he finds out that there are one or two individuals that he talks with who, three years later, tend to be right much more often than other people.

Shockley

You do have to wait that period to get your evaluations.

CREATIVITY IN BUSINESS

Wallis

I have the impression that in the area of creativity—unlike some other fields, including those on which we have had earlier seminars: collective bargaining and the use of the computer— there has been a minimum of contact between academic and business people. My impression is that most of the academic people working on creativity have thought about creative academic people, or scientists, or possibly artists, and that they have barely considered creative people in business or creative organizations.

For that reason, this conference perhaps has more difficulty in communications. But, on the other hand, it is of much greater importance, too; it is more important to start that kind of communication. For example, one of the most useful results of a meeting like this might be—apart from this book—for some of the academic people who have worked on creativity and are very much interested in it to see a new area for research and to study it. My basic point is that, to some extent, our difficulties of communication arise from the fact that academic work has not come to any appreciable extent from business or government or, for that matter, from social work organizations.

Stein

My research on creativity was started in pre-Sputnik days and was supported by the Industrial Research Institute. My experience in the course of eight years of working with research laboratories has resulted in my asking two questions: Does industry want creativity? And, if the academicians found it, would they know what to do with it?

Let me back that with my own experience. The Industrial Research Institute, composed of about eighty-two research laboratories across the country, sponsored research over a period of five years. We come up differentiating between their more and less creative men. We work out a series of techniques for assessing the laboratories, the value systems of the laboratories, and so forth.

Then, when the techniques become available, we find something very interesting. Out of the three laboratories in which we did a very intensive investigation of ninety-six more or less creative men, only one laboratory was willing to go ahead with the next step in the process.

Only one laboratory was willing to take on the prediction problem; the other two laboratories were no longer willing, even on conditions of no cost to the company. (The research was now being supported by the Carnegie Corporation.) They were simply unwilling to allow this next step. Why?

They raised the following objection: It was too costly in terms of time. It does take something like eight hours per man, and they wanted a five-minute test of creativity.

At the end of the final presentation, I was approached by several research directors of laboratories. The only thing wrong with my research was that it took too long, eight hours rather than five minutes. And I was asked, literally, for a five-minute test of creativity.

So you have this kind of problem: When the academician does come up with some kinds of things and then turns to industry and says, "Would you like to test them?"—the academician does not have his own laboratory to do the selection of people—he gets a negative answer. After these experiences with industry, I once threw out the challange that I would be willing to put up a proportion of my savings to a proportion of the profits of the company if they would let me select men and a laboratory and pit that group against any group that management selects.

Not only that, but my experience duplicates the kinds of experiences we got from the men in the research laboratories. They often said, "My God! What does top management want? We have nine million new product ideas here. When will the new products committee pick this up?"

The personality structure of decision-makers in industry, and administrators, is very different from researchers. I think part of this becomes a fantastic problem when the research men in industry complain that top management just does not have the knowledge to evaluate their scientific capacity.

SHORT-RANGE PROFITS
VERSUS INVESTMENT IN CREATIVITY

Wallis

They have an even stronger incentive to get a good new product than the researchers do.

Stein

But they also have what some of the men characterize as the cash-register philosophy of creativity. They do not want creativity; they want to hear that cash register tinkle. And, therefore, a new product may come along—it may be a very worthwhile product; it may be a brilliant idea—but no one in top management can think that it will make *x* million dollars next year.

Wallis

Would you suggest any different criterion than the profitability of the idea?

Stein

Profitability over *what* period of time? That is the question, because there is *immediate* profitability but there is also what will be profitable five or ten years from now. Management has to confront itself with the question of creativity for *what:* What are its aims? What are its goals? Or what are its purposes? What is its image in the total society?

You arrange the men in order of rank and plot the logarithm of productivity, measured in terms of papers per year or patents per year, then you find that, while the median man may have *one,* the top man in your population may have *ten,* and the bottom man, maybe just one every ten years, or none. This gives a distribution which is a cumulative distribution plot on unconventional co-ordinates, but it turns out to be a log-normal distribution, essentially, with a pretty big spread.

IS SALARY COMMENSURATE WITH CREATIVITY?

Steiner

Dr. Shockley, while we are talking about profitability to the firm, could you tell us about your study of the relationship between income paid to creators and their creative output?

Shockley

We used a tool at Bell Laboratories which I worked up in 1945, and perhaps it is being used in other places as an aid to salary control.

We took the population of the laboratory and plotted each man's salary against his age. So any given man at a given date appears on the chart at some point with a certain salary. And at each age, there is then a certain median salary. Next, you take this population and divide it into what I call "merit quartiles."

The question then is this: How much more is the first-quartile man worth than the second-quartile man and the third-quartile man? The measure I took for this was productivity, in a very simple way, so that it could be measured. If the man is a physicist, for example, you count the number of times his name appears in *Science Abstracts,* and you count the number of patent applications filed for the man.

Now, if your salary structure is sound, and you are evaluating these things, you would expect to find more productivity for the people in the first quartile than in the second, more for those in the second than in the third, etc.

We plotted now against quartile number: the top quartile, which was 1, the second quartile, 2, and so on—we plotted log-average productivity in those quartiles.

But if you compare this with salary raises, you find that they occur much more slowly from quartile to quartile—the productivity lines rise from three to five times more steeply.

Suppose that a man can change his creativity, or does, somehow, and he starts producing 50 per cent more than he did before. The result will be that he will move about far enough according to these statistics so that he will get a 10 per cent raise. Or, to put it another way: If you are going out to body-snatch, and you can body-snatch a man who is making 20 or 30 per cent more money than the average for his age, and he really deserves it, you are reaping a big profit. He will produce four times as much, and what extra you pay for him is very small.

Of course, this leaves out of consideration certain organizational questions. Try to make up an organization of these people. Will they get along? That is part of the consideration.

Ogilvy

Then do you adjust your own salary scale and give the top key people ten times the bottom, to prevent others snatching your bodies?

Shockley

Of course not. I am part of a large, well-organized corporation called Clevite, and it has salary structure problems. Obviously, what you try to do is to pay just well enough so you don't lose people. You certainly are not influenced primarily by considerations of justice or of equitable distribution. You behave in accordance with the market at the time.

Stein

Well, I have some data that substantiate your material. My data indicate that the difference in salary between more and less creative men is only $1,500 in the companies that I studied. And you now have evidence that salary is not consistent with creativity, in a sense.

You then check the motivational systems of the men and ask: What are the kinds of things that you would like in order to help your creativity along? Or what motivates you? They say, "Money."

Will industry now provide larger discrepancies and pay better salaries? Will they make *his* salary *much* more discrepant from that of the lesser creative man?

Rokeach

The answer is no, because the creative individual will not lay down his pick and shovel if he does not get a pay raise. His motivations are internal.

Alexander

I analyzed a very inventive research man in one of the biggest steel companies in the country. His salary, when I started to work with him, was $12,000; and I think four or five years later, it was $16,000. The steel company had two large plants, one in this city and one in another city. Another man was in a similar position, making the same salary as he was. As he confessed to me, he told me this tremendous indignation which grew during the years: He felt that he made extreme contributions, not only to the company but to the Royal Air Force, because he developed better steel for airplanes, etc.; and he always felt that he was not appreciated.

Then something very peculiar happened. The other man, who was equally good (my patient was a modest man who always emphasized that "He may be a little better than I. I know more, but he is even more original"), got an administrative job and his salary jumped from $16,000 to $80,000. My patient then collapsed, completely. He said, "Now he is in administration. I don't think he contributes more than I. Probably I contribute something much more basic, but his salary went up." He was not very money-minded, but he said, "I'm not appreciated. What I do is so important and still the other man is much more highly valued." Whereupon he got an invitation from an academic institution and accepted a job for $15,000 as full professor.

WHAT ENVIRONMENT EVOKES CREATIVITY?

Alexander

That brings up another question which I think Mr. Stein touched upon. There are two problems for industry: not only to recognize the creative man but to know how to use him. Let us assume that we *can* spot the creative man. That is only half of it. You might spot creative men and they may not then create, so I think there is a very important problem—a psychological problem, at least in part: How do you use the creative man? What type of emotional climate must you create in order to stimulate and liberate his potential creativity?

There are some general principles which pretty safely can be applied. If, for example, we listen to Mr. Rokeach, then we can find some general principles: for example, that this creative man, after he is spotted, probably will do better if he gets a certain amount of freedom, less authoritarian treatment.

Or, what is even more important, I would almost conclude that we should not give him pinpointed questions, because that immediately interferes with real creativity. Then his wings are already clipped. I once asked a Nobel prize-winning physicist about organization of research. He said that when it comes to discovering the unknown, blueprinting is impossible. How can you blueprint the unknown? You can give him the area, but you cannot tell him, "Now, you invent for me this and this." There are people you can use for that, but they are not the creative ones we are talking about.

RELEVANCE FOR PRACTICAL QUESTIONS

Merton

I would like to try to make the effort to relate the discussion of the last forty minutes to the question initially raised by Mr. Bower.

We have had examples of the very thing that he was asking for; that is to say, the raising of concrete questions, which had possibly not been raised before and which are worth raising. We started with the query: Can we identify men with creative potential?

We then moved to a second and entirely different question: Can we spot the people who can spot creative potential? Can we evaluate the evaluator? We are saying that there is a social role in these organizations which is tacitly understood, and that we ought to focus on this role and its occupants. Who are the men best qualified to select the creative men? The practical importance of this is its multiplier effect. For every effective selector, you are getting x creative men.

We can identify a third type of role for which, as far as I know, there is no term in industrial firms or any other formal organization. I would call him the "evoker" of creativity—not the trainer, but the evoker. He is the type of man who, once in the organization, brings out the best or the greater part of the potential of others around him. Now, once we conceive such a role, we must raise comparable questions: What are the characteristics of the evokers? How do they operate? How can you identify them? I think this is of both theoretical and practical importance. I am not referring, in a disguised way, to the everlasting question of the effective supervisor nor to the familiar question of the trainer, but to the men who, through their social and personal relations with others in their immediate environment, stimulate them to do their most effective work.

Now, whether such men exist in large numbers, who they are, whether *their* potential is being utilized by having an effective role defined for them, would represent questions that are at once academically and practically significant.

So we see that it is not only a matter of translating back and forth between academia and the world of practical affairs, but of recognizing that the same issue can have simultaneous significance for both groups.

COMMUNICATION AND PUBLICATION

Shockley

There is one thing that I find myself doing which is effective and which I am sure other people do.

If you want people to do good, technical work and you want to stimulate them to do this, you put emphasis on their getting out papers which can be published in recognized scientific journals. If they do this, if they have this goal, they produce better work. They produce better work because they are going to face the criticism of their peers. They will find this social medium outside the organization; it is a way of getting a reputation. But this also raises a very practical consideration: They will be able— if they want to—to leave you; it will be much easier for them to do it.

LOCALS VERSUS COSMOPOLITANS

Merton

You may be interested, Mr. Shockley, to hear that that is a specific device corresponding to a more general sociological conception. So far as I know, the two have never been connected. It has been found in all sorts of organizations that you can crudely but conveniently divide the personnel into two broad kinds.

The first kind we call "locals." These are the men who are primarily oriented to the organization itself and make their way within the organization. The second type we call "cosmopolitans," those who are primarily oriented to people outside the organization, either to their profession or discipline or to other groups.

One of the great problems is converting locals into cosmopolitans, for the very reason you mentioned; that is, to insure that they become concerned with the standards which obtain in the wider society of their peers who are more critical, rather than merely meeting the immediate local standards, which on the average—taking organizations across the board—will be less demanding than the standards used in the wider population.

QUANTITY AND QUALITY

Shockley

One of the criticisms I run into is: *"Number* of papers doesn't mean anything." Well, this has been debunked. There is a direct correlation, by and large, between number of papers and quality. I put a chap on the following job: Look for correlation between number of publications and academic recognition. So he looked it up and found that in universities there is a very strong correlation between the amount of stuff people produce, when they achieve tenure rank, and whether or not they get elected to the National Academy of Sciences.

Tyler

I have been a dean long enough to know that this does not at all establish the quality of the papers or the relationship between the quality of the publications and their number (and I am sure Allen Wallis will verify this).

Shockley

Would you say the same thing for Nobel prizes? I am quite sure that there is a strong correlation there. I take the fifty-year index of the *Physical Review,* which is an author index, and I look for men whose names occupy two columns. The first one I find, perhaps, is Luis Alvarez. A little while later on, I find Hans Bethe. They are men you think of, first of all, not as mass producers but as producers of quality and ingenuity. So although I would not argue that you can tell whether a man is good simply by counting the number of his papers, the probability is very high.

Bruner

With regard to this same complaint that "number of papers does not tell you anything": Somebody came up with the bright idea of counting the number of times you are mentioned in the bibliography of other people's papers. When they correlated the number of times you are mentioned and the number of papers you published, the correlation is something on the order of .9.

Meehl

I had an experience similar to this. I never published the data, but when I was chairman of the psychology department, I got interested in this problem of objectifying the assessment of staff. Being the actuarial type I am, I thought: Well, I could count some of this stuff; it's objective.

Immediately, of course, one runs into the question of yardage.

What is yardage? Anybody who has a typewriter can get an article published. So I took counts of citations in the *Annual Review of Psychology,* and I also took simple yardage counts of publications. Then I took a kind of a complex, souped-up measure of national social visibility on the basis of invitations to serve on APA committees, election to office, and this sort of thing. Finally, I took just a little set of ranking spirals of the faculty—not anonymously, for they were willing to go along—of how high-powered they thought each of the others was. The correlations among these were such that, with twenty-six people on the faculty, it could all be accounted for quite adequately by one factor. The *Annual Review* count, as you might expect, was a little more saturated than pure "yardage," although not much more so.

THE VISIBILITY OF VARIOUS CRITERIA

Berelson

Most of you know, I am sure, that there is a great deal of criticism of the graduate school these years, because, allegedly, the graduate school is training people to be researchers and is not training college teachers, or is not training them well enough. A lot of people are asking the graduate school to turn emphasis away from research training and more toward teacher training. I am quite sure in my own mind that a fundamental problem here is simply the fact that research productivity is visible and teaching productivity is not—or is not as visible by a long shot. People can write articles in the journals and get evaluated across campuses by the standards of the trade. But we do not even know who are the good teachers within our own department, much less who is really a good teacher somewhere else, except by a kind of hearsay. There is no objective standard. There is not nearly the kind of objective evidence you can get even by numbers of papers, or with the kind of collaborative evidence that Paul mentioned. If someone can find a way to make good teaching visible beyond one's own campus—more visible in some objective way—then a great deal more emphasis is going to be placed on becoming a good teacher, as against a good researcher.

SUMMARY

Steiner

Let me try to summarize some of these things and see if I can pull together a few notions that seem closely related.

Milton Rokeach said, and Dr. Shockley immediately demonstrated afterwards, that the creative individual works and is sustained in his efforts by intrinsic interest in the problem, by what he perceives to be its significance. Now, what he perceives to be its significance may have nothing to do with its significance to the firm—again, as Dr. Shockley demonstrated, because the significance *he* saw in that problem was a mathematical significance, not the psychological significance which Milton saw in it. Yet this is what enabled him to create, with respect to this problem. Similarly, in the case of creative research people, or people in other staff functions, it seems clear that what they perceive to be the significance of the problem will not necessarily be its corporate significance.

Along the same lines, encouraging publication as a way of fostering creativity may hinge on the fact that this forces the creator to consider the largely "horizontal" significance of his problems, their practical significance in the specific context in which he works.

This, of course, may lead to the interesting paradox that the people who will be most creative in a staff function are people who care the least, in a sense, about the line functions. And, of course, it relates to the problem of moving great creators out of their creative capacity into administrative positions, simply because it is the only channel for advancement.

And that brings me to the final point: to generalize this to non-scientific people. Perhaps the cosmopolitan administrator is the counterpart here of the scientist who sees the scientific or professional significance of the particular problem he is working on and pursues it, not so much for what it can do for the firm, but out of simple interest. The creative cosmopolitan manager may see and respond to the situation as a problem in management, or what have you. He therefore will be valuable to the firm while he is there but is perhaps less likely to stay there, because his interests transcend those of the particular organization.

5

Some Observations on Effective Cognitive Processes

(EDITED COMMENTS)

JEROME S. BRUNER

What I normally do for a living is to take a very detailed look at activities that are usually grouped under the strange word "cognitive": I watch the processes of perceiving and perceptual organization; the strategies by which people attempt to remember things; how they approach their problem-solving. The emphasis is on the process of accepting, dealing with, and transforming information.

I shall deal with the creative act from this point of view, and I shall assume that any kind of activity can be creative: You can cook creatively, you can raise your children creatively, you can run a mill creatively, you can do scientific experiments creatively, or you can solve an ordinary mathematical equation creatively—or stupidly. I shall also assume that not only can any*thing* be more or less creative, but any*body* can be.

When you talk about a sequence of activities that leads to the solving of a problem or the seeing of something in a new way, what is involved is the production of *effective surprise*. I want to use that term in a fairly technical way. Now, once effective surprise has been produced by somebody, it has about it the character of obviousness or self-evidence. "It fits the set of requirements. It's obvious."

Take the instance of Galileo coming up with the beautiful formula that $S = \dfrac{GT^2}{2}$ and solving a whole series of things having to do with distance covered per unit of time by falling bodies. Immediately, this particular surprise has the quality of compacting a tremendous amount of information, simplifying, introducing a transformation on something which before was diffuse and not capable of being dealt with simultaneously.

What we usually stress about effective surprise is that it is improbable, that it is a rare event. But I would like to argue, for the moment, that perhaps it is not its rarity or improbability that is important. It is something else. Several statisticians have been concerned with the distinction between surprise and improbability.

They make this point: When you play bridge, for example, all hands in the game are equally improbable. Now, when you get a hand with all honors, or one with none at all, you say, "Aha! Look what I've got!" You are surprised, but this surprise has nothing whatever to do with the rarity of that particular hand, because all particular hands are equally rare in bridge, as in most other things. What is important about this hand is that it is surprising within a set of constraints, which the statisticians like to speak of as "rule bound." When we speak of *effective* surprise, we speak of something which has not been produced before (and, in that restricted sense, is rare) but also which fills the bill in terms of a *set of rules*. (In this respect, I think we can make quite an easy distinction between the schizophrenic's odd sentence and a sentence produced in the poetic medium by T. S. Eliot.)

This is one of the reasons why I am intrigued with this question of why it is that certain creative men are better than certain noncreative ones in recognizing something as a "hot" idea that is worth following up.

This business of capturing something that has this effective surprise value usually has the function of providing an image or a plan or something that you did not notice before. It needs, as I say, a recognizing audience.

My pet example is the Cavendish Laboratory at Cambridge University. What was there about the Cavendish Laboratory under Rutherford that was absolutely so hot? To be sure, one thing was its rich environment; people were throwing out hypotheses. But I would rather suspect that, in that particular atmosphere, there were some keen recognizers of surprises-about-to-be-born, people who could pick up an idea and run with it like mad. So that, as Lord Rutherford himself said, a laboratory, just like any other physical phenomenon, needs critical mass before you can get off the ground; and this critical mass has to do not only with a certain amount of output within the system but also with the question of an ample number of recognizers and reactors.

Now let me say a little bit more about effectiveness when we talk about it in terms of surprise. We must first distinguish three kinds of effectiveness:

The first is the sort of effectiveness which can best be called *predictive* effectiveness: how to predict future performance or a recurrent regularity in nature, in a business, in the market, in a pool of manpower, and so on.

Second is *formal* effectiveness. Here we are dealing with the kind of thing in which a structure by itself is seen in a new way, without respect to anything that may have to do with predicting something in nature. The field of mathematics, of course, is the seedbed for things of this sort. I mentioned briefly before that when logicians saw that you could take any proposition in formal logic and deal with it in terms of a simple "truth table," this gave them a powerful opening that has nothing to do with anything in nature; rather, it has to do entirely with the structure of a notation. Musicians sometimes have the same kind of insights.

You may say that this has nothing to do with the business world, but I will argue that formal effectiveness is also of great importance. You will see that, in the long run, formal effectiveness helps you in business in terms of representing things. Grammar of discourse is helpful in this way.

Anybody at any age is capable of demonstrating this type of thing. Last year an English mathematician and I tried teaching quadratic functions to a group of third-grade children. We were so encouraged by the results that we took a fourth-grade class through group theory and vector spaces in the next term. We found that you can very quickly get a child to the point of recognizing a well-formed or ill-formed expression in mathematics; you can then go on to work with the mathematics of reference with it, dealing with things in nature. Formal effectiveness is not just the playground of mathematicians and logicians. It is also of tremendous importance in terms of the over-all activity that goes into producing.

The third kind of effectiveness, which is something that principally concerns the arts, is what I call *metaphoric* effectiveness: joining spheres of experience in such a way that you see a kinship that was not seen before. I think, for example, in Faulkner's novel *Sanctuary,* the juxtaposition of Temple Drake, Red, and Popeye—three tremendously different characters who suddenly find themselves in one situation with a common plight—joins together things about which you cannot quite use an objective yardstick but you just *know.* You get the "click": "My God, what an idea!" Or Sartre, putting those three benighted characters into his hell, *No Exit,* having to last out eternity in total incompatibility. In Eliot's *Lovesong of J. Alfred Prufrock,* for another example, you get poor old Prufrock, a sort of combination of an object of contempt and compassion.

What goes on in metaphoric effectiveness? It is clear that this has something to do with activity in the sciences, and probably in any other form of social organization. Frequently, when we look at the activities of people who produce, we discover that their first insights come in terms of a metaphoric rendering of an idea. Niels Bohr once said that the principle of complementarity first occurred to him when he thought about the fact that you cannot look at another person simultaneously in the light of love and in the light of justice. These were incompatible ways of looking, and he went on and said there must be an analogue to this in physics. It turns out that there is, and it's a great hole in the head in some respects.

Now take these three kinds of effectiveness in juxtaposition. What is it that produces an effective surprise and what is it that produces even the ineffective one? What is going on in most cognitive activities?

What is going on, mostly, in producing hypotheses to test is some sort of combinatorial activity, taking a lot of things and trying them out with one another. It is finding the combination that brings off effective surprise or even any kind of effectiveness.

Combinatorial activity is extraordinarily interesting. Mathematically, it has the property that the number of elements and the number of states of those elements that you can combine in a hypothesis are so vast that, if a person tried to combine everything with everything else, systematically ("algorithmically"), he would sit on his backside till the end of time before getting even one-quarter of the way through the possibilities. Obviously, then, this activity does not take place in a way which could be regarded as systematic. (There are certain kinds of problems that we can put on a computer and run off by algorithmic technique. But problems that can be rendered in this way have two characteristics, [a] they are stupid, and [b] they are well understood. To use Norbert Wiener's term, they are labor not fit for human beings.)

So what comes into this combinatorial activity that produces these surprises must be governed not by an algorithm—a systematic technique for getting proofs or getting them in the right combination—but by something which is called a *heuristic*.

Now a heuristic is a technique for combining elements which has the characteristic of being, first of all, very selective selection. And it is non-rigorous: It can never be proved to be a certain way of getting to a solution. So you are dealing with a highly selective program of combining things that can never really render itself completely proved, as having run through the gamut, until you get the right thing.

Now what could be the nature of this heuristic? Here we come to the real question of what it is that people do when they are trying to solve a problem, whether it is putting together a piece of copy or putting together a decent way of running an industrial laboratory. I think first that one tremendously important factor relates to the act of abstraction: *What* features of a situation does a person pick to work with? When you find somebody who has brought off something that is really "hot," whatever the field, you discover that he has looked to the variable and said, "This is good. This is worth betting money on."

Generally speaking, it is not just some aspect that was already there; it is almost always inventing. It is inventing in terms of some larger system which relates to an over-all way of looking at something; that is, a new set of grammatical improvisations, a structured way of relating items to each other.

These systems of looking are the things that tend to be defined. They are the program, the bent to what kinds of things are worth looking at first and what kinds of things are worth isolating. Each of the fields that we look at is characterized by something that can be called a heuristic of its own. There are things which you can speak of as the intuitive familiarity of the chap who is trying to learn how to do it; he has to get up to some point where he has the "stuff," and it is here that the matter of technique tends to be tremendously important.

These heuristics create a problem in terms of selection. It is frequently the case that you cannot know before a person has gone into a field, whether he is going to operate happily and effectively within the set of heuristics that are available there. It is also frequently the case that, by giving a person a little training, you can get a much better sense of whether he is going to be able to operate effectively. This creates a fierce problem. In recent years people have come to us to do research who have backgrounds in mathematics, physics, theoretical chemistry—scientists who look very good indeed. Some of them seem to be able to generalize from their way of operating in those fields, and others jump back and want everything neat and clean. (The one thing they had not noticed, working in the prior field, was that it had been made neat and clean by over 400 years of hard work that has not yet gone into this field.)

I do not know how you predict that in advance, but maybe you could get some measure of intellectual hospitality or open-mindedness. At any rate, until a person has had a chance to spin the heuristics that go on in the field in which he has got to operate, it is extremely difficult to get a rational selection device for him.

What are the general properties of any kind of heuristic that is going to be used as a means of combining possible ideas to create a new idea? One of them that we are very much interested in at the moment is the question of the technique whereby a person can take a long range of observations and summarize them briefly; whereby he can look at a highly successive set of events in simultaneous representation.

We are doing some research on this; I shall tell you briefly about one piece of work. We ask ourselves the question: Can you say something about what happens to a system about which we know a fair amount—perception—when you take away from it its built-in capacity for dealing with things simultaneously and force it to represent things successively? We developed a nice apparatus called a Judas Eye, which has a peephole and underneath it a picture, or an outline drawing, or something of the sort. The subject's task is to move this peephole around in any way that he will and to tell us what is underneath. In other words, he takes something that comes to him successively and translates it into a simultaneous representation.

Of primary importance is the fact that it is exceedingly difficult for the untrained eye to take this kind of successive intake and render it into something simultaneous. There are two tremendous sources of interference, and I think these have some relevance to other activities as well.

First, you get a tremendous exaggeration of any feature that is potentially informational; that is to say, wherever there is a deflection.

Ogilvy

That's the way the early mapmakers drew maps.

Bruner

Exactly. If you ask where the errors come, it is in the size of the capes—they stick way out in the ocean. Or if you look at that famous drawing in the *New Yorker*—the New Englander's view of the United States—Provincetown looks like a sore thumb in the middle of the Atlantic. This is one of the sources of interference.

The second is that the subject will frequently feed back before he can. The secret of being able to operate well is to segment the flow into components and then put it back together again. But before that develops, what may happen is that the subject will get a hypothesis and will be stuck with it: The fish is a flower. From that point on, he has a research model.

The interesting thing about this (and now I come to my next point about general heuristics) is that you can characterize strategies that people use for rendering experience more meaningful in terms of the frangibility or the infrangibility of a strategy: whether the person does something which is corrigible or incorrigible; whether he can correct himself.

There are many incorrigible strategies in this world that we have never taken a proper look at. The main thing I worry about, for example, in case-history method, is that once case-history method has become nicely formed in terms of a theoretical point of view, every exception to the case has a way of being rationalized until it is quite incorrigible, so that the theory or hypothesis cannot be smashed. And the smashability of a theory—a low-level theory, that you would operate with in perception of problem-solving—that very smashability is *the* thing that turns out to be most important.

Not only must there be the possibility of correcting a hypothesis, but the person must have a stop-rule. We have never appreciated fully the importance of stop-rules, but once you take a good, close look at problem-solving, you realize that the stop-rule is as important in human problem-solving as it is on a computer. You cannot go on forever making little epicycles on your notion. You must stop at some particular point and say: Do I want to go on?

Here is a second little experiment, an "experiment-let," if you will, compared with the huge problems of business organizations. We take a picture, an ordinary, garden-variety color picture, and we put it into an apparatus which we call the "ambiguitor" that puts it out of focus. Over four minutes, the machine gradually brings it from totally out of focus into complete focus. We can then get the recognition point—the point in focus at which a person is capable of recognizing the picture.

The first thing you discover is that about 25 per cent of the subjects will go all the way up to the recognition point; the machine will stop; and they will sit there for thirty seconds without being able to recognize what the picture is. If they approached it fresh, of course, they would get it immediately.

What happens? Two things, I suspect. First, the individual adopts a premature hypothesis in the situation, closes off, and then changes his acceptance rule—develops, if you will, an incorrigible strategy: "It should still be a so-and-so, but it has some funny things on it." Let me give you my own personal experience. I got the kids around the lab to develop a set of pictures that I hadn't seen, so I could run through fresh on this.

One of the pictures was of three bicycles in a bicycle rack outside Emerson Hall looking across Quincy Street to the Fogg Museum—a place that I pass practically every day of my life. This picture came on, and about a third of the way through, I thought to myself, "Aha! Very clever. Very, very clever of them. I recognize this one. This is the painting by Renoir of the mother and daughter at the opera for the first night." It had the wheel. It looked like the front of the opera box. And I worked on it and said, "It isn't quite coming clear, but it will come clear." And then I heard the machine stop, and I sat there for thirty seconds trying to figure out what in God's name was this jumble? Then suddenly it snapped.

What we have done as a control under these circumstances is to take a group of subjects and start them at a point well below what most people can recognize, but well above completely out of focus, so that there would not be the temptation to change the nature of the strategy. If I now take the median point—the point at which 50 per cent of the subjects will have it from out of focus or within focus— 96 per cent recognize it by the other group's median point; there isn't that tremendous amount of interference at the change in the characteristics of the strategy.

To recapitulate: First of all, there is the matter of techniques for rendering long, successive things simultaneous; second, development of strategies that can be smashed and stop-rules if you are not sure how they are doing. Third, I suspect there is a terribly important thing that goes on in most problem-solving situations that we can see when we characterize people who perform well as compared to poorly. This is what has been referred to by one of our more picturesque colleagues, a young Englishman, as a "brush-hook" technique—a whole set of brush-hook heuristics. A brush-hook heuristic is a technique for getting rid, at the outset, of things that are going to be ridiculous: taking a look, for example, at what would happen if you pushed them to their limit. (For example, the kind of thing in which somebody comes along and says, "Look, a straight association-theory of ideas will never explain language learning, because if you had to associate ideas at that particular level, the number of thirty-word sentences that a person would have to learn would be about as large as the number of protons in the universe.")

Now the trouble with the brush-hook technique is that, while it does clear out the underbrush, it also sometimes eliminates necessary things.

I could go through a series of things that are characteristic of good synergies. I'm not going to do that. I just want to give you these illustrations, because I think it's this type of thing that can be put into a training regimen. There are things that you can do early in the life of the young human being which makes it possible for him to recognize these things himself. And, very frequently, the process of recognizing the possibilities of doing these things may be important. I think, for example, that the early grades, rather than the training divisions that you run in your corporation, is where this training should be done.

Let me now say a few things that get a little bit closer to this problem of the creative man, the fellow who at least produces enough of these effective surprises so that we can say that he did it once or twice. If you take a look at the successful act when it is brought off, you tend to notice some things that have about them an odd quality of antinomy or contradiction. You know, first of all, in watching good complex problem-solving, that there is always some kind of optimum mix between what might be called enormous *commitment* to a problem and *detachment*. The person is tremendously committed and yet he is able to pull away from the problem, to get away from it.

Now, to me, it is very interesting that the detachment aspect of the thing seems to be helped principally by a person's capacity to deal with the formal properties of the problem (very much like Rokeach's matter of detaching the information from the source). I always remember one remark of the mathematician John von Neumann at the Institute at Princeton. When somebody was joking about someone having been away for a long time, he said, "Oh, he was only away for a weekend—a weekend is any sequence of days including one and only one Sunday." I thought to myself, "Absolutely marvelous. It's a beautiful, formal definition of a weekend." Here, in the midst of a semi-hostile joke, was a man who could look at the formalism of the definition of a weekend. It is no surprise that very many good scientists, good businessmen, and good musicians like certain kinds of games that have this totally syntactic form to them. They do not point to anything; they just live in themselves. This is one of the vehicles for detachment, I suspect.

A second antinomy is some sort of counterpoint between what might be called passion and decorum: you know, passion for a subject, great vitality, and at the same time a tremendous amount of reflectiveness that goes with it, not pushing, not forcing the problem to behave in the way you want it to.

There is a third thing, too, and I might suggest that some of these things are matters of organizational atmosphere. The third thing has to do with the freedom to be dominated by an object that is apparently outside of you. I always have been impressed when colleagues, telling me about an experiment they are doing, say something like, *"It* needs a control group." Or, *"That picture* needs something there." Not that *I* need it, but that *it* is something that has a self-contained life—and yet you are dominated by it. Now, I suspect that this is one of the most valuable ways to reduce anxiety about our endeavors—externalize them. (It is a point Freud made about the poet or the playwright, that somehow the externalization of the internal cast of characters allowed him to deal with them in a kind of objective way.)

The fourth thing has to do with an antinomy between deferral and immediacy. When we have a notion or hypothesis about something or other, we like to have it turn out to be so, and we are eager to grab hold of something and say, "Yes," and stop. But the process also requires that there be deferral. The one thing we know about even the most primitive perceptual system is that once a person thinks he sees what it is (on the tachistoscope, a fast-exposure apparatus), you can start changing the nature of the picture he is looking at and he will not notice the change. Once there is partial confirmation, he closes down the system. So, simultaneously, a man must have the impulse to want to close the system—otherwise he wouldn't be in this game and stick at it—and he must also defer it.

Well, I have had nothing to say directly about business organization, or the creative organization, but I suggest that close analysis of people doing any kind of intellectual work reveals certain common factors. I suggest that it might, in spite of the general pessimism thus far, be worth while to look at the process of producing something. One must not judge by the product. Perhaps it is not possible to look at the process and say what a *creative* process is. But I suspect that, if you look at any problem-solving activity and simply ask what it takes to make this effective in even the slightest degree, there will be some things that suggest fairly basic changes in the way you put together an organization.

Steiner

This presentation is relevant on at least two levels: first of all, in what it teaches or provokes us to think about in terms of the individual creator, and, second, in its implications for extension by analogy to the organization itself. What are the organizational stop-rules, for example? How incorrigible is organizational strategy?

Especially relevant, I think, is the notion of detachment versus "investment"—a company is investing in a certain goal, but at the same time it must be detached enough to go into other areas. What kind of a strange mixture produces this capacity in an organization? Some organizations seem to be fixed endlessly in one particular pursuit, whereas others may jump around too much. What is the right mixture, and how, organizationally, is it attained?

6

Some Studies of Creativity at the Institute of Personality Assessment and Research

(EDITED COMMENTS)

FRANK BARRON

Let me begin by telling you where you can find fuller accounts of some of the studies I shall refer to. First of all, there is my article in the September, 1958, issue of *Scientific American*. The entire issue was devoted to the topic, "Innovation in Science," and my own contribution to the issue was titled "The Psychology of Imagination." That article describes my work on originality up to the beginning of the studies of creativity recently completed at the University of California.

I have also contributed articles on the psychology of creativity to the *Encyclopaedia Britannica* and the *Encyclopedia of Mental Health*. The first of these contains a brief historical account and current overview of psychological research on creative thinking, and the second is a non-technical, theoretical article covering a wide range of common-sense questions. My volume entitled *Creativity and Psychological Health* was published by the D. van Nostrand Company, Inc., in 1963. It is intended for the intelligent lay reader. A compendium of selected passages from that book was published in the *1963 Yearbook* of the Association for Supervision and Curriculum Development, National Education Association. Finally, with Professor Calvin W. Taylor, of the University of Utah, I have edited selected papers from a series of conferences sponsored by the University of Utah and supported financially by the National Science Foundation. This volume was published in February, 1963, by John Wiley and Sons, New York, under the title *Scientific Creativity*. The papers in that volume are addressed primarily to a professionally qualified audience in psychology, education, and industrial and governmental personnel work.

What I shall talk about now is some recently completed research carried out at the Institute of Personality Assessment and Research of the University of California, under the direction of Donald W. MacKinnon and with the collaboration of Richard Crutchfield, Harrison Gough, Ravenna Helson, and Wallace Hall.

Our procedure in all the studies has been as follows: We select subjects for study because they possess to an outstanding degree certain traits we are interested in—in this instance, creativity. We ask them to come out to Berkeley for three days to take part in a wide variety of experiments, tests, and special interviews designed to furnish us systematically with information we need to answer certain questions or test certain theories.

The measurement we have adopted involves first an activity which could be called instrumentation; that is, developing measuring instruments, so that the work we do is replicable and can become public scientific knowledge. The psychometrics themselves are definitely subsidiary to the intent of gaining understanding. That is, we are seeking through repeated measures to establish a body of findings which will tell us something about creative individuals as persons, and then, by inference, about creative processes.

We also try to get at creative processes directly through the use of problems we set the subjects during our "assessments" and by interviews about their life work. Psychometrics, used in this way, are, as James Joyce characterizes Irish art in *Ulysses,* "a cracked looking glass." If you try to hold the mirror up to nature and your mirror is made of correlation coefficients, you are likely to find a shattered image that you must reconstruct considerably. The error variance in even the best of psychological tests is so great that the correlations such tests produce do not give a clear picture of how things work.

We take three main approaches to the criterion, or criteria, of creativity. The first is the purely psychometric definition. We say that a response is original if it occurs with some specified degree of unusualness, such as one time in a thousand, and if it is adaptive to some kind of reality. An example of the use of this criterion is an experiment whose results were published under the title, "Originality in Relation to Personality and Intellect." Here, the sample itself was not selected for creativity. The subjects were Air Force officers, and although they were well above average in almost all the traits we are ordinarily interested in—health, psychological stability, general intelligence— they were not especially selected for creative ability.

We used two main kinds of tests to give us an over-all criterion. One is the sort that is typified by anagrams. You give the subject a word like "generation" and you say, "Make up all the anagrams of this that you can, and you have such-and-such a length of time." In this case, you count up the frequency of the responses suggested and then by determining which ones are most infrequent in the group under study, you assign weights based inversely on the observed frequency. Note that here you have a determinate number of solutions, since there is a completely specifiable set of anagram solutions to any given word. Such a test can of course be scored with complete objectivity.

A second class of tests we have used cannot be scored rigorously but depends upon the judgment of "raters." Paul Meehl's remarks about the importance of having a rater who can discern originality is borne out by our experience with this second class of tests. It so happens that many of our findings on such tests have fallen out rather well with our theory, whereas some other researchers do not get the same findings with the same tests. I believe that the reason our findings make sense is that the test raters who are asked to judge the originality of response are themselves highly selected for originality. One of our raters, for example, was a senior at Mills College who had been endorsed by the faculty as the most creative girl in the college. Another rater won the undergraduate poetry prize at the University of California. We tried as a matter of policy to employ as raters only those individuals who themselves were already known to us to be highly original. Our logic was: "It takes one to catch one."

An example of this sort of test is provided by the Symbol Equivalence Test, one of the tests described in the article mentioned in the September, 1958, issue of *Scientific American*. We presented to the subject certain images such as "haystacks in a field," or "empty bookcases," and asked them to create some equivalent image or metaphor. A common response to "empty bookcases" is "empty mind," or "a deserted room"; an uncommon response is "the vacant eyes of an idiot." The task of the rater is to look at all the responses, not knowing who the subjects are, and simply to rate them on an eleven-point scale from the most original to the least original.

Merton

May I interrupt you? With your technique of relative frequency of responses as a measure of originality, have you gone on to adapt this to the checking of social impressions of originality? That is to say, if you now submitted this list of responses, of which *you* have the known frequency of occurrence, to judges, and asked them to judge which of these are most common and which strike *them* as original, what would be the error factor in what is taken to be original as compared with your objective data on this relative frequency? I ask this because of our earlier conversation, in which you remarked that when you depend on social judgments of originality, they may not at all coincide with the relative rarity of actual occurrence. I think you can adapt this technique to tie it up with this earlier experience.

Barron

That is a very good suggestion. The difficulty is that, outside of a controlled test situation, you rarely can obtain exact counts of responses which would serve as a basis of comparison with ratings. It would certainly be valuable information if it could be obtained.

Let me sum up what I have said about this method of establishing criteria of originality. What we do is take a battery of tests, obtain ratings of the subjects' responses, and use these ratings to identify the regularly original persons in the population we are studying. Our psychometric criteria in the study you have before you were these: (1) The person should, on at least one test (out of eight in this particular study), score in the top one per cent; (2) On all tests, averaging test scores across the board, he should be superior to about 70 per cent of the population. Thus you can establish groups of regularly original and regularly unoriginal subjects on the basis of current test performance.

The second method of establishing criteria is to ask a group of people who are well known to one another (all the members of the senior class at a given college, for example, or all the members of a given military organization) to rank one another in terms of their originality on the basis of observed performance over some period of time.

A third method is to ask persons who are themselves considered to be both highly perceptive and competent in their field to nominate the individuals in their field who are the best of the lot. In our own studies of creativity, we used this method with writers and architects. We thus obtained lists of prominent architects and writers who in the judgment of critical observers were highly original. We then invited subjects who were most frequently nominated to come to Berkeley and participate in our studies. The proportion of acceptances varied in different samples, but they averaged over 50 per cent. Considering how busy most of our subjects were and how valuable their time was, we felt gratified by this response. Besides the question of time, there were of course some objections offered to psychological testing. Among the writers, particularly, there were those who objected to the whole idea of psychological study of their creative processes. Some felt this to be unjustified meddling; others felt that we were doing the study in the interest of a society which was seeking to control them. We were aware of these dangers, of course, and had taken on the job in spite of them. We tried to communicate this awareness to our subjects, and generally we succeeded.

So much for the criteria. We employed several kinds of tests with reference to predictors, and we tried to tap several domains of personal functioning. First, we tested for intellectual aptitudes, both verbal and non-verbal. For verbal comprehension, for example, we used the test that Lewis M. Terman and his associates at Stanford University developed to measure the IQ's of their "gifted children" grown older, the Concept Mastery Test. Then we also used various other tests of specific intellectual aptitudes of a non-verbal character, such as spatial perception. An example is the Gottschaldt Test, which requires the subject to separate simple figures from complex ones in which they are embedded.

We also used personality tests of a standard sort, such as the Minnesota Multiphasic Personality Inventory, which yields scores in terms of such psychiatric diagnostic categories as depression, schizophrenia, psychopathic deviation, and paranoia. Projective tests, such as the Rorschach Inkblot Test and the Thematic Apperception Test, gave us samples of complex symbolic behavior. We also employed tests which measure various aspects of strength of the ego. An example is the California Psychological Inventories, with its scale for measuring such traits as flexibility, intellectual efficiency, responsibility, and the like.

Certain social-situational experiments were also employed, such as the Asch "independence of judgment" experiment. We have found that independence of judgment is highly correlated with the ability to produce unusual responses, to see things differently, to perform creative acts which are carried to completion in the real world. An amusing incidental observation of the degree of independence of creative writers was provided by this experiment; here is a description of the prototypical form of the experiment.

In the prototypical experiment, of which we used a variant, there are ten apparent subjects, nine of whom are confederates of the experimenter. The task is to judge which of two lines on the right is the same length as another line on the left. In the critical trials, the confederates of the experimenter give a prearranged false answer. They are seated in a row and respond aloud one by one. The single subject is seated ninth in the row, so when he hears eight people in front of him giving the wrong answer, the question becomes this: Will he give the right answer, or will he agree with the false consensus?

In the variant we used, one of the items in the test presents two circles of identical area, and the task is to say which of the two is the larger. Under control conditions, where there is no pressure to accept a false consensus, people of course split about fifty-fifty. Under the experimental conditions, they will shift to a 75–25 ratio; that is, three of four naïve subjects will accept the false consensus. This occurs even though there is actually no basis in reality for any prefer-

ence. In the case of the writers, on this item they shifted 82 per cent
the other way; that is, in eight out of ten cases they chose the circle
the rest of the group said was smaller.

There are several possible explanations. One writer reported that
when he saw all those other writers saying it was the one to the
right, he figured that that *must* be the *wrong* answer.

Rokeach

> Did you treat that finding as an indicator of dependence or
> independence?

Barron

> That is a very nice question, because one way of looking at it
> is that the person is compulsively going against the norm. This
> would seem to be rebelliousness or contrariness rather than real
> independence. The other point is that, unless you go a little
> too far, you may not be able to go far enough. Artists always
> have been at pains to make it clear that they are exceptions,
> even the very great ones—William Blake wearing a red bonnet in
> England at the time of the French Revolution, for example. The
> greatest scientists as well are inclined to go out of their way to
> assert their individuality.

Let me go on to some other findings. First, the psychometric finding with regard to measured intelligence. In our highly creative subjects—top mathematicians, writers, architects, and research scientists
—we found a uniformly high IQ rank. Among thirty prominent writers, for example, there were only two subjects who fell below the
average of Terman's sample of gifted children on the Concept Mastery Test. This means that the average IQ of the group was somewhere
between 145 and 155. This is just a guess from comparative data
and perhaps should not be taken as numerically exact, but we can
say quite safely that for achievement of this sort a superior IQ is
necessary. Yet within such superior groups, in almost every study we
have done, IQ—while quite high on the average—has no relationship
within the samples to rated creativity. In fact, with artists we find a
slight negative relationship.

What this means is that throughout the normal ranges of intelligence and creativity, there is a positive but low correlation, in the neighborhood of from .35 to .40, between measured intelligence and creativity, but as you push upward in the realm of creativity, that correlation drops off to zero. And, probably, if you had to generalize and still stick to IQ terms (which, by the way, are used less and less as we get a clearer picture of the complex structure of intellect), you would probably say that beyond 125 or 130, IQ does not matter as far as creativity is concerned. Two kinds of things do matter at that point: one, motives and, two, certain stylistic variables descriptive of personality: the drive to achieve through independent effort, for example, or an emphasis on intuition as opposed to sense perception, in the sense in which C. G. Jung uses those terms. Still another important variable, in part motivational and in part stylistic, is the preference for complex and challenging problems and a liking for the dynamic as opposed to the static.

One last finding from this all too cursory survey of our early results is rather an intriguing one, bearing on what has popularly been considered something of a paradox; namely, the relation of genius to insanity. What we find in almost all samples is that the most creative subjects, on tests like the Minnesota Multiphasic, have higher scores on measures of psychopathology. Combined with this, in some samples (although not in all), we find high scores on a measure of ego strength, although in the general population ego strength is negatively correlated with such traits. This is especially true of schizophrenia; yet we find certain creative writers scoring high on schizophrenia and also high on ego strength, even though the correlation is −.70 in the general population.

Basically, the observation amounts to this: Creative people are both able to and want to transcend the usual bounds of conscious experience, yet they have the ability to behave in a "realistic" fashion while doing so. One function of the ego is to make things regular and to make the world predictable so that we can move in it with security. These people seem to have the ability to break those bounds and to live in a world which is different, and perhaps dangerous psychologically, but at the same time is a world which enhances instability and thus increases the possibility of new combinations.

Discussion

Guetzkow

If you thought of it as a combination of a knack or bent for a little slippage, combined with the necessary editing, then the actual schizophrene has the bent for the slippage but lacks the talent for the editing, and the ordinary man lacks the bent or knack permitting the slippage, but these people have the knack for the slippage followed by the editing.

Barron

Yes, I think that is a good description, although I do not think in those terms. "Slack" or "slippage" may be accurate terms, however, to describe the pathological aspect of what I am here calling "ego transcendence."

Two or three points concerning motivation arose in this connection. Motivation is of paramount importance in actual creation. In terms of the prediction problem, you can certainly spot people who have the set of traits and abilities which conduce to creativity. But whether they will prove productive depends on their motives, or better, upon whether their needs as individuals can be met by the given social milieu so that a viable form for realization of the potentiality of the individual occurs.

There, of course, is where the function of the organization becomes a very important one—how, for example, you interpret to the individual the meaning of his work in the context of his life. The question the creative person might ask of the organization is, "Why am I working here and what are the stakes in this game?" And, moreover, "What are the stakes *beyond the immediate* stakes?" I found Mr. Shockley's remarks about publication intriguing, and I think they are relevant to this point. One must ask on what basis, in his own eyes, the individual stands or falls. Or, as we sometimes put it, who is the jury in your case? Everyone has his own jury, self-chosen.

Another question we ask here is, "What could earn you heaven or what could send you to hell, metaphorically speaking?" Heaven and hell—your personal heaven and your personal hell —*what earns you which?* And if you had to elect a jury to decide your fate, in that sense, who would be on it? Again, to writers we put the questions: "Who is your audience? What kind of persons? Contemporaries or persons in the past?"

Answers to these questions can be very illuminating and give you some idea of the person's value system, his philosophy of life, what basically is activating him. One strong motive we find repeatedly in creative individuals is the drive to make an elegant synthesis perceptually, to take account of *everything*. This applies as well to their own life work, so that they are in a sense cosmologists. For the novelist, for example, the shelf of his books constitutes a kind of world-view, a universe of his own creation.

Ogilvy

Are you disagreeing with Paul Meehl?

Barron

I think not, although perhaps I consider it more likely than he does that current research findings are valuable *right now*.

Meehl

We don't disagree much, but we do appear to disagree a little bit. But I would be inclined to advise everyone here to go with him rather than me, since this is his field of expertise and my acquaintance with it is relatively superficial. I was perhaps somewhat less optimistic than one should be even about the present state of the evidence; although, as Frank says, given a group of persons who are above your cutting scores, there is still not a huge probability of finding a creative individual (although it is still a lot bigger than the probability for somebody who was not so screened in the first instance).

Second, the interests were different, in that I was addressing myself to what might be the present, momentary, tactical maneuvers appropriate in an institution where the decision policy can maximize its odds of getting output. Frank, on the other hand, is primarily interested in what in the long run is more important to all of us, I presume; that is, an adequate understanding of the causal processes, with reference also to the instrumentation that you have to do in the light of your theory about those processes to soup up your psychometrics, so that in the future they will be even more powerful.

I think this is a matter of degree more than of fundamental difference. I don't think Frank contends that from the practical, daily, institutionally oriented decision-policy standpoint, our predictive power is really impressive right now. On the other hand, I will not say that we can't do *anything* in this respect.

Barron

Well, it depends. One must consider base rates, as you well know; and one must consider also the exact selection situation and the prediction situation. If you are a corporation, the question is how much money is involved; if a school, how many applicants you have and how many you can accommodate. I think that our present results are now usable; that is, they have enough demonstrated validity to put them to work. I would venture to say that if you can define a practical selection situation for me, where you can tell whether or not the tests are working, I could set up an appropriate battery of tests which would show worthwhile validities.

Merton

Would you say that you could do a great deal better within practical affairs in identifying one *type* of creative person rather than another? One type might be, let us say, a production manager for Mr. Bensinger or a marketing manager for Mr. Peterson. Would you have less success in identifying that kind of fellow than you would a copywriter for Mr. Ogilvy?

Barron

The main point I would emphasize is this: that you cannot speak *in general* until you know what the job is. You must appraise the selection situation psychologically and in concrete detail.

Often the variables that are not essential to the creative process itself do become important as selectors for this or that kind of task. If you want a creative merchandiser, for example, he may need certain other attributes, such as high personal dominance, that a copywriter would not particularly need. Sometimes the non-essentials, so far as creativity is concerned, make the big difference when it comes to success in a given social role.

Steiner

I just want to comment on this apparent inconsistency between Paul and Frank. It seems to me that there are two important variables. (1) What is the size of the sample the organization can select? If your object is to bring in a hundred or two hundred people every year and to make sure that, of those two hundred, you are going to end up with a half-dozen or so creators in the next decade, then clearly tests ought to be of some help. On the other hand, if you are going to hire one man or two men and it is critical that those two men be creative, then tests are going to be of relatively little help to you.

(2) Also, Paul phrased the alternatives in this way: He said that, at the moment, he would put more credence in the considered judgment of a highly creative person who knew the candidate well. Frank did not really speak to that question; he has not made that particular comparison at all. Usually, in organizational recruiting, no one knows the candidates well. So, once again, this would be an advantage of the use of tests when large samples of people are available.

7

A Case: Observations on the Development of the Transistor

(EDITED COMMENTS)

WILLIAM SHOCKLEY

Perhaps the one thing that I bring to this meeting is a background in creativity in the transistor field. But I thought that rather than trying to give a detailed history that would hit all the aspects that might bear on this, I would try to give a once-over-lightly of about five minutes and then see if these aspects would turn up responsible questions.

Before I start, there are one or two things I feel like saying at this point about why I am here at this meeting.

There are at least two reasons. The decisive one is that I had a personal debt of gratitude to Allen Wallis. If somebody else had asked me to take time to come to a meeting of this sort, I might very well not have done it, simply because I could perfectly well see other things I should be spending my time on.

I will say there's another aspect though, and that is that this is a real stimulating affair. I've enjoyed the discussion and I enjoy the type of thing that goes on. I have more confidence in this group of people than I would ordinarily have and, therefore, my guard is up somewhat less. I can talk about myself more than I would under similar circumstances in groups of this size. So this is something about background.

Now somehow I see myself as a sort of guinea pig in this setup. I qualify as being an intelligent and creative person. I can count patents. I can read what is being said about me. (I have had the unusual experience of reading my biography recently, and there are things which people say about me which I would never have had the nerve to say, you know, myself. But there they are, and I can say I am a pretty creative guy with a lot of originality and effectiveness. Whether I would have said that if I hadn't seen it in writing where I could quote it, I don't know.)

But saying something more about myself here: A lot of things that have been said by some of the people speaking about the psychology of creative people strikes home. I am looking at this reprint which Frank Barron just handed out to us. It says we're "likely to have more than the usual amount of respect for the forces of the irrational in ourselves and in others." I think this is true. And I would think maybe this other paragraph: "They have exceptionally broad, flexible awareness of themselves. The self is strongest when it can regress, admit primitive fantasies, naïve ideas, crude impulses, inner consciousness and behavior, and yet return to a high degree of rationality and self-criticism. The creative person is both more primitive, more cultured, more destructive and more constructive, crazier and saner than the average person." I don't know, but I would be inclined to buy this kind of thing in reading about myself.

Something else in my background is this: I am a person with very mixed self-esteem and I am aware of this. It doesn't solve all your problems to win a Nobel Prize. You still go around wondering if you are any good, every now and then, and you do various things which may not be really necessary for any demonstration, you see. I would have felt somewhat distressed if I hadn't worked out this generalization of the end links in the chain. I enjoy showing off. I have a need to feel I'm making contributions to things.

Well, I thought I would run through things historically.

CHRONOLOGY

I'll start out with 1936, which was the year I came with Bell Telephone Laboratories as a fresh Ph.D. from M.I.T. There was a conversation that I had at M.I.T. which I think may be significant in what went on in my career. It was a conversation with M. J. Kelly —whom many of you probably know by name—who was then research director and who subsequently became president. Kelly talked about the objective of an electronic telephone exchange; that is, where everything is done electronically, with no relays.

Well, then, there's a period of about 1939 to 1940 in the course of which I had some ideas of trying to make a solid state amplifier. (That is what the transistor is.) But I got involved in doing some things like trying to make other amplifiers that didn't have vacuum tubes in them. One of them involved using a piezo-electric crystal. It was a thoroughly lousy idea, I think, but you never can tell. These things may come back if somebody does it better and finds a use for it. But as far as I can tell now, it is a lousy idea. Nevertheless, the intent was right.

From '41 to '45, there was a war, at which time I was a radar designer and in operations research work.

From '45 to '48, I was co-head of a solid state research group. The areas dealt with in the solid state group were formalized by Mervin Kelly. That covered chiefly four general areas: (1) magnetic materials; (2) piezo-electric crystals; (3) semiconductors; and (4) dielectrics of insulators.

Semiconductors are the crystalline materials that transistors are made of; of course, at that time there were no transistors but a number of other useful electronic functions were performed by semiconductors. In particular, copper oxide rectifiers were used to make so-called "click reducers"; these protect the subscribers by limiting the maximum amount of noise that may come out of the earphone in the event of some malfunction of a telephone circuit. All of the subjects selected for areas of research by the solid state group had to do with the transmission of electrical signals over wires and were related directly to major problems of the telephone business. In this area, I had a very free hand.

From 1946 to 1948, I cooked up some additional ideas about amplifiers. These led to certain difficulties; certain new lines of research started, out of which came the transistor.

The first transistor was not an idea of mine. (The point-contact transistor is a different kind of thing.) But at the same time, I cooked up the idea of the junction transistor, which is the patent under which practically every transistor made now is made.

From '51 to '54, there were various kinds of writing and other transistor ideas. I have the patents on at least two other principles, which are important principles in getting amplification out of semi-conductors that are quite distinct from junction transistors.

From '54 to '55, I got tagged at the Pentagon again in the weapons systems evaluation group in an activity which led to the setting up of a corporation group, which some of you may know, is called the Institute for Defense Analysis.

From '56 to '62, I've been involved in a new venture of trying to set up a business. There are about 130 people and we are part of Clevite Transistor, a division of the Clevite Corporation.

SCIENTIFIC ASPECTS OF PRACTICAL PROBLEMS

There are some interesting aspects about this: I think I've formulated a sort of research objective in this activity which I will try to describe by the phrase "respect for scientific aspects of practical problems." That is, if we can't make a transistor of some sort, or if we can't make a process work (after we've done a reasonable amount of messing about and trying), then we turn around and say: What is nature telling us? What does it mean? We forget about solving the problem for the time being. We try to understand the science of what is going on. This I think may represent an important trend in creativity in modern industry, which would not have been appropriate in the time of Edison. At the time of Edison, it was better to try things, because the fundamental understanding was not there. There is now enough fundamental understanding in these things, and once you understand this, it is pretty likely you'll find answers.

Discussion

PRACTICAL ASPECTS OF SCIENTIFIC PROBLEMS

Ogilvy

Who owns the patents you mentioned? Do you get royalties or them or does Bell?

Shockley

Bell owns all the patents, and I can't see a better way of handling it. I would just love to have my hooks in this thing, of course. This is obvious. But, on the other hand, any other scheme would make an unlivable place. I would not like to work in an organization nor try to run an organization in which a man received outstanding awards for his patent contributions.

If you have such an arrangement, you will find six people sitting down in a conference to discuss something, some problem. Now suppose there is a high award for an invention, and I have an idea. I'll say to myself, "Gee, maybe this idea is really an invention, but I don't quite see it yet." So I will keep my mouth shut, I'll go back to my desk, I will work for a day on the thing, and I'll get it written down and witnessed before I bring it out in front of anybody who might be able to out-think me on it.

Peterson

What about the problem of the discovery of the problem to be tackled, as contrasted with the solutions? How do you select problems?

Shockley

Well, you see, in '39 and '40, I think they did a very good job in my conditioning at Bell Laboratories. They stuck me to the vacuum tube department for a while there, but then when I indicated that I wanted to get into more scientific things, no bar was put up to my getting back and doing more basic work in solid state physics.

Well, I then had ideas that you might be able to make an amplifying device not using a vacuum tube. There is a thing called the old crystal detector which some of you are old enough to know about—the galena, cat's whisker—which does the same job as a certain kind of vacuum tube. What De Forest, the father of electronics, did was to take the rectifier and put a grid in it. Now, the cat's whisker, galena detector did a job like a vacuum tube diode, which Edison had a lot to do with discovering, by the way. He put a grid in this which is a handle, a valve handle which gave a valve-controlled electrical flow.

People had an idea somehow that you could stick a valve handle into this crystal detector. That idea was not original with me.

But back in 1940, I had an idea which in principle is sound. It doesn't violate any laws in physics to do this job. In about '45 to '46, I had another idea which was sounder and which now works, though it didn't work then. Now, I'm not saying any more about this because I just suspect that if we get into any of the technical aspects it will take too much time.

But there is an aspect of pattern in there, from '45 to '48, that I think is worth mentioning. Taking this idea of how an amplifier might be made to work based on sound physics, but which so far did not, I persuaded at least three different experimenters, all of whom were competent, to try to do this and make a measurable observation. Nothing measurable came out of this.

It was at that point that Bardeen came up with a physical explanation that there were some new physical phenomena occurring here, not generally recognized, which was preventing this thing from working. This was his theory of surface states, a subject still of active scientific interest in semi-conductors. We started to investigate that aspect, and this led us to new experimental configurations, more understanding of nature, and in turn, in the course of these experimental configurations, to some situations which appeared to give us more control. It was in the course of following those up that Bardeen and Brattain came out with the first point-contact amplifying device, the first point-contact transistor.

At the same time, in part stimulated by these things and stimulated also by some earlier work I had done on how semi-conductors work, I came out with the more generally useful idea of the junction transistor, which was filed as a patent application in 1948. I published extensive papers on the theory in 1949. It was first made to work effectively in 1950.

I reported on this at one of the first international semi-conductor meetings in Reading. It was a non-scheduled paper, and it made so little impression that it never got into the proceedings of that meeting.

Then in 1950—this is an interesting sideline—I got involved with the Pentagon; I was shipped off to Korea in an operations research activity. In the course of this, I got involved with being consultant for the Quartermaster General, and I discovered the proximity fuse situation. And one thing that was perfectly obvious was that what one should try to do was to make proximity fuses which were transistorized.

When I tried to promote a program of that sort, the best electronics man I could find at Bell Laboratories to make a transistorized amplifier to go on a proximity fuse said, "Look, if you could really make a really good junction transistor, this would be an awful lot better than a point-contact transistor." During this period, there had been some more development on techniques and we had another crack at making a junction transistor, and then we made the first really striking transistors. These were announced in 1951, and it was really in '51 that the transistor field took on something of clear and major technical and economic importance. These junction transistors, made as a result of this military stimulus, were of a much lower power, with much higher quality and much higher operating efficiencies, than the then existing point-contact transistors.

Bruner

Do you recall what your own psychological reaction was at the time with respect to the experimental tests? Certain groups and good experimenters had failed and then Bardeen subsequently came up with the reason why you're not getting the effect you should get. You were building a little sub-theory, I gather, from this disparity. But, prior to Bardeen's contribution, how did you feel about your idea after good men had failed to get the effect?

Shockley

Well, I was having self-esteem problems, frustration, confusion, and a whole bunch of things. I was not really depressed about this, but—

Bruner

Did your confidence in the basic conception go under attrition?

Shockley

Well, this took some attrition all right, yes; but all the same, one says, "Damn it all, here are the things of which there is pretty good evidence, and according to these this ought to work, but there is something in here which is messing it up. What is it?"

Bruner

It is a fascinating problem, whether there is any personality trait that distinguishes people who rightly stick to their guns, as opposed to people who stick to their guns unsoundly, when the facts start piling up against them.

Shockley

Well, this junction transistor idea and the patent application were sound. But, in the course of this, we tried various ways of making good PN junctions. Morgan Sparks tried dropping molten N-type germanium on solid P-type germanium; these things came out lousy. I can remember being shaken by some fellow who said the only way to make a good rectifier was to form it while applying voltage when it is being made. The physics of the situation—there was no reason to think it would work —but I can remember after enough failures taking this man's objections a damn sight more seriously than they deserved.

Bruner

Are these colleagues of yours evokers or just co-creators?

Shockley

I am said to be the chief evoker in this; I set this goal and went after it. These colleagues of mine, one way or another, accomplish essential things to make it go. But I can recall one electrical engineer in our group who said, "Well, this other device, the point-contact, might be called a transistor, but if you ever make this junction transistor, it should be called the *per*sistor, because that is what you are doing about it."

Ogilvy

Are you a better creator or evoker?

Shockley

Myself? I do both things. No modesty.

Ogilvy

You keep going back and forth from one road to the other?

Shockley

Myself? I think so. There is only so much you can do yourself with your own hands. I do things which involve pencil and paper and tight quantitative thinking simply because I don't have anyone else that can do these things as well as I can.

I tell people what I think I want. I want a man who is going to work on the best idea there is around. I expect him to take mine into account, and his own, and everybody else's you see. But I have trouble that I can specifically pin onto a couple of kinds of people: the fellow who says, "Well, you told me to do this," and he goes and does a lousy job at it, and it doesn't work. And the fellow who, by God, will not do what I tell him. He's got to prove he can do something which is his own idea.

IMPLICATIONS FOR REWARD SYSTEMS

Merton

Dr. Shockley, isn't this an instance of the type of relation between personality variables and organizational variables? You said earlier that you were opposed to the notion of giving awards to the men who made patentable inventions. You went on to explain that a reward system of this kind could be dysfunctional. The result might be the hoarding of experience, secrecy. This would cut down the rate of innovation in the organization.

Here you are talking about an organizational variable, the reward system, and how it is going to affect behavior. Ten minutes later, when you were asked whether you were a creator or an evoker, you decided that you probably were both. Now, if we consider that as an aspect of your personality, then you are not the type of individual who is secretive. You are willing to share your ideas and to get others to follow them up.

And now we start to raise the question, you see, of the connection between types of personality and types of reward systems. Some men would tend to be fairly secretive under any reward system. They can be found in the history of science. They are the men who would not make their ideas available until they had worked them out as fully as they could, even if the reward system was not of the kind that you mentioned. Every time we get down to concrete cases, we find that we cannot even describe the case adequately without examining the interplay between personality and organizational variables.

Shockley

Let me say that, in my own case, I'm conscious of the points you make, and I'm conscious that I may actually make an evaluation at a moment as to what I am going to do. That is, if I'm in a discussion and I have an idea which I might bring out, I may actually go through this evaluation and say: What am I likely to add to make the discussion go? What will this add to the organization? What will I get out of it if I do it another way? And then I come to a decision, and what has gone into this decision, I don't know. I might decide in that case to be secretive, either for selfish reasons or because I think that this one will lead the whole discussion more astray; we might not get to the end and then for more straightforward organizational reasons it wouldn't pay off, you see.

NO "SWEEPING PRINCIPLES"

I would comment on one aspect about a lot of what has gone on here yesterday and today: I distrust, by and large, the availability and applicability of any great number of sweeping principles. I lean more to being a believer of low cunning and expediency. As an illustration: How do you go about starting a scientific job? Certainly you have the people who read everything; they don't get anywhere. And the people who read nothing —well, by and large, they don't get anywhere, either. Or the people who go around and ask everybody, and the people who ask nobody. I say to my own people, "Well, I don't know how you start a project, but maybe you can ask your boss. See if he knows someone in another company whom he can phone up and ask. Or go and look at the literature. Or step out and do an experiment." You see, there is one principle here, and that is that you don't first start on something which is going to take six man-months before you get to the answer. You can always find something in which, in a few hours of effort, you will have made some little steps, so there is certainly some kind of a small step before a big-scale effort—well, that's such an elementary general principle, but short of ones as elementary as that, I'm not sure I have much confidence that you can enunciate too many of them.

8

A Creative Organization

B. E. BENSINGER

The United States businessman has always been dependent on new ideas for survival and growth, but never has he been more determined in his search for new ways of doing things than today. We in Brunswick are no different from many other companies in America and, therefore, we are extremely happy to be able to exchange ideas with other businessmen, educators, and researchers on a subject which is so vital to the progress of American industry.

The theme for the seminar as I understand it is "The Creative Organization." In attempting to translate this theme in terms of Brunswick, many questions come to mind. Some of these are:

———Is Brunswick a creative organization? If so, what makes it so?

———Have Brunswick's successes been those of creative efforts? If so, what are some of these creative contributions and how have these been made possible?

———Does Brunswick hinge its future on creativity?

Most of you have heard of Brunswick's unusual performance in the past few years. In 1957, when I spoke before some financial people in Missouri, I reported sales of 122 million dollars and net income of under 7 million dollars. When I projected substantial earning gains for future years, some appeared to be skeptical, for, after all, Missouri is known for the famous slogan, "Show me." Three years later, in 1960, Brunswick reported sales of 360 million dollars and a net income of 38 million dollars.

Because of this unusual performance, we have often been called one of the nation's postwar "glamor corporations." We are not particularly moved by this description. The word "glamor," it seems to me, has a rather shallow and temporary connotation. After all, how many of the glamor-girl movie stars of the 1920's are remembered today? Brunswick plans to be around for a long time, and we prefer to think of ourselves as a growth company, moving forward on a rising tide of new ideas and a sound creativity-oriented management.

We all know that competition is actually increasing rather than decreasing and that the stepped-up pace of modern innovation is putting a severe strain on us as a company. When we hear of "innovation," it rings a familiar bell. We hear many clamoring for new or redefined goals, but when examined, many of these goals are not new; they are merely ones previously known by management and now forgotten. "Innovation" is confused with "creativity." Too frequently that which is new is only different, not better. We in Brunswick do not believe in constantly making change for the sake of change, but we strive to better every aspect of our business.

We also believe that ideas cannot be plucked from the brains of our team and dumped immediately into the mainstream of our business with any real hope of success. We try to improve our management efforts on the basis of long-term gains. It follows naturally then that we believe in laying careful groundwork before concocting new ideas and translating these ideas into action.

We do not confuse analytical or judicial thinking with creative thinking, but we feel that both have a real place in the scheme of things at Brunswick. Both seem to come into play in the efforts of every segment of our organization, among the engineers and designers, production people, and marketing people. In a short space, I cannot give a definitive picture of our creative organization, which within a short time has undergone stupendous transformations, but I shall try to give a thumbnail sketch of some creative efforts at Brunswick in each area—Engineering and Design, Production, and Marketing.

FURNITURE FOR THE FUTURE— CREATIVITY IN ENGINEERING AND DESIGN

We may first look at the engineering and design field, where we certainly can point to many creative examples. Let me cite one.

For years, most people thought of a school chair merely as something to sit in and a doctor's examining table something merely to lie on. But we've changed all this.

We have pioneered new concepts in furniture for schools as well as for physicians' offices and clinics. In schools, we shunned the shackles of tradition and came up with entirely new concepts that represented a revolution in terms of the school room as you and I remember it. We unhinged the desks from the floor and made the classroom a "living room for learning." We introduced beauty and function into furniture and made it quite flexible. We introduced bright colors and attractive plastic for the seating materials. These were durable, stackable, and rearrangeable. Our original classroom design concepts have been universally accepted by others. We are improving them all the time and intend to continue to do so.

Our efforts in the medical field are comparable: As modern as medicine is today, so is the professional furniture for the doctor designed by Brunswick's Aloe Division. The line consists of examination and/or treatment tables with matching cabinets and accessories. Instead of accepting preconceived ideas, we discarded the ultraconservative ideas manufacturers long thought should be incorporated into medical treatment furniture and came up with a fresh, original concept in furniture that incorporates beauty with the most advanced ideas of function, construction, and materials. If you were to talk to our manager at our manufacturing plant, he would say, "Our product improvement never ends. We guarantee everybody will get more than we claim in our advertised prices." So thus, with over-all superiority in advanced design, quality, and function, our furniture, for both schools and physicians' offices and clinics, is destined to become the "furniture for the future."

IDEAS INTO INDUSTRIES—CREATIVITY IN PRODUCTION

Just as we have tried to set the stage for creativity in design, we have made inroads into the production field with creative efforts.

Some of our successes in the production field are epics that parallel Horatio Alger. The illustrations I might cite are ones where one man had a unique idea, believed in it enough to spend most of his time and energy developing it, and eventually saw it pay off for himself and Brunswick. But this was only the beginning in these instances, for these men built teams that embraced a theory of dissatisfaction, teams that are forever reasonably dissatisfied with what they have. The observation of Oscar Wilde, that "Discontent is the first step in the progress of a man or nation," is certainly appropriate here. When I walk through the plants, where automatic machinery is used for production, I get the feeling that this machinery is obsolete when it has been on the line for a mere two months. These people seem to live by one of Kettering's old sayings: "Just the minute you get satisfied with what you've got, the concrete has begun to set in your head."

The manufacture of hypodermic needles and clear plastic tubing for medical use seems simple enough in our highly developed medical society. Yet for years, "the best obtainable" caused problems for doctors and hospitals.

Do you realize how many "shots" are taken yearly by us Americans? Do you realize that Americans take two billion hypodermic injections annually, an average of almost one per month per person? With the mounting frequency of injections, three hazards to health are involved in their use to combat disease: (1) the danger of cross-infection; (2) the possibility of violent fever reaction from foreign proteins known as pyrogen; and (3) the degree of pain in administration. All of these are eliminated by the use of our Roehr disposable needle.

Obviously, if an intravenous needle were used only once, it would be safer, for there would be no danger of cross-infection from an improperly sterilized needle. And if the point could be really sharp, like a razor blade with no burrs, it would cause the patient no unnecessary pain; and if the needles could be produced cheaply enough, the hospital staff could perform other duties in the time formerly devoted to cleaning, sharpening, and sterilizing needles. When we examined the manufacture of hypodermic needles, we found that the methods developed 60 years ago had changed little. Needles were being manufactured one at a time.

Before launching production, we set out to discover what the market could bear from the standpoint of cost. We worked doggedly on the product and method of production until the costs were brought low enough to introduce and compete successfully with conventional, non-sterile needles. Today we manufacture 300 needles at a time and produce 2,000 different types and sizes of hypodermic needles. In fact, Japan, the second largest producer in the world, takes a month to produce what we produce in a week.

The story of our plastic catheters is a comparable one. It all started with an idea that catheters could be made more simply and cheaply. Experimenting continuously with vinyl-based pigment, our people pursued experiments with various formulae and extraction processes until they found a way to make catheters continuously from clear plastic, glassy smooth inside and out. Besides improving the manufacture, they dispensed with many connecting problems normally encountered, and these catheters can now be connected to other tubing without special adapters.

This seemingly simple technique has made older catheters obsolete, from the standpoints of both cost and variability of use. Like the Roehr disposable hypodermic needle, it is economical to discard our Argyle catheters after a single use, thereby eliminating the hazard of cross-infection.

We talked of the disposable hypodermic needle and catheter, but what caused these ideas to spring into industries? It was the eager acceptance of challenge. It was the constant search for different and better ways of doing things, as a result of the dissatisfaction and restlessness of mind of each member of the team. In brief, it was the application of amazing ingenuity to tough problems of production.

BATTLE FOR BOWLERS—CREATIVITY IN MARKETING

The bowling business has been built by creative efforts. As we all know, businesses today not only are confronted with the problems of day-to-day operations which have an impact upon current profits, but must look ahead into the future and determine a course of action for the achievement of future objectives.

This takes *vision*. It was this kind of "looking ahead" that enabled a small group of us being regularly quite "early in the game" to set long-range objectives and revamp our organization for action. It was this kind of foresight that enabled us to envision a new and bigger market for bowlers.

Almost from the beginning, bowling had been a man's sport. The majority of the installations were in an environment not at all conducive to family participation. We realized very early that bowling had to come out of the basement, into an atmosphere of high respectability, to give it universal popular appeal. To be successful, we realized the following conditions must be met:

————The environment of the game had to be improved.

————More regular bowlers had to be created.

But *vision* of a potential market and what was necessary to build that market was not enough. Additional creative efforts were necessary. By this, I mean sheer *determination*—determination to meet our competition and produce a successful automatic pinsetter; and *resourcefulness*, that would enable us to apply every creative effort to seek out and obtain the proper financing, and the imaginative engineering required for an outstanding automatic pinsetter. Of course, coupled with these aspects of *determination* and *resourcefulness* is proper *timing*, which is of the essence.

This is the story of how we utilized these creative efforts of *vision, determination,* and proper *timing* to set out the favorable financing and engineering efforts to get an automatic pinsetter built and a new industry established.

1. The first efforts were those of our creative engineers who produced an automatic pinsetter which proved to be a superior and economical prototype.

2. These creative engineering efforts proved an excellent asset to us when we approached the Murray Corporation to assist us in the financing required for the production of these pinsetters. We were fortunate in working out the Brunswick-Murray Automatic Pinsetter Corporation to develop and produce the pinsetter. It was agreed that Murray would supply the financing and Brunswick would handle the distribution, installation, and servicing.

3. Stimulated by the success of our financing, Brunswick engineers accelerated their efforts and field-tested the pinsetter by the end of 1954. It was ready for production a year later.

4. In the meantime, our sales force persuaded many operators to "hold the line" and buy pinsetters from Brunswick instead of renting machines from our competitors. The salesmen booked 50 million dollars' worth of sales before the first machine was delivered.

5. In 1956, the Otis Elevator Company, to which Brunswick and Murray had subcontracted manufacturing, turned out the first batch

of pinsetters. By this time, our competitors had already installed some 9,000 of their machines.

6. Meanwhile, Brunswick and Murray were finding their relationship somewhat less attractive. Mr. Gould, President of Murray Corporation, who felt that his credit line might be pushed to the limit, called for revision of the basic partnership to enable Murray's share of the revenue to be higher. I realized the solution to this proposition was not an easy one. To pay Murray some 18 million dollars in a period of tight money, and to satisfy Otis that Brunswick's credit was good and it was safe for Otis to go on manufacturing the machine, was quite a trick. I approached the C.I.T. Financing Corporation and persuaded them to take a look at the pinsetter. I finally convinced them and ended up with 55 million dollars' worth of credit; later this was increased to 95 million, and today it is almost 160 million. We at Brunswick then borrowed 27 million dollars to pay Murray's share of the pinsetter affiliate and repay its bank loan.

7. The next step was a severance of ties with Otis which had been producing a pinsetter for us. We established our own 200,000-foot factory at Muskegon, Mich., and produced our own machine. More recently, we have started installing our own pinsetters, which also had previously been done by Otis.

It is difficult for me, at this time, to spell out the details of these interesting experiences, but I can assure you that our original *vision* coupled with the *determination, resourcefulness,* and proper *timing* carried us over the hump.

Simultaneous with our establishment of the pinsetter, we endeavored to enlarge our market by continuously attempting to get more regular bowlers and improve the environment of the game. As a result of our constant "battle for bowlers" and a tremendous number of creative marketing efforts, in 1960 the American Marketing Association presented Brunswick with its top award for original sales efforts, along with IBM, American Motors, and General Foods.

"Getting our heads together," not necessarily in what you know as formalized brainstorming sessions, but in informal, idea-producing sessions, our marketing managers came forth with a number of creative marketing efforts.

As early as the 1930's, we tried to bring more women into the game. You all recall the efforts of the cigarette industry in trying to alter folkways and mores in order to enable a girl to smoke with respectability in society. Just as they did, we resorted to Hollywood and its stars to assist in our efforts to gain popular appeal and universal acceptance of women in the bowling field. We created, developed, and produced films in which actresses and movie starlets were shown bowling, and much of our publicity was aimed in this direction.

Since then, we have launched at least a dozen different programs that would appeal to women. One such idea was introducing bowling fashions. We showed that girls do not have to be built like lady wrestlers in order to bowl. Drawing upon our earlier experience in founding the American Bowling Congress, we helped organize the Women's International Bowling Congress to build a new generation of bowlers. We helped organize the American Junior Bowling Congress. Officials of this group traveled the country convincing educators that bowling was well and good.

Television, which was keeping prospective bowlers at home and appeared to be a real threat to the entire industry, was turned to our advantage. In attempting to mold the new image of bowling, we used television to bring the sport into the people's homes.

Architectural research provided new designs for bowling establishments that made them true assets for growing suburban communities. We emphasized the appeal of color in our lines of bowling equipment and transformed the bowling establishment into a community center for the entire family. Bowling has now become part of our way of life.

As was implied earlier, ambitious growth goals require that a corporation's entire resources be geared to the creation and development of products which will strengthen present markets or create new markets and will provide the sales and profits necessary to meet growth objectives. This we have done, in a creative fashion. We created new attitudes to a fine old sport. We created a new environment which appealed as a recreation center for the family. We created a new and ever-growing market, through creative marketing efforts.

THE BRUNSWICK APPROACH

What approach does Brunswick use to spur this creative activity? We do utilize the venerable suggestion box, but to date we have not resorted to the stereotyped and planned creative approaches advocated in many circles. We have not drifted into the free-wheeling, idea-association techniques such as "group think," "buzz sessions," "imagineering," and the popularized "brainstorming." Nor have we insisted that our people adhere closely to the individual techniques of "attribute listing" of Professor Crawford; "area thinking" of Professor Arnold, or "input-output." Even though our people are constantly at work at idea production, we have not set forth any specialized training programs on "imagineering" or creative thinking.

However, even though we have shied away from formal creative sessions, we try to provide a relaxed atmosphere that will help people unlock their mental storehouses. As I mentioned earlier, we believe very strongly in laying careful groundwork before ideas are put into action. This has not necessarily been a "1-, 2-, 3-step affair," but it has followed a somewhat general approach in most instances.

DETERMINE NEED

In most instances, when we have marshaled our forces for growth, the philosophy of a now retired Vice-President of U. S. Steel was used as a basis. He said, "Give me a need and I will develop the market. Give me a market and I will develop the product." It was with this idea that we developed our approach to creative ideas and growth. For example, when we thought of the field of school furniture, it was a matter of simple arithmetic to compute the necessary classroom count by projecting the record birth rate and rapidly rising school enrolment. When we probed other areas of universal need, we saw one right on our doorsteps in the field of recreation. Never before in history had people had so much money and so much free time in which to enjoy it. There were strong forces at work that had brought about this unprecedented wealth of spare time, over and above that required for earning a living. It was these kinds of studies that we resorted to. We studied the situations analytically to help pinpoint our direction of growth.

DETERMINE PROFITABILITY

Once the need was determined, a second important aspect was asking ourselves, "Would it be a profitable venture?" Without adequate profit, I am sure we would have never come this far. The same applies to any other business within our economic system.

SET OBJECTIVES

After we had determined that a venture would be profitable, we clearly set our objective, whether it was gaining a new bowling market or coming out with a new product.

ASSIGN TO IMAGINATIVE MANAGEMENT

Once the objectives were set, the problem was placed in the lap of our imaginative management. Our Brunswick management team is not a stereotyped one, nor are we of the "standpat" type. I am a profound admirer of conservative counsel; we in Brunswick seek it and value it, but it is not what has made Brunswick a "go-go" company. I place much higher values on imaginative and creative efforts in coming out with new and better ideas for our advancement.

CREATE IDEAS

We have no formal brainstorming sessions or planned approaches, as I indicated above, but our management has constantly set forth a multitude of innovations—innovations that were not merely changes but were improvements in production, design, engineering, and marketing.

PUT IDEAS INTO ACTION

Of course, ideas in themselves are not enough; our final aim is to get these ideas into action. We have created the atmosphere in which these new ideas can be realized. We do come up with many ideas that are unworkable, but the ideas we have used are ideas from our imaginative team and this has helped make Brunswick the corporation that it is today.

CONCLUSION

In conclusion, let me say that never before has the need for creative management been so great. As we look at the sixties, we find that our economic growth is not as rapid as it should be—our profits are being squeezed unmercifully and competitors are constantly challenging our position. It is evident that we need to redefine and elevate our goals and our performance as managers. We must develop, produce, and market more products at a fair profit, and to do this, we must encourage the best creative efforts of people who are handling each aspect of our business, design, engineering, manufacturing, and marketing. I believe these are true goals for men who make industry run, and that most managers of industry are willing to accept such challenges.

Discussion

Ogilvy

Brunswick sounds like a glamor stock to me.

Bensinger

I said there has been some deflationary attitude.

Bower

Why were you so late in getting the machine, relative to American Machine & Foundry?

Bensinger

We were stupid. That is a fair statement, too, although it is easy to rationalize a lot of things after the fact. At that time, there were ample pin boys. We sampled our customers, and found that most proprietors did not want an automatic machine because they knew it would cost a lot. When AMF came out with their first machine, with no competition, they charged 14¢ a line. A pin boy then was getting 8¢, 9¢, or at the top 10¢. In our effort to hold the line, we promised the customer that we would not come out with a machine on this basis; if we did, we promised that it would not cost him any more than his current pin boys.

As I have said, we were short of cash. We had spent a lot of money in design, engineering, and development of the school furniture line. It took three years after the war before the government removed the restrictions on building, so we did not have much business either. We weren't so well heeled to go into this, so we sloughed off. We wanted to watch what the other fellow was doing, which was AMF. Just before they did start their first production, we bid—because there were patent involvements —$700,000 for a machine in Camden, N. J. They bid a million and got it. It never was worth a darn; they have never used it, but that is the frantic way in which unsound business judgment sometimes is utilized.

But to answer your question directly: There was no real good reason, other than that management made a wrong decision, in my opinion, not to pursue this more vigorously, so they beat us. They put out nine thousand. We only put out two thousand the first year. I think the year we put out our two thousand, they put out six or seven, but in three years we caught up with them, and we have maintained the annual majority of installations in this for years.

CREATIVITY OF A DIFFERENT ORDER IN BUSINESS

Peterson

We have been talking about creativity as though it were a homogeneous thing. We have heard about the need for freedom, permissiveness, etc., and yet our own experience tells us that in many business situations, unless you have a fairly clear goal, you want something by a given date to fill a stated need, nothing much happens. For example, we were working on electric eyes for seven or eight years before competition really gave us an incentive.

Perhaps we should break down creativity into various types. Much of what goes on in business is not the creativity that many of these gentlemen are talking about—not fundamental understanding, basic breakthroughs, etc., but just minor adaptations of things you know how to do. Maybe we are putting too much into one basket by talking about creativity. I have a feeling that 90 per cent of what businessmen would call creativity is really a different kind of creativity from what many of you have talked about.

Bensinger

I agree; Brunswick has a couple of research engineers who are working way out ahead. Nobody bothers them. We get checks and reports on their creativity, but so far it has not resulted in anything tangible. This same team though—it is now eighteen or twenty people—did produce something we have been able to use in our defense division. I suspect that we will take a close, hard look and limit this a little. I know, Franz, you say you should let a man just think ad infinitum, but when you have budgets, profits, and other things to meet from a business point of view, a management point of view, you cannot always do what you would like to.

Peterson

I never talked to an engineering department that didn't argue that if they just got more freedom and more time, and could put their feet up on the desks, everything would be wonderful. Almost everyone feels this way. What comes out of this is: The more fundamental the knowledge that is needed, the truer this probably is. But the more directed your goals are, the less true.

Meehl

But the similarity between creativity in science and creativity in the kind of work that you were describing, I think, is quite evident; that has to do with the discovery of the need. You referred to the fact that your first step was to identify a need. And we are told time and time again by the scientists that one of their first steps is to find the problem.

Now, in the realm of the sciences, if the problem is not brought to your attention by some practical urgency, you evolve the "sense of the significant problem" that we have heard about by detecting a gap in the preceding thought; by detecting an anomaly in the finding that is not coherent with pre-existing thinking, or by making a derivation from preceding thought. The interesting question to me, as I listened to your account, is how you in business go about discovering need—which could be, I think, a formal parallel to the situation in the sciences where you try to define the problem in order to get on with the business of solving it.

Now, could you tell us a little about how you have gone about discovering these needs? It does no good to say that you must have some degree of limitation on this freedom, because that already assumes that you have the target. How do you arrive at the target, how do you identify the target?

Bensinger

It gets back to the philosophy of the corporation and the particular fields any corporation is in. We had to select certain major fields: health and science, education, and recreation. It is the philosophy of the management that if we can cater to needs in a way that will make peoples' lives healthier, happier, fuller, and more complete, then we will have met these needs and in turn we will get our volume and our profit back.

When you analyze any particular field of endeavor within, say, the recreational area, or the health and science area, it is not difficult to find the need. For example, in the case of the Roehr needle: People were getting injections in a very inefficient and costly manner. The reason Roehr made a modest success before we got hold of this is that he saw this need. He saw an opportunity to expand, develop a better needle, a better syringe, and make it disposable, which he pursued.

It is not difficult to find needs. Take anything you want that I know something about, and I can define a need; for example, an outboard motor. We own Mercury (Kiekhaefer) Corporation. Now, the creation of the outboard, which goes way, way back, again stems from the need for a propulsion unit in a boat. Now there is something new that has been added, like latakia in tobacco. The latakia that was added in the boating propulsion field is what is known as a stern-drive unit. Again an analysis was made. Was this a genuine need or a whim of the public? When it was determined that it would probably be more than just a whim, that it might take over a major portion of the outboard motor business, Kiekhaefer, our subsidiary corporation, determined to move ahead two steps over the stern-drive unit of Outboard Marine. I don't know if I have answered your question.

9

Several Findings of a Transactional Approach to Creativity

MORRIS I. STEIN

Creativity is a process that occurs in an individual who exists in a social context. Both the more complete understanding of the creative process and the increased probability of accurate predictions as to who will or will not manifest creative behavior, therefore, depend on our knowledge of the individual's environment, his psychological characteristics (including his developmental history), and the transactions between the two. I shall present several findings of an ongoing study.

The data to be presented later are based on sixty-seven Ph.D. chemists, employed in three different industrial research organizations. These men were divided into two groups: one group of thirty-three "more creative" and another group of thirty-four "less creative" individuals. The two groups were established on the basis of ratings obtained from their superiors, colleagues, and subordinates. Both groups represented approximately the upper and lower 20 per cent of the men rated in their respective companies, but they were equal in formal education as well as other characteristics. On the average, they were in their middle thirties; they had been in their respective companies for approximately five years; and they had an almost equal number of patents and publications. The two groups did differ from each other in supervisory level and "work area." A larger proportion of more creative men came from the upper supervisory echelons (which may well reflect how industrial management rewards creative individuals with increased administrative responsibility that may draw them away from their research), and a larger proportion of them were also involved in what for industry may be described as long-term or basic research. The manner in which the data we obtained vary as a function of both supervisory level and work area, does not concern us at the present time. Rather, the discussion will be concerned solely with differences related to "more" and "less" creativity.

Environmental Characteristics

To gather data on the environmental factors that may be related to creativity, a questionnaire[1] was developed in which a central position was held by the concept of "role"—the expectations that the industrial research environment has of the individual researcher. Previous experience in our pilot investigations had indicated that the industrial researcher was expected to fulfill five major roles in an industrial research organization—scientific, professional, administrative, social, and employee. A series of items relating to these roles was constructed and presented to the men under a variety of conditions. However, before turning to the data, let us turn to the definitions of these roles.

THE SCIENTIST ROLE

As the "scientist," the industrial research chemist, like all scientists, is expected to "discover, systematize, and communicate knowledge about some order of phenomena."[2] In his role as scientist, the individual undertakes activities not because they will benefit anyone who may be considered his client, but because they will result in more knowledge. "Scientists, in the purest case, do not have clients."[3]

In fulfilling his role as scientist, the individual conforms to the ethos of modern science which, as described by Merton,[4] involves the following four institutional imperatives or constraints. (1) Universalism: Source and claims for truth are to be subjected to "pre-established impersonal criteria." (2) Communism: This refers to the fact that "the substantive findings of science are a product of social collaboration

---

[1]M. I. Stein, *Manual for Surveys of Research Administration and Environment* (Chicago: Science Research Associates, 1960).

[2]E. C. Hughes, "Psychology: Science and/or Profession," *American Psychology,* August, 1952, p. 7.

[3]*Ibid.*

[4]R. K. Merton, *Social Theory and Social Structure* (Glencoe, Ill.: The Free Press, 1949).

and are assigned to the community. They constitute a common heritage in which the equity of the individual producer is severely limited." (3) Disinterestedness: Science demands objectivity and has no place for the personal and subjective motivation of the individual. (4) Organized skepticism: This last institutional imperative involves "the suspension of judgment until 'the facts are at hand' and the detached scrutiny of beliefs in terms of empirical and logical criteria . . ."

THE PROFESSIONAL ROLE

Overlapping with the scientist role is the professional role. As a professional, the industrial research chemist has been trained in a specific tradition and "only members of the profession are treated as qualified to interpret the tradition authoritatively and, if it admits of this, to develop and improve it."[5] This statement holds true for both the professional and the scientist. What distinguishes the two is that the latter is concerned primarily with increasing knowledge and in communicating with his colleagues, while the former earns his livelihood by giving what Hughes has called "esoteric service" to a client.[6] The client for the industrial researcher is "the company." By accepting a position with a company, a researcher both implicitly and explicitly accepts the tasks of working on problems related to the products that the company produces. But the company is not only the researcher's client. It is also his patron, in that it provides him with the financial security, the equipment, the personnel, etc., to carry out his work. It is this client-patron role, the company vis-à-vis the researcher, that puts certain restraints on the fulfillment of the scientist's role for the industrial researcher and is manifest in the following imperatives: limited communism, focused truth, selflessness, communication with lay personnel, and vested interest.

THE ADMINISTRATIVE ROLE

In terms of this role, the industrial researcher is expected to guide, lead, and supervise the work of other scientific, professional, technical, and non-technical personnel. While the researcher may be expected to fulfill the other roles early in his career, the degree to which he is ex-

---

[5]T. Parsons, "A Sociologist Looks at the Legal Profession," *Essays on Sociological Theory* (rev. ed.; Glencoe, Ill.: The Free Press, 1954).

[6]Hughes, *op. cit.*

pected to fulfill this role generally varies as a function of the research-er's time in a company, his experience in industrial research, or the level of his accomplishments.

THE EMPLOYEE ROLE

The fourth role of the industrial researcher is the employee role. It is to be distinguished from the scientific and professional roles in that their adequate fulfillment adds *new* information to the system of industrial research, while the fulfillment of the employee role pertains to the flow of already existing information and to the maintenance of the system as an ongoing enterprise. The industrial researcher shares this role with others in the organization and it involves the following factors: consistent productivity, financial awareness, efficiency, ac-cepting status position and adjusting to authority, and regularity and flexibility in the performance of his duties and responsibilities.

THE SOCIAL ROLE

The social role refers to the behavior patterns that an individual is expected to manifest in his interpersonal relationships with superiors, colleagues, and subordinates. The individual's social role varies as a function of his position in the organization's status hierarchy. The higher the status, the more immunities and privileges accrue to him, and he may even be able to alter the role so that it is more congruent with his personality. At lower levels in the hierarchy, however, the individual may feel that it is impossible to alter the role to suit his needs.

The social role differs in one very critical respect from the roles considered previously. For the scientist, professional, and employee roles, there are usually either written or spoken codes and regulations with which the individual may acquaint himself. But for the social role, the prescriptions are not codified and often not verbalized. One learns about them through personal experience, or the individual may be in-formed about them by close friends. At times when they are verbalized in a professional discussion, they may be denied, for the social role includes the "irrational" factors in the social process with which the scientist does not want to concern himself, especially since he may not be too adept at fulfilling them. Yet fulfilling the social role adequately is in some situations a prerequisite for establishing smoothly functioning communication networks that may facilitate his work and often gain for the individual the *opportunity to be creative.*

The above definitions of the roles were used as the background of a theoretical framework, and a series of thirteen items was developed to gather data from the chemists about the extent to which each of the roles was important to them at the time they first came to work for their companies; those they felt were most important to them at the present time; which of the activities was most important for success in the company; and which of the activities should be rewarded if creativity was to be promoted. Top-level administrative personnel of the industrial research organization also indicated how important these different activities were, insofar as they were concerned for success and creativity in the company.

Analysis of the researcher's responses to the role items under these varying conditions indicated the following:

1. The scientific role was more important to the more creative men at the time of the study than for the less creative men.

2. The less creative men saw themselves as fulfilling better positions of subordinate status in either scientific or professional roles than was true of the more creative men.

3. Furthermore, the less creative men said that when they first came to the company, they had felt that it was more important to them to assume positions of subordinate status in either scientific or professional roles than was true of the more creative men. While there may be errors in recall, one cannot overlook the possibility that self-selective factors may also have been involved and that those men who had been regarded as less creative some five years after they had first joined the company had not seen themselves when they accepted employment as having any interest in other than subordinate roles.

4. For the more creative men, there was higher agreement between what they felt made for creativity and the capacities they possessed.

5. As we studied the relationship between success and creativity as a function of supervisory levels (including data obtained from top-level administrative personnel as well as from the researchers themselves), we found that as one goes up the administrative ladder there is greater agreement between what makes for success and what should be rewarded for creativity. One of the activities on which there is greater emphasis as one rises administratively is, as one might expect,

administrative. But what is more important is that at the lowest supervisory level of research personnel, there is the greatest discrepancy between success and creativity, reflecting the possibility that the newer research people encounter greater "culture conflict" as they move from the university to the industrial environment. Or, as one of our researchers said, "It may take four years to get the academic Ph.D., but it takes another four to get the industrial Ph.D."

In summarizing these data briefly, it may be said that the more creative men see themselves as possessing skills and abilities that are more congruent with the demands and requirements of the industrial research environment than the less creative men. Furthermore, they see themselves as possessing greater skills and abilities to develop new information for the industrial research organization than the less creative men.

PSYCHOLOGICAL CHARACTERISTICS

In order to study the psychological characteristics of the more and less creative men, we selected a variety of areas, intelligence, problem solving, and personality characteristics. As our studies progressed, we frequently adapted new techniques for our investigation; consequently, we do not have the same number of subjects for all of them and therefore the data need to be dealt with cautiously. It should be pointed out, however, that these data are consistent with data obtained in other studies.

INTELLIGENCE

As with other psychological factors, so with intelligence as measured by intelligence tests; a rather wide range of intelligence test scores have been obtained in other studies of creativity. Similarly, in our study we found that there were no statistically significant differences between the scores of the more and less creative men on a test of verbal intelligence that dealt with analogies.

Wallis
What was the range in their intelligence measures?

Stein
We used the MAT—the Miller Analogies Test—which you can

convert very easily in terms of IQ. It is a high-level verbal analogy test. The maximum score is 100, and their mean scores were in the 80's. I don't know what the exact conversion is.

Wallis

So there is a relatively narrow band there. It was a top 5 per cent.

Stein

Oh, yes, in terms of percentage of population, we got a top 5 per cent.

Wallis

So that the lack of any correlation between that measure and creativity within that sample is not surprising.

Stein

No; in a highly selected population, you do not find this kind of differentiation.

PROBLEM SOLVING[7]

It was impossible to study the problem-solving processes of our chemists as they worked on their day-to-day problems. Therefore, our approach was to gather data by studying their behavior as they went along solving a rather difficult experimental problem. In this problem, the men were presented with a machine that contained on its face a circular array of lights and buttons. When a disk with various arrows was placed between the lights on the face of the apparatus, it was possible to indicate to the men that the lights were interrelated in some way. The men were not shown the nature of the relationships, for they had to learn them. They then had to demonstrate that they had learned these relationships by pressing only a designated set of buttons which would eventuate in the lighting of the center light. (It is impossible to do justice, in this brief time, to the complexity of the problem. An indication is the fact that about one hour is required to instruct the subject and for him to study the practice problem.)

The results of this experiment indicated that our two groups of men

---

[7]A more complete discussion of this may be found in S. I. Blatt and M. I. Stein, "Efficiency and Problem-Solving," *J. psychol.*, XLVIII (1959), 193–213.

are distinguished from each other not in their capacity to solve the problem but rather in the *process* through which they sought their solutions. (It was possible to study their problem-solving processes by virtue of the fact that every button that was pushed marked a moving tape.) Our more creative men spent more time and asked more questions that were oriented to analyzing the problem. Our less creative men, on the other hand, spent more time and asked more questions that were oriented to synthesizing the information they had. Our observations suggest that the more creative men were "feeling out" the problem, attempting to understand it, to become one with it; and, after they understood what they were about, they then integrated what they had learned. Consequently, they spent more time analyzing the problem and less time synthesizing the information they had. Our less creative men appeared, at times, to be engaged in battle with the machine; they looked as if they were going to wrench the solution from the problem, to dominate it; they "went after" the answer even before they knew the structure of the problem.

The contrast in the behaviors I have just described is reminiscent of the descriptions given of mathematicians' solutions to problems. Among mathematicians, it is sometimes said that he who arrives at the more elegant solution to a problem has the edge on creativity. It is the search for this type of elegance which seemed to differentiate the more from the less creative men in our study.

PERSONALITY FACTORS

In addition to studying intellectual and cognitive characteristics, our research was also oriented to investigating the personality characteristics of the chemists. Here the data indicated that the more creative men were more autonomous, more dynamic, and more integrative than their less creative colleagues, and they also saw their attitudes as more different from others.

In a test of autonomy that we used, we found that the more creative men were more autonomous; in contrast to some of the previous discussions, I would describe the men as autonomously detached, rather than hostilely alienated, from their environments. They do not waste energy in fighting the environment; they will leave it or become cosmopolitans, in the sense of not belonging to any single organization. They really belong to the profession called the science. The more creative men in this study, possibly because they were employed in industrial research organizations, placed higher value on practical matters and utility. They also placed more emphasis on harmony and form and less on mystical values and acceptance of the church as an institution than their less creative colleagues. The less creative men were more authoritarian in their attitudes than were the more creative men. The more creative men were less anxious than the less creative men we studied, although there is some suggestion that in those work areas which involve more basic than applied research, the more creative may tend to be a little more anxious than the less creative men. By the same token, the more creative men gave more evidence of psychological well-being than did the less creative men. Finally, in a test designed to gather evidence on the men's own perceptions of their needs and motivating factors, it was found that the more creative men were more oriented to achievement and acceptance of their own inner impulses, while the less creative men were more oriented to avoiding situations in which they might be blamed for their activities or in which they might feel inferior.

In summarizing the psychological findings that differentiated the more and less creative individuals in our study, it may be said that our more creative subjects made more complete use of their potentialities; they enjoyed understanding problems, and they might even seek them out. They were persons who were free to question and not afraid to deviate from the status quo; they were not tradition-bound. They were open to their internal and external experiences; they were autonomous men who devoted themselves conscientiously to their work. They sought understanding and possessed an aesthetic sensitivity which helped them in finding solutions. They were not the victims of preconceived ideas nor were they bound by absolutes; rather, they were capable of utilizing their hypotheses in a fashion that enabled them to attend to and integrate the external forces in their environments.

AUTOBIOGRAPHICAL FACTORS

The third area of our investigation was a study of the life histories of our subjects. We hoped that these data would not only enable us to understand better their current psychological status, but also prove helpful in identifying creative individuals relatively early in their lives.

Here are some of the findings that differentiate the more and less creative individuals: A larger proportion of more creative than less creative men came from homes in which emphasis was placed on scholarship and science. Furthermore, we found that a larger proportion of the more creative men had had parents who set goals for them. In their interactions with their parents in childhood, we found that a larger proportion of the more creative men regarded their mothers as inconsistent and their fathers as providing them with satisfactory male models to be emulated in certain respects later in life.

Limiting ourselves to these few findings, we would suggest that the inconsistency experienced by the more creative individuals may have disposed them to deal with external matters by drawing more heavily on their own resources than was true for the less creative individuals. But at the same time, the more creative individuals were provided with direction for their energies in terms of the value system of the home, and had experience with a male figure in the home which prepared them for dealing with other males later in life.

These, then, are some of our results to date on the social, psychological, and biographical factors that differentiate more and less creative Ph.D. chemists employed in industrial research. Our current efforts are devoted to exploring the different types of individuals who can be creative (since the material presented above is based on over-all group results), the different types of environments that exist in industrial research organizations, and how they either impede or facilitate creative activities. Finally, we are also investigating the possible value of the findings just reported for the prediction of creativity of students as they undertake a program of higher education that may lead to an engineering career.

The last point I wanted to make was that the more creative men have had a more complex early life than the less creative men, and I think this is what disturbs their homeostasis in some way and gives them a different orientation toward growth. I would have to add that the mere complexity alone is not sufficient; it is the reaction to the complexity that is important. For example, when you take groups of more and less creative men with the same, self-rated complexity of background, the more creative men say that they found their complexity stimulating or challenging. The less creative men felt it discouraging and depressing.

Discussion

THE LINE BETWEEN CREATIVITY
AND SCHIZOPHRENIA

Alexander

Can we go back to Mr. Barron? I found it most interesting that he discovered, in creative people, a coincidence of strong schizoid trends plus great ego strength—a rare combination of things.

I find a very interesting corroboration of this finding, which is probably not as precise as his, but was very convincing for me. For some other reason, I compared a modern abstractionist artist's product with a schizophrenic's painting, and some similarities were extremely strong. I projected a schizophrenic product which I got from the mental hospital and, beside it, the corresponding modern artist's painting, which I selected. I then asked my audience to select which was the mental patient's work and which was the great artist's work. There was quite often great confusion, which created, of course, a very strong reaction. The implicit conclusion was that modern painters are schizophrenics.

Ogilvy

A French psychiatrist has reached the same conclusion.

Alexander

Yes, but I did not. If you study more carefully, you find exactly that difference which you described. You will see that in the artist's work only is there a certain sense to the madness. There is more organization, more integration. The other is more—let us say—dissociated, to use an ugly, technical expression. There is no cohesion.

Of course, I do not know the explanation, but it is very easy to think of this: The schizoid feature means only a great amount of tolerance, in the case of the artist, for unconscious material. A great novelist, a Dostoevski or a Balzac, has a communication with his own unconscious which is extremely great, almost as great as in the schizophrenic. (The schizophrenic understands himself very well. A famous old psychoanalyst, Ferenczi, said that if a patient brought a dream which he could not understand, he went to the mental institution, selected a good schizophrenic, and got the answer from him.)

What happens in the man who has ego strength and also communicates with his unconscious? I think the causal connection is that, because their ego is strong, they can tolerate the onslaught of unconscious, threatening material.

Barron

Yes, I would interpret it that way.

Merton

So would I. The one guy has relatively undistorted derivatives because he cannot hold them down, and the other has some distorted derivatives because he can afford to accept them.

Alexander

Van Gogh's case, for example, is quite clear. In his very crazy periods, when he was extremely disturbed, his painting deteriorated. As long as he was schizophrenic or manic-depressive, but could still control and integrate, he did the greatest art. When his optimal balance broke down, then you had all the wild, incoherent intrusion of unconscious material.

INTENTIONAL "LOOSENING OF THE EGO"

Barron

One other thing should be added; many creators deliberately attempt to bring about in themselves certain altered states of consciousness, similar to psychosis. One of the most common means for bringing this about is the use of drugs, such as hashish or opium. Recently, psychologists have been studying this process experimentally by the use of such drugs as lysergic acid and psilocybin. It appears that what happens when the ego is weakened by biochemical means is that defenses are reduced and one finds surging up from the unconscious all the material that usually is shut off at the border between conscious and unconscious. What creative persons can do, apparently, is to permit such usually censored material full conscious expression. They can do this, because their ego is strong and they can tolerate a degree of disorganization without suffering damage to their capacity for integration.

Steiner

Are there organizational counterparts to this? Can you identify some companies whose management is so strong and secure that they can tolerate a certain type of disorder or other element within the company that normally would be thought of as disturbing? And at the other extreme, do you have companies that are so completely disorganized that they are always disturbed and disrupted?

Overt criticism of management might be a similar variable. You might get a great deal when management is simply bad, less where management was even worse but involved strong sanctions against it, and more again when management was secure enough to tolerate and capitalize on criticism. I wonder if there is any way to institutionalize this; in some sense, to put this kind of ego strength into a company or into one unit—to let the id go mad, so to speak. What do you do, organizationally, to produce that kind of thing?

Barron

Social organizations larger than companies may provide us with some illustrations of this. Consider nations, for example. The capacity we are discussing is an important determinant of national adaptability and flexibility. Premier Khrushchev's revelation that Stalin was not the good guy after all, but a bad guy, is perhaps a relevant example of the breaking of a national taboo. It was an iconoclastic act, the breaking of an image. The dead Stalin was killed, in a sense more significant than physical murder. I recall predicting at the time that there would be a tremendous gain in impetus from that act—the release of a lot of energies that previously were bound up in the rigid, tyrannical system of Stalinism. And I think that is actually what occurred. The Soviets thus increased their flexibility and response repertory, and they increased their objective freedom as a consequence of it. Points of crisis in other countries can perhaps be studied fruitfully in these same terms.

IO

Nurturing Innovation in an Organization

MARVIN BOWER

In every organization, most people conceive new ideas worth fashioning into innovations. But most of these ideas are never born. Of the new ideas that are born, most die soon after birth. And of the ideas that do live, most are trampled to death in infancy or fail to achieve sufficient maturity to carry through into an effective innovation.

These conclusions about the low birth rate and high infanticide of ideas are drawn from nearly thirty years of helping progressive managements of leading companies effect change in most industries in the United States and a good sampling in the United Kingdom and Europe. But since ideas are so murderously dealt with in even the best-managed businesses, it follows that progressive companies throughout the free world have enormous opportunities to become better innovators—and in the process to increase their contributions to their economies and their profits for shareholders.

A Case Example

Let me illustrate these conclusions with an experience of a colleague who was making an integrated cost-reduction study for a large petroleum company; an integrated study is one that cuts across departmental lines so as to identify cost relationships. The consultant noticed that what seemed to be a fairly high grade of lumber was being used between lengths of oil well pipe to protect the pipe and keep it from shifting during shipment on freight cars.

A foreman was asked whether the lumber was not more expensive than was needed. "That's what I always thought," he replied, "but when I asked my boss about it he told me it was the job of the purchasing department to buy lumber and that we had better keep our noses clean." Analysis that went across departmental lines quickly disclosed that no one had questioned the purchasing department about the grade of lumber. The department readily agreed that lumber two grades lower would serve equally well. The annual saving was $40,000.

A dock foreman who heard about that incident said to my colleague, "I hear you are interested in lumber. I have wondered for ten years what they do with the lumber we use for the same purpose on pipe barges for our offshore drilling—the stuff never comes back." Investigation showed that when the pipe was unloaded on the offshore platforms, the used lumber was simply thrown into the ocean. By returning the lumber to shore for re-use, and by reducing its grade also, there was an annual saving of $70,000.

INNOVATION IMPEDIMENTS AND OPPORTUNITIES

These simple cost-saving innovations are not fundamental, but they do illustrate many of the underlying reasons for a low birth rate of new ideas followed by a high infanticide. Based on behind-the-scenes observations and on a good many thousand confidential interviews concerned with effecting change within business and governmental organizations, we have seen a number of impediments to innovation emerge, as well as a number of specific, positive steps that can be taken to stimulate innovation in any organization.

CAUSES OF THE LOW BIRTH RATE OF IDEAS

Analysis, observation, and confidential discussions with firing-line executives lead me to believe that there are four primary reasons why ideas are not born or die almost at birth: (1) inertia in mentioning the idea; (2) fear of criticism if the idea is offered; (3) feeling of futility about the likelihood that the idea will be well received or acted on; (4) lack of early attention to the idea.

INERTIA

Most people with even a low level of imagination have ideas streaming through their minds. Many of them they discard or don't even capture as the ideas pass through. But many of the ideas do take shape, and then the individual is faced with deciding whether to mention it to someone for reaction or action or to let it pass into the limbo of forgotten things.

Most people don't mention ideas due to lack of time, initiative, or even interest. For this simple reason, most ideas fail to get born even after they are fully conceived. The organization and the economy are the losers.

FEAR OF CRITICISM

When an idea is conceived and captured as it streams through the mind, the typical individual will not give it birth if he feels that it will result in criticism for him. After all, no one knows that he has conceived the idea and the easy course of action is simply to say nothing about it. Over the years, my discussions with executives frequently produce statements such as these: "They don't want new ideas around here"; and "I am not going to stick my neck out by suggesting something like that."

Top-management executives never cease to wonder why management consultants—who are outsiders—can often draw worthwhile ideas from down-the-line executives more easily than top management executives themselves. Part of the reason is fear of criticism. The management consultant, who occupies an independent, objective, and non-authoritarian role, can be made the repository of ideas without fear of criticism or ridicule by someone who can affect the man's career. The moral of this for the organization is to create an atmosphere that encourages freedom of expression, by avoiding unwarranted or unreasonable criticism.

FEELING OF FUTILITY

The individual who has conceived an idea will not give it birth if he feels—on the basis of his past experience or that of others—that his brainchild will be ignored or permitted to die from lack of nourishment. If a person has overcome both inertia and fear of criticism to give birth to an idea, he wants something to happen; and if either his past personal or vicarious experience convinces him that nothing *will* happen, he takes the easy course of letting the idea pass into the limbo of the forgotten.

No reasonable person expects *much* to happen as a result of most ideas that he puts forth. The realistic person recognizes that the idea may not be new; it may not be applicable, suitable, or timely. But if the feeling of futility is to be overcome, he expects at least a reaction, even if there can be no action.

It has been my observation that reasonable and realistic innovators are satisfied with reasonable explanations of why their ideas cannot be acted on at all or cannot be acted on at that particular time. The mere recognition that the effort has been made and appreciated is about all that is necessary to overcome the feeling of futility.

LACK OF EARLY ATTENTION

Many ideas die shortly after they are born because they fail to get a sponsor or because they get lost in a welter of other ideas and activities. A person gives birth to an idea by telling someone else about it. In an organization the idea will usually be given to someone who, it is hoped, will do something about it. This will often be the individual's superior. Or the idea may be given to one of his peers for testing purposes. The person who receives the idea, of course, typically places less value on it than on several related ideas of his own. Typically, he is busy with day-to-day activities and may fail to give the idea consideration.

In addition to listening to the idea, the receiver must in turn make one of several decisions. He may conclude that it is worthless and decide no action is called for. He may decide the idea has value but not be sure just what course of action to follow. He may decide that the idea cannot be acted on for some time. Or he may decide that the idea has sufficient value to give it a high priority and take action on it immediately.

Unless the receiver makes the last of the possible decisions, the idea is likely to get lost in the shuffle and be forgotten—perhaps by both parties. So unless the originator of the idea continues to be its sponsor or the receiver of the idea becomes its sponsor, the organization takes no action and the value of the idea is lost. The least the receiver can do is to tell the person what the decision on the idea is and why.

The receiver of the idea may also find that it stimulates his thinking to get another and related idea; that is, there is a proliferation of ideas. This then requires the receiver of the idea to decide which of the several possibilities shall be followed up and acted on, if any. Again, there is the potentiality that the original idea will get lost.

The realities of an organization inherently provide a cruel climate for an idea at birth and, as a consequence, most ideas expire through neglect, inattention, and lack of sponsorship.

STEPS FOR INCREASING THE BIRTH RATE AND REDUCING THE DEATH RATE OF IDEAS

Any organization, department, or other unit of an organization can increase the idea birth rate and reduce the death rate. The steps suggested for achieving these objectives emerge from my observations in creative organizations where innovations are well nurtured. These steps can best be taken on an over-all organization basis, with the motive power coming from the chief executive; but the individual in charge of any department or other unit can provide leadership for increasing innovation within his unit.

My observations indicate that there are four primary ways for expanding an organization's ability to innovate:

1. Develop a fact-founded, objective approach to solving problems and making decisions.

2. Separate long-range planning from short-term execution whenever feasible.

3. Foster a desire to improve and a dissatisfaction with the status quo.

4. Create a working atmosphere within the organization that leads to freedom of expression and to openness among people in their dealings with each other.

It will be noted immediately that these steps are simple to state but difficult to translate into the daily functioning of an organization. Full achievement of these objectives in any organization takes years of effort. But I have served many organizations where these approaches to managing the business are deeply imbedded, and I have observed the power of these hidden competitive weapons. Once built in, their value is incalculable.

A FACT-FOUNDED, OBJECTIVE APPROACH

I find there is a broad range among businesses in the way that their executives go about making decisions. At one extreme is the highly structured organization where people down the line await the word from higher up. "Theirs not to reason why." In such an organization innovation is minimal.

At the other end of the scale is the organization which has learned that the theoretical approach to problem-solving and decision-making is also the most useful and practical; that is: (1) Define the problem and the objectives to be achieved; (2) determine the various solution possibilities; (3) analyze each possibility by getting the facts concerning each; (4) make an objective choice among the alternatives. This may be termed the "fact-founded" approach to problem-solving and decision-making. This is decision-making "by the book"; but it really works.

The fact-founded approach produces not only the best solutions and decisions but also the greatest number of innovations. There are two basic reasons: First, objectivity reduces fear of criticism and, second, the search for alternate possibilities automatically provides an opportunity for new and original alternates to be suggested. In fact, the superior who wants to encourage innovation will say to his subordinates: "Can't we try a little harder to find a possible solution that no one has yet come up with?" He will stretch his people's minds.

In between the authoritarian approach and the fact-founded approach to problem-solving and decision-making are many shades of non-objectivity. Innovation declines in quantity and quality as emotion, personal politics, arbitrariness, and caprice are introduced into the process. The man who gets "clobbered" a few times soon learns "the party line" and gives up making innovative suggestions.

The president of General Motors Corporation referred to its approach to problem-solving as "the General Motors attitude of mind." In an appearance before a United States Senate Subcommittee, Harlow H. Curtice, then president, gave a statement on "The Development and Growth of General Motors."[1] During the course of his testimony, he said:

Now we come to the second fundamental reason for the success of General Motors—our approach to problems. It is really an attitude of mind. It might be defined as bringing the research point of view to bear on all phases of the business. This involves, first, assembling all the facts; second,

[1]Appearance before Subcommittee on Antitrust and Monopoly, U. S. Senate Committee on the Judiciary, December 2, 1955.

analysis of where the facts appear to point; and, third, courage to follow the trail indicated even if it leads into unfamiliar and unexplored territory. This point of view is never satisfied with things as they are. It assumes that everything and anything—whether it be product, process, method, procedure, or social or human relations—can be improved.

I have tried to think of a single term to describe this attitude, and I think perhaps the closest is the inquiring mind.

It may appear to be boastful, but I truly believe that in General Motors we have developed to a unique degree this attitude of the inquiring mind. We are always seeking ways to make things better and do things better. In fact, as you may know, we have long had a slogan, "More and better things for more people."

I believe that this attitude of mind is a great asset of General Motors or of any organization that will take the time and pay the price to develop it.

The fact-founded, objective approach to problem-solving and decision-making virtually guarantees a high level of innovation in any organization.

SEPARATING PLANNING AND EXECUTION

There is increasing recognition that innovation can be stimulated through revision of the organizational structure to separate long-range planning from execution.

The man who is immersed in day-to-day operations does not have time for getting, nurturing, or sponsoring ideas, nor for seeing them through to maturity. He will not be blamed for not innovating; he will be blamed for not meeting sales quotas or production schedules. Separation of long-term planning has a number of advantages:

1. The planner can be held *accountable* for innovation. Experience shows that, although getting ideas cannot be demanded, responsibility to innovate does step up innovation.

2. Specialization of planning work permits better selection of the right man for the job. The creative thinker can be put in a position where his creativity has a greater payoff than as an operating executive.

3. The planner has time to do contemplative thinking. But he must not be too far removed from operations, or he will not get the stimuli needed to generate ideas.

For these and other reasons, American industry has tended increasingly to follow this trend. This has led to the growth of staff work, starting with the production scheduling supervisor and the market research specialist and coming on down (or up) to executive vice-presidents in charge of development and vice-presidents in charge of diversification and new product development. In the latter categories, the executives are charged with responsibility to innovate in basic corporate strategy.

A judicious use of this approach will step up innovation, provided, of course, creative thinkers are put in the jobs.

CREATING A DESIRE TO IMPROVE

Another direct attack on stepping up innovation can be made through definite steps to create a desire to improve and a dissatisfaction with the status quo. Here the General Motors attitude of mind again comes into play.

Johnson & Johnson has attained leadership in the surgical dressings field through establishment of a value system that "expects" improvements throughout the business, from research right on through production and sales. In fact, that company's innovations are customer oriented. There is an expectation—starting with the chief executive— that products will constantly be improved to serve customers better, and that costs will be constantly reduced without sacrificing quality.

Such a pursuit of increasing excellence typically starts with a demanding chief executive or department head. But the "demands" are made through constructive leadership, not through "clobberings" or crackdowns. The fear of rolling heads typically will not inspire innovation; it kills off ideas before or at their birth.

Some companies have achieved success in making innovation a definite responsibility. One outstanding leader in its industry requires that the yearly plans every executive makes for his department or section shall include specific ways to increase the effectiveness of his operations and simultaneously cut their cost. It is surprising how the requirement for improvement does bring it about.

The du Pont Company has developed in its executives at all levels a deep desire to improve the activities for which they are responsible. This has produced a dissatisfaction with the status quo that provides a constant challenge to existing methods. It appears that this working atmosphere in du Pont, which so successfully nurtures innovation, has its origin in an orientation of the entire business to research, the staffing of many key positions with scientists, and a real dedication to fact-founded problem-solving and decision-making. Moreover, the company is managed by an executive committee made up of men who have little day-to-day work; they are planners, thinkers, and analysts with responsibility to challenge and innovate at the highest level.

The history of du Pont points up the fact that these and other innovations in the management of that great enterprise had their origin in the *need* to innovate in order to change the basic dependence of the company on gunpowder. The leadership that brought about such innovations also took pains to insure that there was a succession of leadership dedicated to innovation. This philosophy is characterized in the company's slogan, "Better things for better living—through chemistry."

The Procter and Gamble Company started a chain of innovation many years ago by agreeing to provide a specified number of weeks of work each year to its factory workers. This required a regularization of work that in turn involved major changes in approach to marketing, inventory control, and other activities.

Thus, successful innovation stimulates other innovation and builds up the *expectation* that innovation must continue.

FAVORABLE WORKING ATMOSPHERE

Innovation thrives in an atmosphere that stimulates people to express themselves freely and to deal with each other in an open, non-political manner. The atmosphere must, at the same time, be a demanding one. The "soft" atmosphere, with low performance standards, nurtures ideas little better than the monolithic structure with the authoritarian chief executive.

But an atmosphere that best nurtures innovation will typically come as a byproduct of efforts to achieve other objectives. The favorable atmosphere is most frequently a byproduct of a determination to make decisions and solve problems through a fact-founded, objective approach.

So my analysis of the creative organization convinces me that if there is one single way to increase the innovating capability of any organization, it is through a determined effort and an effective program to establish the fact-founded approach to solving problems and making decisions. This will provide the foundation on which the other stimulants can be erected: separation of long-range planning and execution; dissatisfaction with the status quo; and development of a working atmosphere that stimulates freedom of expression.

Then every executive can *require* more innovations from his associates and can take other positive steps to increase the idea birth rate and decrease the idea death rate. Everyone will benefit: the economy, employees, stockholders, and the innovators themselves.

Discussion

Steiner

You have done a very clear job of spelling out the conditions that do or do not characterize a creative organization. Do you have any feeling, from your years of experience, about what conditions are most likely to give rise to such a company; that is, new companies versus old companies, little ones versus big ones, or companies in fiercely competitive industries versus more monopolistic industries? Can you make any generalizations, at present, about what seem to be the conditions that produce such an organization?

Bower

Well, I mentioned the du Pont Company, which began its creativeness as a matter of necessity. I think that his is one characteristic. They *had* to be creative in order to live. And so this again gets back to the notion that creativity can be fostered by the demand of the total situation. The new and small business creates a total demand more automatically, but that demand can be built into the large business.

Steiner

Would you extrapolate that and say that, as a company becomes more successful and more profitable, it is less likely to be creative?

Bower

Yes, innovation becomes more difficult with success. Its continuance requires better programming and better leadership for the large organization than for the small one. But experience shows that a momentum for innovation does develop, which good leadership and good programming can continue.

Steiner

I am trying to draw the parallel between the individual and the organization. It is clear that, at least in the case of individuals, exhortation usually does little to make them more creative; you have to change the conditions that give rise to it. I wonder if there are any conditions, within management control, that could be imposed upon an organization in order to make these characteristics emerge, other than just telling them, "You ought to do this."

Bower

I think that if I were doing it, I would start out with creating an atmosphere of objectivity—which I think would have a great backlog effect. Of course, this whole thing usually starts with the creativity of an individual. I think you find in General Motors that Alfred Sloan was a great policy maker, and people have been trying to get him to tell the General Motors story. Such history as there is on it shows that he was a great policy maker, a creative thinker at the policy level. We refer to Kettering as a creator in the product sense.

Alexander

Are there examples of creative organizations which are in a sense monolithic, where the leader is an extremely original, creative individual and the organization is built to implement his creative ideas? That would be a case in which the individual members are not creative, so that the organization is only an instrument in the hands of a creative man. There are examples of great military leaders, extremely creative individuals, where just this type of organization existed, where nobody had anything to say. Napoleon is one. Alexander the Great is another. De Gaulle was this type, and under certain conditions he might have been one.

Bower

I can think of two petroleum companies where that is true, for the very simple reason that the big profits and success in the petroleum industry come from big policy decisions that can be executed on a command basis.

Alexander

Ford, for example—originally not such a creative leader—conceived a new kind of organization: selling the automobiles to his own workers. That was a novel idea, I think, and he carried it out.

Bower

Yes, and I guess the history of that would show that the situation caught up with him, and he didn't maintain sufficient flexibility as an innovator. He lost touch with his situation, and it caught up with him.

"FAILURE OF NERVE"

Bruner

Mr. Bower, I am puzzled by one thing. Looking at industry from the outside, what strikes me is not so much a lack of innovational capacity as a failure of nerve. Let me take two industries and ask what really is at the base of the problem. Let me take, for example, one company that you mentioned—General Motors. We know perfectly well that General Motors has within its stock in trade in its engineering departments modes of propulsion; techniques, for example, of arranging the polarization of lights between headlights and windshields so that nobody would be dazzled. Yet all these things, in existence for over ten years, have not been adopted. If you talk candidly to General Motors executives, they will tell you this.

At General Electric, where I know the situation a bit better, there is the same kind of thing. Somewhere along the line, it is not the capacity to innovate new ideas for how you put together a product, but the nerve to take a go at a consumers' market. If I

were to name one area where inventiveness is needed, it would
be how you get a decision on things it is in your power to do;
how to recognize that supply creates the demand and that supply
of a better product would very likely produce a demand for a
better product.

Bower

I think it is nerve. Now, what I'm saying now has nothing to do
with disclosing any knowledge of General Motors. General
Motors is currently stepping up its share of the market and every
time that the market goes up 1 per cent, its nerve is bound to
decline probably by 2 per cent. Competitors of General Motors
say that all GM would have to do is move from third to fourth
gear and they could take over another 10 per cent, because they
have been working at this inquiring mind for so long that they
have the power to do it. They don't dare do it under antitrust.

Bruner

In home appliances, they will tell you that they are producing
by principles that were relevant thirty years ago and that a whole
infrared technology could be introduced—the toaster, heater,
refrigerator, and the rest.

Bower

I don't know the answer to that, but there is a tremendous lag.
You are talking about situations where they say there is no lag;
they could put it in very quickly if they wanted to. Is that right?

Bruner

They want to, but what keeps them from doing it? Why are
they frozen in this antique posture? Why are they not matters
for public debate? For example, if there is a question of holding
back a technology—and this includes use of our technology
for defense as well—if there is an issue here that has to do with
the organization of our economy and our society, where is the
timidity that keeps somebody from speaking out on this? As I
say, looking from the outside, I am struck more by the failure
of nerve in the situation than I am by the lack of innovation
and capacity of American industry, which we know is enormous.

Wallis

This issue is likely to get us off the subject of the conference.

Bruner

I wonder. We were called to talk about creativity and it seems to me that this involves the instrumentation of ideas.

Bower

One of the reasons why people's ideas are not taken up is that they do not tie in with the then goals of the organization, and one of the ways of keeping that person from being discouraged is to say, "Sorry, pal, this isn't the time to do it. It's a great idea but we can't take it now." And this is an important part of innovation in organizations. If everybody just innovates all over the place, the organization isn't going to achieve its goal.

II

Some Approaches to Innovation in Industry

PETER G. PETERSON

I cannot emphasize enough the kind of creativity that most of us in business deal with. It is most often *not* fundamental innovation; it is most often relatively minor rearrangements of things that have already existed. In the language of science, we are most often dealing within the state of the art, rather than with the basic kind of research that Dr. Shockley refers to when he talks of inventing transistors.

Thus, I will spend my time on the kind of innovations that I think take place most often in business—something other than basic innovations. I make this distinction because it seems to me that the process that leads to effective innovation differs considerably depending on whether we are talking about basic or minor innovation.

On how to get ideas, I have been interested to hear that something we worry a good deal about in business is apparently something that you in academia have also done a lot of worrying about; namely, how much *structure* and *freedom* produce the optimum amount of creativity?

David Ogilvy and I have a mutual friend in advertising who has a point of view about how to get *effective* advertising. The point he makes is that we should be interested in creative advertising per se. We should be interested in *effective* advertising. I think this is true of all business. The essential criterion must be effectiveness in terms of sales and profits.

This man goes on to argue that the way to get effective advertising is to structure it in the following way. You should break an advertisement into two different processes, (1) *what* to say, and (2) *how* to say it. The way to get a good ad, therefore, is to approach these problems in that order.

After watching this process work for a few years, I concluded that it apparently violated some fundamental principle of the process of creativity; much of the advertising created by this process seemed quite dull, unoriginal, and not effective.

So, on the one hand, one of the things I think we worry about in business is structuring the problem so much that we come up with dull answers. On the other hand, I have observed many situations in business where you provide so much freedom that you come up with brilliant answers to the *wrong* problems. The thing I worry about is how to structure the situation enough so that people solve problems that you want them to solve, without structuring so much that you somehow freeze the very process that you are trying to encourage.

Dr. Merton used some phrases that struck home with me when he mentioned people who were evokers of creativity. I think most top managements probably feel that if they have a role, it is probably this one more than the other.

I would like to say something about top management's role in creativity. To hear some of us businessmen talk, you would think that the *only* reason companies innovate is because it is economically attractive. I would argue that, in many cases, it is also a matter of taste; that is, a certain kind of leadership could not run any other kind of a business, while other kinds of leadership (which incidently are quite profitable in many cases) put their emphasis on efficient operation, doing what the other fellow does, only doing it better at lower cost. And there are companies of this type that are extremely profitable.

So we should not conclude that, in order to be profitable, you have to be an innovator. To be sure, innovations often contribute very importantly to company profits, but I think it is often a reflection of the taste and personality of the leadership of the business.

Back to the subject of structure and creativity. One of the things that we have found useful in fostering creativity is to get kind of compulsive about being dissatisfied, stating the dissatisfaction, and trying to state it articulately enough that people understand the general dissatisfaction. Then, wait and see what happens.

With respect to getting ideas translated into *action,* I have observed two or three problems, both in the advertising business and at Bell & Howell.

Sheppard Mead has a concept he calls "the glob." He explains that whenever a large group gets turned loose on an idea, it cannot stand the sharp corners that characterize most new ideas. A sharp corner is unfriendly, and by the time the large group is through rounding it off it is often a "glob." So one of the things we try to avoid is getting too many people working on an idea so that all of its originality gets torn from it. One of our people in marketing puts it this way: "This is an idea that started as the Queen Mary and by the time it was launched, it was a leaky rowboat." This is a great danger in the creative process; if you get too many people involved, what made the idea fresh in the first place may be emasculated.

The second barrier to getting effective ideas translated into action is the *inertia* that most of us have to change. Almost every novel idea that I have ever been identified with has had the usual set of objections at the outset. It won't work; it shouldn't work; it can't work; it never has worked; it never will work; etc., etc. I cannot pretend to discuss the psychological aspects of this problem, but I have the view that *even* if people are open minded, the human mind is often limited in its ability to appraise the effectiveness of a new idea through a rational or analytical process.

Thus, before we let an idea get emasculated, and before we let any thoroughly rational appraisal of the idea convince us that it will not work, we ask ourselves another question. Is there any way that we can *experiment* with this idea at low cost? It is my view that experiment is a most powerful tool for getting innovation into action and probably is not as widely used as it should be in American industry. Quite often, if we really try, we can test the effectiveness of an idea through experimental approaches on a very low-cost basis.

One other thought on getting ideas into action. I don't know if you were as impressed in listening to Mr. Bensinger today as I was, but I think his talk illustrated something important. I think the concept of *energy* is something perhaps that we should talk a little more about.

Mr. Bensinger talked today about what happened on the automatic pinsetter. I am sure you were impressed with the fact that this project got done largely because someone at the top said it was *going to be* done. You recall the series of barriers that he presented to us today, a very imposing list of barriers that would have discouraged most people. In my experience, one of the big reasons that ideas never get into action is that most people lack this grim determination and the tremendous energy that it takes to make these ideas work.

I should like to illustrate two or three ideas by tracing their history through our company.

First, let me try to illustrate this notion of articulating dissatisfaction and then seeing if this somehow doesn't lead to an answer. We compete with a certain very fine company in Rochester which has about 96 per cent of the business in color film. Because of this, they are in a position to spend substantial amounts of money on advertising equipment that in turn uses the film. It is an exhilarating experience for those of us not in the film business.

A part of our problem is that we can never compete with this company on the basis of *weight* or quantity. One of the objectives, one of our needs we keep trying to answer, is how to make a *unique* impression with a limited number of dollars. The second thing that occurs to us very quickly is that we cannot possibly hope with our limited funds to reach everyone; therefore, we keep asking ourselves: Is there a way we can effectively reach a certain segment of the market?

We were doing conventional things. We were not reaching any particular groups of people with ideal impact. We were not making the quality impression that we wanted to make. We stated and re-stated this dissatisfaction, and I am sure that it was by stating the problem so often that we finally came up with an answer.

One Saturday morning, my two-year-old son turned on the television set at the most unlikely hour you can imagine—11:30, on a Saturday morning. On the screen came one of the most provocative documentaries I have ever seen, called "The Face of Red China." In a period of one hour, it certainly changed some of my stereotypes of Red China. I thought to myself what a tragedy it was that something like this had to be seen at such an unlikely hour. It was not until two days later that it suddenly occurred to us that here perhaps was precisely something that met Bell & Howell's requirements from a commercial standpoint. Leaving aside the question of public responsibility in business, why not have a company sponsor controversial public-service programs in prime evening time?

We went to the networks and found that, thanks partly to fortunate timing, they were very receptive to the idea. Mr. Van Doren and the quiz scandals that took place just about that time helped, I am sure.

We found, however, that within the company many questions were raised and quite understandably. For example, who on earth is ever going to watch television of this type? Second, are you ever going to sell a product in this kind of serious atmosphere? It is a serious program and "everybody knows" you cannot sell products on serious programs. Third, everybody knows that you cannot sell products in a controversial atmosphere. Quite the contrary; if you are controversial, you are going to hurt your company.

We could have intellectualized these problems to death, and if we had listened to all the reasons why it would not work, everyone would have dropped the idea right then. But some of us had a personal conviction that much of this was folklore. For example, there was really almost no evidence to suggest that controversy really hurt companies. It often takes only a few letters to bother company presidents. But in terms of systematic evidence, I found none that said that companies engaged in controversy got into trouble where it counted, in the profit-and-loss statement.

But rather than just talk this problem to death, we said, why don't we try one or more of these shows and see what happens? And we built into this an experiment in which we tried to get a measurement of the various things that would not work, such as how many watched it, who watched it, did they get upset at the company, how did they feel about buying the products, etc.

The group participated in setting up the experiment and some of the criteria. Once the results were in from the first shows, it was perfectly obvious to all of us that most of these things were not true.

For some reason that is not clear to me, many of us in business seem to want universal love from the market. The truth of the matter is that often we sell to only 5 or 10 per cent of the market, and I think I could argue that if we could get just 10 per cent of the people delighted with us, that is probably as much as anyone could hope for, even if the 90 per cent are not entirely happy with us. But what this experiment showed was that the vast majority of the people, who normally do not trouble to write letters, thought it was a fine idea to have a company willing to discuss controversial issues.

The point I am trying to make is that if we in business can get the concept of the experiment built into our thinking and thereby get *evidence* on a lot of these "can'ts," "won'ts," "shouldn'ts," etc., more of our good ideas will be translated into action.

Another problem in marketing springs from the earlier problem. Because we are not a large company, we cannot afford to take massive risks in spending X million dollars promoting something without knowing whether it will be effective or not.

One day a friend of Dr. Alexander's came in with an idea that, on the surface, was "preposterous." Those who have read the Harvard marketing casebooks will know every reason why this idea will not work: Why not sell a $150 movie camera outfit by *direct mail?*

Those who have not had the benefit of business school training will not appreciate how "ridiculous" this idea was. In the first place, any fool knows that an expensive product must be demonstrated to be sold. This is a marketing axiom. Any fool knows that nobody buys a durable item unless he can compare alternatives, models, etc.

Rather than say to this, "Gentlemen, this idea is preposterous," we tried to build in this notion: "Let's examine some reasons why it might work." One of the reasons that made sense was that only about 30 per cent of the product in our business is bought on credit. And this involved a lot of credit buying. Another reason was that a direct-mail package could put all the various elements of movies together for a convenient purchase. Then we asked the key question: "What would it cost us to try out this idea?" The cost was only about $10,000. The point is that we could have spent $100,000 worth of time over-intellectualizing this problem.

If you were to show this direct-mail piece to a hundred marketing experts, nine out of ten would tell you that it is preposterous; it just will not work. Here is an outfit of movie equipment that sells for $150, and all it says is: Shoot the show; get a couple of rolls of film free; if you don't like it, send it back; if you do like it, 24 months to pay, and an attractive combination of lights. The startling thing is that this one method of selling has been extremely successful and is now a basis of an important new business at Bell & Howell, in which we have set up a subsidiary devoted exclusively to selling by direct mail.

It is possible for us all to get a little pompous about the power of an intellectual, rational approach to an idea that is often extremely complex in terms of what makes it work.

There is another specific idea that I would like to treat, a marketing idea, not only because it is something I know something about, but because there has already been a good deal of discussion about development and research at this seminar.

The idea is dissatisfaction; how do we articulate it? Those who know anything about the durable-goods business will appreciate the fact that one of the common patterns in this industry is for each manufacturer successively to give his dealer larger and larger sales hypodermics to buy products. This goes on until it is unclear whether the dealer is buying the hypodermic or whether he is buying the product.

We sat down and said we were unhappy with this system, for a number of reasons. In the first place, marketing costs keep going up, and everybody is giving dollars away, which they could be spending in other ways. Second, the effect of this kind of promotion is extraordinarily short run in nature; the dealer tends to be motivated by this promotion versus that promotion, and very little is done to build one brand over the long run. Could anybody think of anything that would in some way achieve two objectives—one, to be low in cost and, two, to build a longer-term relationship between Bell & Howell and its dealer organization? And there we left it. We structured it and no more than that.

About two weeks later we were having lunch and, as is very common today in industry, someone was discussing the price of our stock. But I can just remember our sitting there and saying, "Stock."

Now why has no one ever thought of that before? Why not make dealers stockholders in Bell & Howell? Instead of giving them money, which doesn't achieve anything, why don't we make them stockholders and build a longer-term relationship? We have done this for two or three years now, and we are finding that, at about a third of the cost of cash incentives, we are able to achieve a much more permanent effect and a much deeper impact.

I think I have pretty well concluded from my experience in the company that, for most business problems, you do need some structure. Talk about freedom probably gets pretty wasteful, in terms of most of the problems that we need to sell in business. I am talking not about our basic technical research but about most of the problems we face. There is something to gain by defining problem or need in reasonably specific terms.

The second thing that I have learned is not to let too many people mangle an idea, to make sure that we do *not* emasculate it.

The third is to have an appropriate humility toward our intellectual ability to appraise new ideas. There is a lot of talk about how intuitive people are, yet I would hate to have a statistical batting average of most of us in business if we were to rely on our intuitions. If there is one approach that we have found useful, it is that of always asking, "Is it possible to have a low-cost experiment? Is it possible to set up a model of some sort and try it out?"

Most of us at Bell & Howell are far more impressed with one piece of behavior in the market than with many hours of intellectual rationale for a new idea.

Dr. Bruner's question about the delay in putting infrared technology in toasters is quite an indictment of business, and it may be true. This problem comes up at Bell & Howell every once in a while. As you probably know, most products that are introduced on the market are rather minor changes from year to year, and built into the existing product is an enormous, a staggering, investment in tools, know-how, dies, and equipment. One of the characteristics of basic technological change is that the start-up cost, so called, is truly enormous, because you then have to start all over again, let us say, with your tools. Whereas a product change in a camera might cost us $100,000, a major innovation might cost us $4,000,000.

I suspect that one of the reasons these changes do not take place is that in computing what it costs to make the change versus how much more they will sell, management decides they are better off not making the change. It is not necessarily just a conspiracy—although it may be in some cases—but there is a reason for it. Do you believe that?

Discussion

THE SMALL-SCALE EXPERIMENT

Bruner

I believe it. And then comes the question whether there are ways in which industry, given the fact that it is capable of developing new ideas, can find some manner of making it possible for technology to move ahead in spite of this. I was intrigued by what you said about experimentation. Isn't there some means of operating experimentally for tryouts, to see whether there can be a gradual transition whereby you do not lose your entire investment?

Peterson

Yes; and which can measure the impact. Let me give you an example from Bell & Howell. Have you heard of zoom lenses? One of the great advantages of being new in a company is that you are thoroughly unaware of what cannot be done. I thought a zoom camera was something that you used for football games. That was my image—an extraordinarily expensive object. One day I was in the lab, and there was a zoom lens. I had never seen one in my life, and I put it up to my eyes, and—well, it is a very dramatic thing.

They explained to me that this was not applicable to consumer products, because it would cost a fair amount of money and so on. I asked, "What would it cost to make a camera for me— just one—with a zoom lens on it?"

"Just one? Do you mean a crude modification? I think we would probably spend $500 on it."

I said, "Well, suppose we do that, because my rates come pretty high; it will cost at least $500 for us to continue this discussion for another hour or two, so let's just do this."

I took this camera home. At a dinner party that night, I put this zoom lens on the piano, and I asked everybody coming in if they wouldn't participate in a very sophisticated piece of market research; namely, to put the camera to their eye. To the man, the reaction was extraordinarily enthusiastic: "My, this is marvelous, I've never seen anything like this in my life." We did this for about $500. So you are right; if more industry would try out new ideas on a low-cost basis, perhaps their expectations of what the market will bear would go up.

Shockley

The approach that Peterson is talking about is one that I would recognize in a researcher in the laboratory: "Can't we do something quick and dirty and cheap?" It may not be high-grade, it may not be accurate, but, by God, get some kind of feel for the problem in a practical way. This, I think, is in an area of "art."

Peterson

Someone once said: All data are more or less imperfect in the initial stages. The evidence is usually terribly imperfect; namely, some person rationally trying to think the thing through.

Shockley

This is worse than the lousiest experiment.

Peterson

I think it is worse than a quick and dirty experiment, in most cases.

THE RISKS OF CHANGE

Stein

Something is missing here. Both Mr. Peterson and Mr. Bensinger have presented some fascinating information on how they created needs in the public. Therefore, I wonder if the hesitancy of big industry to introduce big changes is really economic. Is it an institutional factor? Is it the orientation of management? Or what is it?

Peterson

I find that much of our activity (and I'm not saying this is to our credit) is essentially defensive in nature. It is what I call "share of market" tactics. This fellow did this, so you must fight back by doing the same kind of thing.

But given that no one else does anything, you might be able to make an economic case for the fact that you are better off not taking some of these big steps, because of the risks of major innovation; not just the cost, but the risk of being wrong on top of that.

There are thousands of case studies. A classic example of this is in the airline business. Pat Patterson of United Airlines is on our board. I have heard him talk about supersonic jets. He has just invested several hundred million, I believe, in Mach 1 jets. He is the first to admit that anyone who has a Mach 2 or Mach 3 jet will get more business, as was the case with the current jets over the piston planes. But the prospect of *his* starting this thing and junking three or four hundred million dollars is also extremely hard to digest; and understandably so, I think.

What sometimes happens is that suddenly someone who does not have this kind of commitment—no inventories or tools, or a lot of money and doesn't know what to do with it—does it, and then the whole equation changes. The question then is not, "How much does it cost?" but "Where are you if you *don't* do it?"

Bower

It should also be said that the chief executive, like any other innovator, will be open to criticism. He is afraid for his job and everything else. Read Part II of the General Dynamics study in *Fortune*. There was a risk decision that cost more hundreds of millions of dollars than Mr. Patterson is faced with—and loss of job.

But, on a small scale, if everything is going along all right, there is loss of nerve, and fear of criticism. Why take the risk if I don't have to? As Pete says, if no one is breathing down my neck, why should I innovate? Not just for its own sake. There is a combination of economic factors that bear on the individual, just like any other innovator.

ORGANIZATIONAL FACTORS

Merton

Don't Peterson's examples bring out some issues we did not have time for earlier? He is saying that it is first necessary to diagnose the character of different organizations and their products before you start talking about the creative organization. Because, as organizations differ in the character of what they do, what they produce, and what they achieve, you are going to get very different conditions for creativity.

Take some of these examples and do a little translating. If you happen to be in an organization where a major innovation involves a capital investment of $50,000,000, you obviously have a very different condition from one in which the pilot run costs $500. That is one variable that will affect the rate of effective innovation.

Beyond that, he told us that this also depends on things outside the organization—its environment and the market—and that the responsiveness of organization A to innovation is a function of what organization B is doing. In an effort to diagnose the more or less creative organization, therefore, one should diagnose the environment of which it is a part, the kind of competition it is subject to.

The third implication, I think, of what Peterson said is one that Veblen had a lot of fun with when he was in his heyday. He called it "the penalty of taking the lead." His essential idea was this: Once you innovated and had a capital investment in the innovation, you were in a bind for some time to come. Your competitor—whether it was Germany competing with the USA or another firm competing within the same economy—could get the jump on you, because he started with the next technological step. He might miss out on Mach 1, but he could make it on Mach 2.

The gist of what he has been saying, at least in the latter part of his discussion, brings us back to consideration of types of organizations in relation to creativity and types of environment that affect creativity of organizations.

CONDITIONS FOR CREATIVITY MAY VARY BY CULTURE

Hauser

I am a guest of the conference; I am puzzled by something that concerns both Bower's and Peterson's papers. There are undoubtedly many situations in organizations, both environmental and specific, in which creativity and innovation can and do occur.

But if we go back 25 or 30 years there was a lot of conviction that the type of environment, and the type of organization, in the USSR was entirely inimical to creativity and innovation. A monolithic organization which we said would not work in American industry seems not to have done too badly, with USSR rocketry and nuclear activity.

The point I'm trying to introduce is that I think much of the approach we may be taking, and have taken, in this country is essentially a limited, ethnocentric approach to this problem. There are many cultures, many environments, many organizational setups in which innovation may occur, and what you might bring together in this kind of a seminar—partly because of the fund of knowledge that is so pathetically poor as yet—might lead you to conclusions about creativity that would be just like those the blind men arrived at with the elephant.

Peterson

If you want a wonderful example of a monolithic structure, I think you should discuss the Polaroid Company, which we admire as much as any company in the business. If my sources are accurate, this organization is led by a great man with enormous personal resources, enormous personal creativity. I read a comment by one of their senior research people one day about how they define research projects, what areas were they going to go into. The person said, "With Dr. Land around, that is no problem." I think you are right, and that there are some great success stories built on a handful of people.

Bower

I agree that, if you have an innovator at the top and he gives the right order, you can carry out the innovation all right. I guess the USSR puts the heat on, but they put the heat on one thing and then get it out.

Wallis

If they had invented or conceived the ideas of rockets, it would be more impressive.

Hauser

It wouldn't be any more impressive to me than the fact that they've got one now that works. It seems to work better than the one we've got.

Stein

You mean their Germans are better than ours?

Steiner

Those Germans don't come from too permissive an environment either.

Bruner

I want to pursue this continuum of maturity within an industry. There are times in which it is quite plain that an industry is in an economic bind; where, in spite of all the innovative activity, in spite of all of the good will, it just cannot break out of the economic barrier where it is overcommitted to a particular technology and where it cannot be rescued. Under those circumstances, I rather suspect that innovative activity does not consist in lathering up your executives to be creative, but in becoming a little bit creative on the legislative side and making it possible for the industry to move ahead by removing certain kinds of restrictions that exist in public law.

We have gone to one kind of model in thinking of creativity, which stems from the notion that you should select people who are—I shall substitute a phrase for creative—who are not stupid. Non-stupid people will do it.

What happens when an industry gets mature? You don't have that many degrees of freedom. It is not just a question of intelligence, will, good heart, good faith, and the rest of it. There are arrangements at a level which has nothing whatever to do with selecting people, but rather with institutional inventions; it has to do with legislation and the rest of it, and I would hope that before we finish we can try to locate precisely those areas—let me just call it "beyond heartbreak"—where you cannot do it by having someone try a little bit harder. The businessman is over a barrel, in certain respects, in a society which was not geared for the rate of technological development that we are now experiencing.

Steiner

Is this mature state of your organization equivalent, in some sense, to the incorrigible situation that your individual finds himself in, and might it need the same preventive?

Bruner

No. Let me give you an example of what I mean by this. I am on the Research Advisory Board for General Electric, and one of the problems that has been bothering the company on the research side is the fact that there is a library full of stuff invented here—big, blue-gray notebooks full of ideas—and many of them do not get into use. The question is, why not? Couldn't we be doing something more about it? If you talk to the man who is Director of Marketing at GE, a very clever man, he will tell you that there are certain kinds of things that they cannot do, just because of sheer size. So what they have seen is the nibbling away of the high-quality, small, high-fidelity set to little companies like KLH, which started little and is now bursting its gussets. It burns them up internally.

GE is an organization which cannot use all the innovations that it has paid for; excellent people are now chewing out their guts and are ready to go back to M.I.T., as a result. What do you do about a company when it reaches this critical size, for example? Can you do something?

Peterson

I can only assume in the case of General Electric that they have an alternative use for their money that returns more to them, whereas KLH does not have that situation developing. Most companies I know have two or three times as many innovations at a given time than they can use, but they try to rank them in terms of return.

Neil Borden's study at Harvard showed what happens to innovation. He pointed out that, with many innovations, it is often several years before the customer is ready. There are many case studies of companies going broke stimulating generic demand, which is very expensive, whereas men with a great sense of timing—who are kind of like parasites, you know, waiting for the right time—just jump in at that point. It is quite rational if you try to maximize your profit. It may not be very gratifying in terms of being an innovator, but it might be rational.

12

The Creative Chef

DAVID M. OGILVY

In my advertising agency I have a fancy title: I am called the Creative Director. Sitting here among you psychologists, I feel like a pregnant woman at a convention of obstetricians. If any of you professors would like to come into my agency, I can offer you thirty-five writers and forty artists to study. Their job is to create seventy-five new advertising campaigns every year.

In leading this team of creative people, I have been influenced by an experience I had in a previous incarnation, thirty years ago. I was a chef at the Hotel Majestic in Paris. Henri Soulé of the Pavillon tells me that it was probably the best kitchen there has ever been.

There were thirty-seven chefs in our brigade. We worked like dervishes, sixty-three hours a week—there was no trade union. From morning to night, we sweated and shouted and cursed and cooked. Every man was inspired by one ambition: to cook better than any chef had ever cooked before. Our *esprit de corps* would have done credit to the Marines. I have always believed that if I could understand how Monsieur Pitard, the head chef, inspired such white-hot morale, I could apply the same kind of leadership to the management of my agency.

To begin with, he was the best cook in the whole brigade, and we knew it. He had to spend most of his time at his desk, planning menus, scrutinizing bills, and ordering supplies; but once a week he would emerge from his glass-walled office in the middle of the kitchen and actually *cook* something. A crowd of us always gathered round to watch, spellbound by his virtuosity. It was inspiring to work for a supreme master.

(Following Chef Pitard's example, I still write occasional advertisements myself, to remind my brigade of copywriters that my hand has not lost its cunning.)

M. Pitard ruled with a rod of iron, and we were terrified of him. There he sat in his glass cage, the *gros bonnet,* the arch symbol of authority. Whenever I made a mistake in my work, I would look up to see if his gimlet eye had noticed it.

Cooks, like copywriters, work under ferocious pressures and are apt to be quarrelsome. I doubt whether a more easygoing boss could have prevented our rivalries from breaking into violence. M. Bourgignon, our *chef saucier,* told me that by the time a cook is forty, he is either dead or crazy. I understood what he meant the night our *chef potagier* threw forty-seven raw eggs across the kitchen at my head, scoring nine direct hits; his patience had been exhausted by my raids on his stockpot in search of bones for the poodles of an important client.

Our *chef pâtissier* was equally eccentric. Every night, he left the kitchen with a chicken concealed in the crown of his Homburg. When he went on vacation, he made me stuff two dozen peaches into the legs of his long underwear. But when the King and Queen of England were given a state dinner at Versailles, this roguish genius was chosen from all the *pâtissiers* in France to prepare the ornamental baskets of sugar and the *petits fours glacés.*

M. Pitard praised very seldom, but when he did, we were exalted to the skies. When the President of France came to a banquet at the Majestic, the atmosphere in our kitchen was electric. On one of these memorable occasions, I was covering frogs' legs with a white *chaud-froid* sauce, decorating each little thigh with an ornate leaf of chervil. Suddenly, I became aware that M. Pitard was standing beside me, watching. I was so frightened that my knees knocked together and my hands trembled. He took the pencil from his starched toque and waved it in the air, his signal for the whole brigade to gather. Then he pointed to my frogs' legs and said, very slowly and very quietly, "That's how to do it." I was his slave for life.

(Today, I praise my staff as rarely as Pitard praised his chefs, in the hope that they, too, will appreciate it more than a steady gush of appreciation.)

M. Pitard gave us all a great sense of occasion. One evening, when I had prepared a *soufflé Rothschild* (with three liqueurs), he took me upstairs to the door of the dining room and allowed me to watch President Paul Doumer eat it. Three weeks later, on May 7, 1932, Doumer was dead, not from my *soufflé,* but from the bullet of a mad Russian.

(I find that people who work in my agency get a similar charge out of state occasions. When a crisis keeps them working all night, their morale is high for weeks afterwards.)

M. Pitard did not tolerate incompetence. He knew that it is demoralizing for professionals to work alongside incompetent amateurs. I saw him fire three pastry cooks in a month for the same crime: They could not make the caps on their brioches rise evenly. Mr. Gladstone would have applauded such ruthlessness; he held that the "first essential for a Prime Minister is to be a good butcher."

M. Pitard taught me exorbitant standards of service. For example, he once heard me tell a waiter that one of the *plats du jour* was finished—and almost fired me for it. In a great kitchen, he said, one must always honor what one has promised on the menu. I pointed out that the dish in question would take so long to cook that no client would wait for a new batch to be prepared. Was it our famous *coulibiac de saumon,* a complicated kedgeree made with the spine-marrow of sturgeon, semolina Kache, salmon collops, mushrooms, onions, and rice—rolled up in a brioche paste and baked for fifty minutes? Or was it our still more exotic Karoly Éclairs, stuffed with a *purée* of woodcocks' entrails cooked in champagne, covered with a brown *chaud-froid* sauce and masked with game jelly? At this distance of time, I do not remember, but I remember exactly what Pitard said to me: "Next time you see that we are running out of a *plat du jour,* come and tell me. I will then get on the telephone to other hotels and restaurants until I find one which is offering the same dish. Then I will send you in a taxi to bring back a supply. Never again tell a waiter that we are fresh out of anything."

(Today I see red when anybody at Ogilvy, Benson & Mather tells a client that we cannot produce an advertisement or a television commercial on the day we have promised it. In the best establishments, promises are always kept, whatever it may cost in agony and overtime.)

Soon after I joined M. Pitard's brigade, I was faced with a problem in morality for which neither my father nor my schoolmasters had prepared me. The *chef garde-manger* sent me to the *chef saucier* with some raw sweetbreads which smelled so putrid that I knew they would endanger the life of any client who ate them; the sauce would mask their condition, and the client would eat them. I protested to the *chef garde-manger,* but he told me to carry out his order; he knew that he would be in hot water if M. Pitard discovered that he had run out of fresh sweetbreads. What was I to do? I had been brought up to believe that it is dishonorable to inform. But I did just that. I took the putrid sweetbreads to M. Pitard and invited him to smell them. He did so and, without a word to me, went over to the *chef garde-manger* and fired him on the spot. The poor bastard had to leave, then and there.

In *Down and Out in Paris and London,* George Orwell told the world that French kitchens are dirty. He had never worked at the Majestic. M. Pitard was a martinet in making us keep the kitchen clean. Twice a day, I had to scrape the wooden surface of the larder table with a sharp plane. Twice a day, the floor was scrubbed and clean sawdust put down. Once a week, a bug-catcher scoured the kitchen in search of roaches. We were issued clean uniforms every morning.

(Today I am a martinet in making my staff keep their offices shipshape. A messy office creates an atmosphere of sloppiness and leads to the disappearance of secret papers.)

We cooks were badly paid, but M. Pitard made so much from the commissions which his suppliers paid him that he could afford to live in a chateau. Far from concealing his wealth from the rest of us, he drove to work in a taxi, carried a cane with a gold head, and dressed, when off duty, like an international banker. This flaunting of privilege stimulated our ambition to follow in his footsteps. He understood the panoply of power.

The immortal Auguste Escoffier had the same idea. When he was *chef des cuisines* at the Carleton in London before the first German war, he used to drive to the Derby on the box of a coach-and-four, dressed in a gray frock coat and top hat. Among my fellow cooks at the Majestic, Escoffier's *Guide Culinaire* was still the definitive authority, the court of last appeal in all our arguments about recipes. Just before he died, he emerged from retirement and came to luncheon in our kitchen; it was like Brahms lunching with the musicians of the Philharmonic.

During the service of luncheon and dinner, M. Pitard stationed himself at the counter where we cooks handed our dishes to the waiters. He inspected every single dish before it left the kitchen. Sometimes he sent it back to the cook for more work. Always he reminded us not to put too much on the plate—*"pas trop!"* He wanted the Majestic to make a profit.

(Today I inspect every campaign before it goes to the client, and I send back many of them for more work. I share M. Pitard's passion for profit.)

Perhaps the ingredient in M. Pitard's leadership which made the most profound impression on me was his industry. I found my sixty-three hours bending over a red-hot stove so exhausting that I had to spend my day off lying on my back in a meadow, looking at the sky. But Pitard worked *seventy-seven* hours a week and took only one free day a fortnight.

(That is about my schedule today. I figure that my staff will be less reluctant to work overtime if I work longer hours than they do. An executive who recently left my agency wrote in his farewell letter, "You set the pace on doing homework. It is a disconcerting experience to spend a Saturday evening in the garden next door to your house, carousing for four hours while you sit, unmoving, at your desk by the window doing your homework. The word gets around.")

I learned something else at the Majestic: If you can make yourself indispensable to a client, you will never be fired. Our most important client, an American lady who occupied a suite of seven rooms, subjected herself to a diet which was based on a baked apple at every meal. One day, she threatened to move to the Ritz unless her apple was always burst. I developed a technique of baking *two* apples, passing their flesh through a sieve to remove all traces of core, and then replacing the flesh of both apples in one skin. The result was the most voluptuous baked apple she had ever seen, and more calories than she ever suspected. Word came down to the kitchen that the chef who was baking those apples must be given tenure.

A Scotsman in a French kitchen is as rare as a Scotsman on Madison Avenue. My fellow chefs, who had heard tales of my ancestral Highlands, christened me *Sauvage*. My closest friend was an elderly *argentier* (silver cleaner), who bore a striking resemblance to the late Charles C. Burlingame. His most cherished memory was a vision of Edward VII (Edward the Caressor) floating majestically across the sidewalk to his brougham after two magnums of *entente cordial* at Maxim's. My friend was a Communist.

Managing an advertising agency isn't all beer and skittles. After fourteen years of it, I have come to the conclusion that the top man has one principal responsibility: to create an atmosphere in which creative mavericks can do useful work.

In the early days of my agency, I worked cheek by jowl with every employee; communication was easy. But as our brigade grows bigger, I find it more difficult. How can I be a father-figure to people who don't even know me by sight? I now employ 497 men and women.

Once a year, I assemble the whole brigade in the auditorium of the Museum of Modern Art and give them a candid report on our operations, profits and all. Then I tell them what kind of behavior I admire, in these terms:

> I admire people who work hard, who bite the bullet. I dislike passengers who don't pull their weight in the boat. It is more fun to be overworked than to be underworked. There is an economic factor built into hard work. The harder you work, the fewer employees we need, and the more profit we make. The more profit we make, the more money becomes available for all of us.
>
> I admire people with first-class brains, because you cannot run a great advertising agency without brainy people. But brains are not enough unless they are combined with *intellectual honesty*.

I have an inviolable rule against employing nepots and spouses, because they breed politics. Whenever two of our people get married, one of them must depart—preferably the female, to look after her baby.

I admire people who work with gusto. If you don't enjoy what you are doing, I beg you to find another job. Remember the Scottish proverb, "Be happy while you're living, for you're a long time dead."

I despise toadies who suck up to their bosses; they are generally the same people who bully their subordinates.

I admire self-confident professionals, the craftsmen who do their jobs with superlative excellence. They always seem to respect the expertise of their colleagues. They don't poach.

I admire people who hire subordinates who are good enough to succeed them. I pity people who are so insecure that they feel compelled to hire inferiors as their subordinates.

I admire people who build up their subordinates, because this is the only way we can promote from within the ranks. I detest having to go outside to fill important jobs, and I look forward to the day when that will never be necessary.

I admire people with gentle manners who treat other people as human beings. I abhor quarrelsome people. I abhor people who wage paper warfare. The best way to keep the peace is to be candid. Remember Blake:

> I was angry with my friend;
> I told my wrath, my wrath did end.
> I was angry with my foe;
> I told it not, my wrath did grow.

I admire well-organized people who deliver their work on time. The Duke of Wellington never went home until he had finished *all* the work on his desk.

Having told my staff what I expect of them, I then tell them what I expect of myself:

I try to be fair and to be firm, to make unpopular decisions without cowardice, to create an atmosphere of stability, and to listen more than I talk.

I try to sustain the momentum of the agency—its ferment, its vitality, its forward thrust.

I try to build the agency by landing new accounts. (At this point, the faces in my audience look like baby birds waiting for the father bird to feed them.)

I try to win the confidence of our clients at their highest level.

I try to make sufficient profits to keep you all from penury in old age.

I plan our policies far into the future.

I try to recruit people of the highest quality at all levels, to build the hottest staff in the agency business.

I try to get the best out of every man and woman in the agency.

Running an agency takes vitality and sufficient resilience to pick oneself up after defeats; affection for one's henchmen and tolerance for their foibles; a genius for composing sibling rivalries; an unerring eye for the main chance; and morality—people who work in advertising agencies can suffer serious blows to their *esprit de corps* if they catch their leader in acts of unprincipled opportunism.

My success or failure depends more than anything else on my ability to find people who can create great campaigns, men with fire in their bellies.

While I wait for Dr. Barron to synthesize his clinical observations into formal psychometric tests, I have to rely on more old-fashioned and empirical techniques for spotting creative dynamos. Whenever I see a good advertisement or television commercial, I find out who wrote it. Then I call the writer on the telephone and congratulate him on his work. A poll has shown that creative people would rather work at Ogilvy, Benson & Mather than at any other agency, so my telephone call often produces an application for a job.

I then ask the candidate to send me the six best advertisements and commercials he has ever written. This reveals, among other things, whether he can recognize a good advertisement when he sees one, or whether he is only the instrument of an able supervisor. Sometimes I call on my victim at home. Ten minutes after crossing his threshold, I can tell whether he has a richly furnished mind, what kind of taste he has, and whether he is happy enough to sustain pressure.

I will tell what I have learned about the creative process from my own experience. The majority of businessmen are incapable of original thinking, because they are unable to escape from the tyranny of reason. Their imaginations are blocked.

I am almost incapable of logical thought, but I have developed techniques for keeping open the telephone line to my unconscious, in case that disorderly repository has anything to tell me. I hear a great deal of music. I am on friendly terms with John Barleycorn. I take long, hot baths. I garden. I go into retreat among the Amish. I watch birds. I go for long walks in the country. I take frequent vacations, so that my brain can lie fallow—no golf, no cocktail parties, no tennis, no bridge, no concentration, only a bicycle.

While thus employed in doing nothing, I receive a constant stream of telegrams from my unconscious, and these become the raw material for my creative work. But more is required: hard work, an open mind, and ungovernable curiosity.

Many of the greatest creations of man have been inspired by the desire to make *money*. When George Frederick Handel was on his beam ends, he shut himself up for twenty-one days and emerged with the complete score of *Messiah,* and hit the jackpot. Few of the themes of *Messiah* were original; Handel dredged them up from his unconscious, where they had been stored since he heard them in other composers' work, or since he had composed them for his own forgotten operas.

At the end of a concert at Carnegie Hall, Walter Damrosch asked Rachmaninoff what sublime thoughts had passed through his head as he stared out into the audience during the playing of his concerto. "I was counting the house," said Rachmaninoff.

If Oxford undergraduates were *paid* for their work, I would have performed miracles of scholarship and become Regius Professor of Modern History; it wasn't until I tasted lucre on Madison Avenue that I began to work in earnest.

In the modern world of business, it is useless to be a creative, original thinker unless you can also *sell* what you create. Management cannot be expected to recognize a good idea unless it is presented to them by a good salesman. In my fourteen years on Madison Avenue, I have had only one great idea which I was unable to sell.

I have observed that no creative organization, whether it is a research laboratory, a magazine, a Paris kitchen, or an advertising agency, will produce a great body of work *unless it is led by a formidable individual.* The Cavendish Laboratory at Cambridge was great because of Lord Rutherford. The *New Yorker* was great because of Ross. The Majestic was great because of Pitard.

It isn't everybody who enjoys working in the atelier of a master. The implication of dependence gnaws at their vitals, until they conclude

> To reign is worth ambition though in hell—
> Better to reign in hell than serve in heaven.

So they leave my atelier, only to discover that their paradise is lost. A few weeks after one of these poor fellows departed, he wrote: "When I left your agency, I was prepared to feel some sadness. What I felt was distress. I have never been so *bereft* in all my life. This I suppose is the price one has to pay for the privilege of having belonged to an elite. There are so few of them around."

Few of the great creators have bland personalities. They are cantankerous egotists, the kind of men who are unwelcome in the modern corporation. Consider Winston Churchill. He drank like a fish. He was capricious and willful. When opposed, he sulked. He was rude to fools. He was wildly extravagant. He wept on the slightest provocation. His conversation was Rabelaisian. He bullied his subordinates. Yet Lord Alanbrooke, his Chief of Staff, could write:

I shall always look back on the years I worked with him as some of the most difficult and trying ones in my life. For all that, I thank God that I was given the opportunity of working alongside of such a man, and of having my eyes opened to the fact that occasionally such supermen exist on this earth.

Discussion

Peterson

I think Dave has raised a very important point about a trend in industry to the so-called professional manager. Having spent five years in the advertising business, I think he is absolutely on the right track in insisting on creative advertising as the most important product. In industry we are tending to develop a kind of sterile professional manager who has no emotional feelings about the product, who does not "love" the product. He doesn't create anything, but he kind of manages something in a rather artificial way. And when I hear Ted Bensinger talk about bowling, and what he has done for bowling—he has a feeling for this thing, as Ogilvy has a feeling about advertising. I was just wondering whether we have put enough emphasis on what he is talking about—our emotional commitment to great cooking, or great advertising, or great something.

Ogilvy

It's the opposite of detachment.

SIZE AND DIVERSIFICATION

Steiner

The conception that the greatest chef would be the most effective leader in the kitchen is creatively sound, but isn't it restricted to businesses or organizations which have one clear-cut professional skill? Take a clinic; obviously the greatest physician would be the most inspirational leader. Yet, what would you say about General Motors, or the University of Chicago, where there is no one, clear-cut professional skill; there is no one dimension?

Ogilvy

It is a bad institution, because it has excessive diversification.

Steiner

That is one answer. How do you make such an institution creative, short of saying: Let's divide it up?

Ogilvy

Divide it up.

Peterson

To the point Dave made of "break up the companies": this is interesting. We recently had a long-range planning consultant take the outstanding growth companies in America, and we also asked him to take those companies that were vastly diversified, that had grown largely by acquisitions of various sorts and stock manipulations of various sorts, and trace their growth. We got about fifteen or twenty of these case studies, and we saw a very interesting thing.

In almost every case, in these vastly diffused organizations, the men at the top had no particular emotional commitment to a product or to a concept; they did not understand the product, the companies are financial holding companies. These companies go up, and then inevitably they start going down. It gets out of control. The top management doesn't know enough about the businesses to know when they are in trouble. They don't know how to get out of trouble. I think there is a real good point here: If you diversify too much, the leadership cannot give the business this sense of excellence and imagination.

Ogilvy

I won't take diversified companies as clients. I always find them sick at the top.

FUN

Bruner

About fun: I have never visited a lab that was worth a damn where the people weren't having a lot of fun, usually rather ribald fun. I remember one episode. A great Hungarian friend of mine, now dead—George Pacek, a physicist—went as a young man to Niels Bohr's laboratory. A very serious young man, he was there for about two weeks and he was absolutely disgusted. People were always playing practical jokes on each other. He went to old Uncle Nick—Niels Bohr himself—and he said, "I'm leaving to go to work at another laboratory at Syracuse. I don't find people serious enough around here." Bohr took him aside and said, "Young man, there are some subjects that are so serious that you can't be serious about them."

This is one thing that bothers me about this creativity pitch. It is absolutely the killer of joy. Would you say to a man, "Say, chap, are you being serious? Are you being creative?" You would freeze him.

Wallis

There is a cultural difference, though, in this business of having fun. During the war, I ran a group that had two main categories of research mathematicians in it. Roughly half of them were Vassar graduates and half were from Hunter. The Hunter girls never smiled at anything. We got just as much work out of them and they were just as original. The other crowd would not, under any circumstances, including really critical deadlines, appear to take anything seriously.

Bruner

I should say women are an exception to this.

Ogilvy

With us, it is the sad, lugubrious dogs who are sterile and blocked and do nothing. It is the exuberant fellows who produce —the unstable ones.

MEASURING AND REWARDING CREATIVITY

Bensinger

You said that one of your writers was more creative, developed many more good ads than the rest, and that you have a sort of scattered, remunerative scale. How do you keep this team in balance—when you have a fellow way up here and there is a gap?

Ogilvy

I don't. It is very unfair, and it bothers me and keeps me awake at nights. There are some people we wish we could pay everything we've got to. It happens to be me, but nobody else. I have my feet in the trough, but these other fine creative people do not get nearly enough. I am trying to spread it more every year. I can't do it at once, but I am giving the top people more and the bottom people less.

Alexander

I have some prejudice against this fervor to quantify and measure goodness, productivity, effectiveness in human beings. When I was a nine-year-old boy, I was extremely hit by the idea of comparing people, telling who is better. One day, I went to my father, who was a professor of philosophy, and asked him who was greater, Newton or Darwin. He very patiently took me aside and said, "My boy, that is a foolish question. If you ask who is a better tennis player, you can prove who can be such. Who is a faster runner, that you can also ask; but how can you measure Darwin's accomplishment with Newton's? The one worked in one field, the other in another field; he had certain assets which the other did not have and they are entirely different, and why should you try to measure?" And it is pointless to measure. Of course you can't. Creative activity is not a race-track.

About a year later—that did not impress me, it was too theoretical—I went to him and again I asked a similar question: "Father, who was the greater poet, Goethe or Schiller?" Then he looked at me disgustedly and very tersely said, "I don't know. I didn't measure them."

That did it, and since then I have never forgotten that that is *not* a meaningful question. It is a destructive question. We have heard of measuring people by how many articles they publish. That is a measure, but it is meaningless. The question is how good the article is.

Ogilvy

I disagree with your father, anyway for business. I would have to say: What did you produce yesterday? I believe Rutherford and Maxwell were measurably greater, more productive, more creative than A, B, and C at the University of X.

Alexander

But who is greater, Maxwell or Faraday?

Ogilvy

That's not the point. I am putting the elite at the top and studying them, the creative leaders.

Alexander

And why do we want to measure? That is the question.

Ogilvy

I have to decide what to pay them.

THE IMPORTANCE OF MONEY

Steiner

Why did you leave the Majestic Hotel?

Ogilvy

In pursuit of money, which I believe to be the main force in my life. I wanted to be a professor, as a boy at Oxford, and I knew I was going to be, but I didn't do well. Looking back, I know that if I had been paid for my grades, I would now be the richest professor of history at Oxford. I am unable to work except for bread.

Barron

I'm glad you didn't make it, because then you wouldn't have been here this morning.

Steiner

I think on the note of the importance of salaries, it is appropriate to turn our consideration to the graduate school.

13

Creativity and the Graduate School

BERNARD BERELSON

I have been feeling very sorry for myself the last day-and-a-half, as one after the other the sentences that I was going to say have been said by someone else. I've been consoling myself with the thought that, although everything that's true has been said so far, not everything that has been said is true, and I might be able to make that distinction this morning.

Now I find myself even sorrier, having to follow Mr. Ogilvy. Those of you who are old enough will remember that the old vaudeville bills were so arranged that, after the star attraction, they usually closed out the show with a dog act while the audience gradually left the theatre, and I feel that I'm put in somewhat of that position now.

I think you'll hear echoes in these lines of things that have been said in the earlier sessions. I thought last night I'd put a gloss on this paper and keep pointing to them as I went on, but I decided not to do that for both good and real reasons.

In any case, I am comforted somewhat by the observation that Carlyle made once to the effect that the essence of originality is not that a thing be new, but that it be one's own. And that line seems to me a very good introduction to what I am about to say. So it says here:

By this time, I had assumed that the central term "creativity" would have been defined for us. Indeed, I should have been surprised if it had not been defined several times. In any case, we non-specialists in this subject are glad to leave the troublesome questions of definition to the experts. I suppose a few words need to be said at the outset about what I think I'm talking about.

I feel about creativity the way St. Augustine felt about time: I know just what I mean until I have to define it. As a quick and rough indication, however, I mean simply the production of important new ideas and/or of new ways of doing things—usually, though not necessarily always, good or correct ones. Thus, creativity can range from literary excellence to scientific discovery, from the professional application of intellectual ideas to the administrative organization through which a new development is brought about.

At first glance, it may seem strange to address oneself to "the graduate school as a creator of creativity." Everyone in academic life knows the reputation of the graduate school as an effective stifler of creativity: how it rigidifies intellectual boundaries; how its disciplines quarrel over jurisdictional lines harder than the carpenters' union; how it forces the young into conformity with narrow criteria of scholarship as the price to pay for the coveted degree; how it rejects anything "truly creative" if it is not also "sound"; how it treats deviants from the true scholarly line; and how it resists change itself. But even if such charges are part of the picture—and I would grant that they are a part, as they are of any human institution, including notably the intellectual circles in which such charges are themselves most frequently made—they are not all of it by any means. An inquiry into the matter may tell us something about both the graduate school and the nature of creativity, at least in the modern world.

For these brief comments I have a single theme. If the question is: What does the graduate school have to do with "the creative organization"? the answer is: It is an institutional invention to promote organized creativity. That is partly its weakness, but it is much more its strength, as I shall try to indicate.

It is important to start the inquiry with an elementary distinction by type of creativity. The graduate school does not pretend to deal with literary, artistic, or musical creativity, in the sense of producing novelists, poets, dramatists, composers, painters, or sculptors; what we call the creative arts. (We don't call the other the creative sciences, you know.) In other fields, the subject is *there*—the physical, biological, and social world. The appropriate disciplines study the subject but do not need to *create* it first. For the moment, we need only note that while it may be too much to say that we shall never be able to train for such creativity, it is probably not too much to say that we do not now know how to do it. This difference between the creative arts and the creative organization will run through my remarks, and I ask myself: How is it that the graduate school feels it is creative in some fields and avoids these creative arts fields, and what are the differences, and what can we learn from that?

Within the province of the graduate school we have to make another elementary distinction, by magnitude of creativity. Some men have been *truly* creative in the intellectual disciplines; they have been creative by historical standards, which means that they started a great deal that took many other men a long time to finish. In this category, we would place such men as Newton, Darwin, Adam Smith, Einstein, Marx, Freud—those intellectual giants who get the most space in the encyclopedias. They exhibit what we usually mean by genius. I suppose the best general rule fitting their emergence—the rule that explains almost all the variants—is simply to say that *no one* can be *that* creative and then cite the few exceptions.

Now, such men might not be able to live, let alone survive, in the university atmosphere. In the modern world, it is enough if the foundations can recognize them early enough, support them, and leave them alone. Certainly, the graduate school cannot train men to such levels of creativity, so we can dismiss them with but one important point that will be echoed later; namely, that the maker of the intellectual revolution is never around at the end of what he started, and the revolution seldom ends where he intended it to. Lesser men decide that, and they are from and of the university.

From the geniuses down, however, graduate (and in some cases professional) training is to an increasing extent the route to prominence and position, if not to creativity. This is certainly the case in the physical and biological sciences, in medicine, and in engineering. It is an extremely rare event when an intellectual contribution is made by a non-professional. It is even the case in the behavioral sciences. In a review I conducted a few years ago of leading contributions made within the preceding twenty-five years, only two non-professional authors appeared, Chester Barnard and Benjamin Whorf. And most linguists today, I understand, are doubtful of the Whorfian hypothesis, although it would certainly be classed as creative at the time. It is more likely to be the case in history, though my impression is that most prizes go to professionally trained, academically disciplined men. It is also my impression that this is more and more the case in literary criticism, as the universities and the world of the little magazines come to have more and more to do with one another— more movement back and forth, more literary men in the institutions of higher education. It is less clearly the case in philosophy, although theological training is a complicating factor here. And it is barely beginning to be the case in business, although legal training is a complicating factor there. As I have said, it is not at all the case in literary and artistic fields.

What is the reason for this range in the contribution of graduate training to new ideas and new ways?

To begin with, some people think that the sciences and related fields benefit from a kind of definitional vested interest, in that the specialists within a field are the sole judges of what is creative and hence can disregard any external criteria. According to this position, economists consider that only economists can judge economists, and the rest of us are placed out of bounds at the outset. This is part of what is usually referred to in graduate school debates as undue specialization, by those who want to be in on such judgments.

But this argument does not seem true as it stands; indeed, it seems closer to false. In the long run, science must justify itself to the outside society by its works, and it has. The physicists and engineers have made the bomb and are exploring space. The biologists and medical men have prolonged life and made dramatically effective inventions in diagnosis, drugs, and surgery. The economists presumably are helping to stabilize the business cycle. The psychologists have succeeded in making individual discriminations on a mass basis, as in testing, and may even be able some day to do something about mental disturbance—and if they cannot, the biologists will. It is precisely by the standards of the larger community, in the long or even in the middle run, that such fields prove themselves as creative. If anything, this is not the case with the so-called creative arts, which are much more likely to be judged by the experts themselves, the critics, and where, on the whole, second- or third-rate stuff is more likely to come to public acceptance.

Another difference in this range of fields has to do with the familiar concern about individual work as against teamwork. There is, of course, the legend that only the individual can be "truly creative." The corollary is that as the sciences have usually gone over to what is called team research, but what at this conference we shall term a creative organization, they have become less creative as a result. This particular line of argument comes close to the heart of the issue, and is worth pursuing.

First, without taking anything away from the individual's creativeness in the arts, let us elaborate it a little, for the sake of the facts. It is true, of course, that a committee could not have written Shakespeare's plays or Beethoven's symphonies, just as it is also true that a single individual cannot perform them—only a team can. Moreover, there is too little recognition that when we look at the process of production in the case of several creative artists, we find the effort of multiple persons, which if it occurred in the sciences would be called team effort.

Thomas Wolfe needed Maxwell Perkins to edit him nearer to intelligibility. Flaubert got the story of *Madame Bovary* from a friend, read the manuscript pages to him on weekends, and rewrote accordingly. Numerous playwrights, including the greatest ones, have taken their plots from others. According to T. S. Eliot himself, "It was in 1922 that I placed before Ezra Pound in Paris the manuscript of a sprawling, chaotic poem called *The Wasteland,* which left his hands reduced to about half its size, in the form in which it appears in print" —a report reminiscent of what happens to any number of doctoral dissertations and research reports in the graduate school. So it would seem that at least a little qualification should be given the traditional belief, most recently enunciated by Mr. Gregory Peck in speaking of film production, that "It's no longer a pure art when it becomes a group effort."

Is the difference one of inspiration? This is hard to define, let alone to document. If this is indeed the fact, then there are a number of deviant cases off the main diagonals. The American sociologist Samuel Stouffer once said, "The brooding imagination puzzling over a multivariate distribution which just came off the IBM machine, and seeking order in apparent chaos, is creating as truly as the maker of a sonnet. The goals may be different, but the scientist's eyes, like the artist's, are oft in a fine frenzy rolling." And on the other side, the English poet and artist William Morris once observed that "Talk of inspiration is sheer nonsense; there is no such thing. It is a mere matter of craftsmanship." And the German poet Rilke believed that "Work is the *only* real way of bringing back inspiration." (The mention of Rilke here tempts me to give Franz Alexander the answer to the question he asked sixty-one years ago. The answer is that Goethe is a greater poet than Schiller. I wish someone had told you that earlier!)

Not to prolong this commentary unduly, and not to put too fine a point on the matter, it appears to me that the major distinction between fields where graduate study does and does not make a central contribution comes down to one thing: method. Those fields that have a method that can be articulated and taught do well in the graduate school and, in such cases, graduate training does lead directly to creativity. Those fields that do not have a method do not do so well. Thus, the sciences get along best; fields like history, moderately well; and the creative arts, not at all.

This, of course, is where the cumulation of knowledge comes in. By virtue of the improvement and the transmissibility of objective methods of securing knowledge, later generations of scientists can build on, validate, revise, and surmount earlier ones, even the greatest innovators of an earlier time. Every high school student today knows what it took the genius of Euclid first to find out. (And if we give Bob Merton the chance, he can spell out for us the history of the famous observation that a midget on the shoulders of a giant can see farther than a giant.) And this is precisely the way in which the great innovation by the creative genius is reshaped, in these fields: by the application of method. Freud started a great deal that will in the end be finished by ordinary Ph.D.'s and M.D.'s, and in the course of completing the task, they will almost certainly discard a great deal of what is most Freudian.

So the existence of a Darwin has meant that today's ordinarily able biologists can go further. But the existence of Melville or Twain does not mean that today's American novelists can do better; in fact, of course, they do not. Indeed, I am personally inclined to think it the case that, if the criterion is approximation to the best of its kind, short of genius, the average well-trained man from the graduate school earns a better mark in his field than the average good creative artist does in his.

(If I had time here, I would spell out what seems to me to be another important difference between these fields; namely, the difference between complexity and profundity. Science is complex and the humanities are profound. Methods work well in complex fields and less well in profound ones. One might even push to see whether there are ways of moving the problems of the fields of profundity, by breaking them down, into fields of complexity where we can handle them.)

The graduate school's distinctive contribution to creativity, then, is in spreading the *possibility* and, in the end (on the average) the *fact* of creativity to many more people than hitherto. Its distinctive contribution is not to the few A+ geniuses—it might even be bad for them—but to the men from A down to, say, B−. It makes the B− into B, the B into B+, the B+ into A, and the A into a better A. And in the course of this, these people revise the work of the great genius and make his occurrence in a way less likely—and perhaps even less necessary as method grows.

Now, this is by no means a negligible or unimportant contribution, for the whole enterprise in these fields—the whole creative organization in producing and applying objective knowledge—is geared to just such people. We need them to do the numerous jobs required, the replications, the negative experiments, the false trials, the exploratory attempts, the methodological tests, all leading to another creative breakthrough even as they validate the last one. Without such people we would not have had, at least not as soon and as well as we did, the the bomb and space exploration, the vaccine, the sample survey, personality and intelligence tests, analyses of primitive cultures, and much more. Indeed, without them, most of us would not be here, for most of us *are* just such people.

And, largely thanks to the graduate school, our contribution to creativity is particularly important in the modern world. Someone has said that 90 per cent of the contributors to humanistic scholarship who ever lived are dead, but 90 per cent of the contributors to science who ever lived are now alive. If those figures are even roughly correct, they signal the importance of this type of creativity in the present day. Genius we shall always welcome, but trained intelligence in such amounts and over such scope of subject matter is something new under the sun, to be highly valued as such. As Pasteur said, "In the fields of observation, chance favors only the prepared mind."

Nor is the game over by many means. As the reach of method gradually informs new fields, primarily business organizations, this type of creativity will become ever more important there.

I summarize with a final comparison with the creative arts which I think puts the thing in a nutshell. A. E. Housman once said that writing poetry is "either easy or impossible." Graduate training, at its best, is just the opposite: It is hard, but—and this is a big *but*—it *is* possible.

Discussion

WHAT MAKES A GOOD GRADUATE SCHOOL?

Steiner

> I noticed you didn't say anything about what the good graduate school is like, as against the bad graduate school. Do you have any general conclusions on that score—not: Which ones are they? but: What makes them good? What makes them creative?

Berelson

> I'll give you the traditional answer to that, and then I'll give you my personal answer.

> The traditional answer, of course, is that the great graduate school is the school with the great men on the faculty—Harvard and others. My prejudice, my conviction, is that the great graduate school is the school with the best students, which isn't always quite the same thing.

> When we were talking about selectivity of personnel, I thought about companies going to M.I.T. to get the bright, young physical engineers, and so forth. Usually people leap to the conclusion from that—and that certainly is, on the average, the thing to do— to go to the M.I.T.'s, Harvard's, Chicago's, Columbia's, because the people on those faculties train people better. But I am more inclined to think that the M.I.T.'s yield the best people, because the reputations of those schools get the best people to start with.

> I think that one of the recommendations that I have for a graduate school that is of Grade B quality and wants to move into

A—quality is: not to try to buy good faculties—that's very hard to do and it takes a much longer time—but to buy good students and to build one's own school more rapidly that way. These things weave together. The best students go to Harvard, because they can work with Jerry Bruner there; but I think that it is the quality of the man who comes that tends to give the quality to the graduate institution.

While I think there are devices that make some graduate schools more efficient than others, I cannot think offhand of any major organizational devices that would make a graduate school better with inferior input and personnel.

Merton

This comes so close to my own prejudices that I am inclined to elaborate them a little bit. What you say about the faculty of graduate schools and the student body is a special case of what is found in organizations of every type. I would resist the temptation to say it is *either* faculty *or* students. I would further resist the temptation to start with one or the other.

The interactive process involves both the key personnel in an organization and the new recruits, once you have begun a benevolent cycle. Once you get a substantial degree of effective originality in an organization, this becomes visible to the larger community and affects the standing of the organization. This then leads to the self-selective recruitment of abler people, both students and faculty. This self-selective recruitment further accelerates productivity. You get a cycle going for a time that is self-reinforcing. The important thing is to see this process as an interplay between the different kinds of personnel in an organization, their achievement, and the further recruitment of new, effective personnel.

The question is often badly put in the case of the graduate school or any other organization: Is it A *or* B? It can start with either. The decisive break occurs when visibly superior performance occurs in the organization. Then the process is almost self-sustaining.

Steiner

Can it also start with neither? That is, can it start via "marketing," in this sense: Can you simply convince people that you have both, without either being true, and thereby start getting some together?

Merton

I would like to see a case of that kind.

Ogilvy

Does it not start with the head? There is an old saying, "The fish stinks from the head." Or as Emerson, I suppose, said, "Any institution is the length and shadow of one man." Find your Rutherford.

Merton

There is a germ of truth in the notion of the "corporate image" —not in the vulgar sense, but in the sense of the imagery of an institution. Once that becomes positive, even though there are weak spots within it, the weak spots can be strengthened because of the processes of self-selection of people who want to identify themselves with an institution or an organization that matters. It is an interesting sociological pattern. The public standing of an organization is important because it sets in motion those selective tendencies of recruitment that repair the deficiencies. Once you get off on the right foot, it is effective in helping you to get further with your job, which helps explain the paradox of occasional discrepancies between the actual state of an organization and its reputation.

AN EXPERIMENT

Steiner

We are going to take Pete Peterson's suggestion: We have been doing a lot of very expensive conceptualizing, and now we shall do a cheap and fast experiment.

Wallis

Bill Shockley asked that we take five minutes to do a little experiment. He told us yesterday he had asked people in his organization to give him little memos on creativity in their organization, and he has two very short ones here. One of them, he says, is from the most creative man in the organization—which, I take it, is really the second most creative man—and the other is from the least. He wants me to read them—he doesn't want to for fear his voice will reveal some clues—and we'll just get a vote as to which is which.

I shall call the first Mr. Yellow and the second Mr. White, since those are the colors of the papers. Mr. Yellow's is simply headed, "Creativity at Shockley Transistor," and it is in outline form:

A. Measures of Creativity
   1. Difficulty and significance of problems undertaken
   2. Number of publications and technical developments of laboratory
   3. Standing of laboratory in the profession
B. Factors Promoting Creativity
   1. *Constant participation of the director in the research planning of the laboratory.* This provides an organizational unity of effort and prevents fragmentation in the research areas separately prosecuted by the individual senior staff members, who may have little contact with each other. This is the case in a number of laboratories.
   2. *Quality of research personnel.* For the laboratory to be creative, it must be staffed by creative people. The attracting and retention of these is a central problem of management.
   3. *Significance of problems.* The problems undertaken must be of a nature to inspire the staff. Mediocre problems inspire mediocre work. Routine development work must be linked in some way to fundamental problems, if first-class intellects are to remain interested.
   4. *Frequent inter-staff discussions.* Ideas are initiated by staff members who may be bystanders as far as the particular discussion is concerned.
   5. *Contact with others in the profession.* This is not as frequent as it would be if the laboratory were located in the New York metropolitan area.

6. *Publication pressure.* The effort required to reduce results to writing often requires catalysis by administration. The aim of publication influences the shaping of the research itself into avenues worthy of publication.

Here is the second one (Mr. White):

Question: Are we creative?

Answer: I think yes.

Question: Why are we creative?

Answer: Creativity, in my opinion, is caused by an interplay of the human mind and the conditions under which it expresses itself. The first condition for creativity is therefore the existence of potentially creative minds in an organization. A dull personality will never create anything, even in the most favorable conditions. The second necessity for creativity is an atmosphere which is favorable for achievement. Three factors can be seen which are pertinent for the formation of a creative atmosphere in science. These are: freedom, stimulation, and availability of personnell and equipment necessary to carry out new ideas. (In case it is relevant, "personnel" is misspelled, with a double "l.")

All these conditions can be found in our organization and are, in my opinion, the basis for its unquestionable creativity.

Ogilvy
One is the top and one is the bottom?

Shockley
Yes, one is the top. The other is—maybe not the bottom, but is a man who may not make the grade.

Merton
How wide a spread is there between them, by any criteria that you would want to use—whether it is salary or your measurements?

Shockley

Well, you can use the quantitative measure. I would guess, in terms of significant publications that these men have produced something in the order of maybe five to one, maybe ten to one.

Merton

I will go out on a limb—those two documents do not represent the full spread. The difference between them is primarily a difference of style, a difference in tone, and not in content. If you did a close comparison of the content of the two documents, you would find the overlap in substantive content to be of the order of 80 per cent. In the one case, it is filled out in more detail and in the other, is put a little more vaguely. If the issue had not been put as it was, I would not have seen that much of a spread between the two.

Wallis

How many think that Mr. Yellow, the one I read first, is the better one? (Two votes.)

How many think it is the white one? (Twelve votes.)

Ogilvy

No opinion.

Wallis

There were at least two of no opinion, weren't there? Of course, there would have been more, had we offered the alternative of no opinion. Merton announced that that would have been his.

Shockley

The vote is correct.

14

Remarks on Developments in Professional Education

W. ALLEN WALLIS

Everybody knows that we need creative individuals. But we also need to make individuals creative. There are many leading graduate departments that have outstanding people but are not outstanding places for graduate training. Some of them do not turn out a number of students proportionate to the number of good faculty that they have.

The need is to give these individuals incentive to identify their own self-interest with the success of the organization. David Ogilvy made it clear that he has ways of doing this in his advertising agency, but even there I wonder whether the people work all night because he is around with a whip making them produce, or whether they would not do pretty much the same anywhere, unless the atmosphere was positively hostile to it. Certainly in a university, there is no way to make people do what they are hired to, much less do more, day and night. Yet the number of faculty members who loaf or fail to show up for their classes is so trivial that we never think about it.

It is also very important to give people the feeling that David Ogilvy mentioned, that they are part of an important, pioneering, and successful organization. It helps to have the people feel that their organization is the greatest, even if they know that it is not recognized as such. They will see that there are lags in reputation and work all the harder to overcome the lag, and that is a healthier attitude than the smugness that can come with recognition.

Universities have the problem of giving enough freedom to faculty members to advance their standing in the profession outside their organization. They have to write and publish and participate in activities that often do not have direct value to the school. This is especially true of professional schools. More than half the faculty in the Chicago Graduate School of Business have degrees in other fields than business —anthropology, sociology, mathematics, economics, and psychology; many things they want to do, say, as anthropologists are not related to the things a business school does, but if the anthropologists are not able to stay in the center of their own profession, they will not be willing to stay very long in a place like ours.

Insofar as there are people of high caliber whose personal interests are nearly identical with those of the school, the situation is ideal. To a considerable extent, that can be arranged in a professional school. If you need to create a new field of study or a new approach to our established subject, you find somebody with a burning desire to revolutionize and reform the subject or to introduce a new field and work it out properly. The ideal situation is illustrated by Barney Berelson's coming to our school to work up the behavioral sciences. We have built by getting key people who were highly creative and who saw in our operation a chance to do something in their own professions. John Jeuck came to us from the Harvard Business School and a lot of interesting things have developed in his area, marketing, a field so shoddy as to be a major problem in most business schools. Business mathematics—the use of higher mathematics and computers in business, not compound interest and discounting—hardly existed as a subject until we brought in people from Harvard, Standard Oil, the Burroughs Corporation, and other places, who thought they could identify their professional interests with our activity. That has been one approach to developing a creative organization.

My comments come very close to what Ogilvy said, except that the top administrator in an academic institution has no real authority and must defer the important decisions about whom to hire, and what the curriculum will be, and whom to promote to tenure, to the cumbersome machinery of faculty voting. Everyone knows that the dean cannot fire him or tell him exactly what to teach or influence his research or his decision to organize a McKinsey Seminar.

These restraints raise in my mind a question about the permanence of creativity in academic organizations. They may cause the cycles we typically find in the history of academic organizations. They may cause those cycles we typically find in the history of academic departments and professional schools, the long periods when they are as strong as the linguistics department at Harvard apparently is and as the sociology department at Chicago was. There are exceptions. The departments of economics and anthropology here at Chicago have been excellent since the beginning. On the other hand, the Business School in the late '20's and early '30's had the best faculty any business school has ever succeeded in assembling (unless the one we have now is better, as I naturally hope and think!), but decay set in and it diminished to insignificance.

About six years ago, when we had an opportunity to build up the school here, we had to think about exactly what a business school is and what its purposes are, because business is not a profession in the same sense as medicine and law, yet it has a great many professional characteristics. This led us to look into the history of professional education in other fields and we found an amazingly similar pattern in field after field.

Professional education starts as apprenticeship outside the academic walls. The boy gets a job as a clerk in a law office or goes around with the doctors in a hospital or works in a business to learn a job. Gradually, universities assume the training job, by moving apprenticeship systems into the degree requirements. The case method that currently dominates most business education is essentially a kind of vicarious apprenticeship that tries to do for students exactly what business does for them when they get there. We tell students, "Go get a job; you'll learn a lot more in two years about how business does things than you'll ever learn in any university."

We have found that, as the profession evolves, people soon get dissatisfied with apprenticeship education in schools. The people that come out may be prepared to meet the standards of the profession ten or twenty-five years ago, but they are not up to date on current practice nor moving ahead of it to make innovations.

Then the schools turn to basic scientific materials. The medical schools in Germany pioneered in the pattern that came to dominate medical education throughout the world; full-time university professors, specialists in scientific subjects with a very extensive background in the sciences that underlie medicine, were put in charge of teaching. A similar movement took place in engineering. The two leading engineering schools, Cal Tech and M.I.T., are among the leading institutions in basic science in the world—and so are some of the medical schools. And this is clearly the pattern of development of business education.

Is that what you had in mind?

Discussion

Berelson

That is exactly the answer I wanted, and I wanted to hear it again, because it harks back to what I tried to say about the development of methods and the spread of creativity via methods. You can see that in a lot of established fields now, in most of the arts and sciences and in the usual graduate school in fields like medicine. Business is a special case only in the historical sense that parts of business today have reached the point at which the spread and training of methods make direct contributions, but parts of their activities have not yet.

For example, my impression is that in the last couple of decades economics within business has come into a very important position, and there a technique is involved, at least in certain parts of economics. And businessmen turn to the specialists. On the other hand, I think that in human relations in industry we are a couple of decades behind in that development. But it is coming and people are working on it; in the end, presumably a "science" or a profession will be much advanced over where we are now. (And even in the more creative sense, in the sense of the creative arts, this is beginning to be the case.)

And, in a sense, this is an anti-Rutherford point, because a lot of people who are not Rutherfords today are making great advances in science without the genius of the great innovator. That is one of the things we call progress, I suppose.

SIX FACTORS IN CREATIVITY

Barron

You are talking here about subtle craftsmanship, for the large part, though not entirely. A lot of what you specify is simply the kind of discipline that a good craftsman has. The additional thing that must be added, the originality, greatness, etc., comes from another source.

Perhaps it would help our problem of description if we recalled the research on factorial structure of creativity done by J. P. Guilford and his associates at the University of Southern California. Guilford found, after extensive factorial investigations, that creativity could be boiled down to factors which are relatively independent of one another.

One is sensitivity to problems. Another is fluency of ideas and associations. A third is adaptive flexibility. A fourth is spontaneous flexibility. A fifth is originality, and a sixth is the evaluative capacity.

People differ among themselves very much in the patterning of these factors. What you try to get, in order to help in prediction, is *differential measurements* of these abilities, because not everyone is high in all of them, nor does every situation call for all of these. For example, much of science requires what Guilford calls convergent thinking: solving problems which are already set, in terms of the history of the work up to that point, by applying known principles in a thoroughly reasonable and adaptively flexible manner. Yet other problems may require divergent thinking abilities, such as spontaneous flexibility and originality. A person with one pattern of abilities may be best for one kind of problem, while a different pattern is required for success in another sort of problem.

15

Observations on Organizational Factors Affecting Creativity

(EDITED COMMENTS)

FRANZ ALEXANDER

I would like to pick up three topics which I could demonstrate through personal experience. Two of them were raised by Mr. Peterson: commitment and experiment; commitment working against creativity, and experiment being the great weapon or implement of creativity.

As to commitment, Mr. Peterson spoke of financial commitment—a company overinvested in Mach 1; therefore it cannot go on to the newer product, Mach 2. But there are other forms of commitment which appear entirely different and yet work the same way. These are emotional commitments: previous ideas, prevailing beliefs, pride of those who advanced those ideas. The status quo forces are very strongly supported by all kinds of commitments. Every commitment favors status quo, if I may make such a generalization.

Experimentation, of course, is the counterforce.

The third topic—the difficulty of selling ideas—was only mentioned *en passant* by Mr. Ogilvy, but it alerted me as something to which I can say a few words.

When I heard Mr. Shockley's autobiographical statements and the excellent little autobiography from Mr. Ogilvy, I went back in my memory. (This is free association—you know, we are trained for free association in our field.) Immediately, it occurred to me that if I look through my own research activities, I experienced all these factors. I cannot do quite as well as these gentlemen—so dramatically—but I would like to mention a few autobiographical data which bear out these points.

I did my first experimental research as a medical student in Professor Tangl's physiological laboratory. He was an excellent disciplinarian; he insisted that all his assistants should know physics, chemistry, and higher mathematics. This was his primary requirement, which, in a medical school, is unusual. Otherwise he was, I would say, somewhat pedestrian, but very exacting and a very good methodologist.

I went to Professor Tangl and said to him, "I want to test out the idea that brain function requires energy, contrary to current beliefs. I want to show that brain activity will increase oxygen consumption."

Whereupon the professor immediately sent me out, saying, "This issue is already settled. Atwater and Benedict in America put students into calorimeters while they worked on mathematical problems and while resting. There was no difference in their metabolism. That is settled."

Again, he said no. Then he turned around. Academic freedom, you know, was very great in those days, even under the kaiser, maybe greater than in a democracy. So he said to me, a medical student, "If you pay for the dogs, you can do it."

So I paid for the dogs. The result of the experiment was positive. The dogs, under the stimulation of strong light, consumed more oxygen. I then cut the medulla oblongata and gave the dogs artificial respiration, then curare, so that the muscle system was eliminated. Stimuli coming from the upper brain centers could not penetrate. The experiment was well done and it was a great success.

A year later, a then famous textbook of physiology came out by Zuntz, a famous German metabolic research man, and there I saw, "Professor Tangl has proven recently . . . ," not even mentioning my work. I was very upset, and I took the book to Professor Tangl. (Priority in those days counted much more than it does today. Today I would not care.) I showed him the book and said, "Professor, have you seen that?"

He was very embarrassed and he said, "Oh, in the next edition, it will be corrected."

Five days later he fired me. That is how I came to psychiatry; otherwise, I would still be sitting in the physiological laboratory. My wife still hates the fact that I sacrificed fifty dogs for this experiment. She loves dogs.

Now my second experiment, or research, or, let us say, innovation, occurred when I came to this country. I became convinced that the isolation of psychoanalysis is a cultural lag. It developed in Europe where Freud was fighting with the doctors, but here the isolation had no historical roots. Psychoanalysis is needed in psychiatry, and there is no reason why it should be isolated and taught at special institutes. It belongs to the departments of psychiatry, in the schools of medicine. This can be done, but everybody's reaction then was, "It cannot be done. You are a Utopian. You are an idealist, etc."

Well, the Chicago Institute [for Psychoanalysis] was founded and the Chicago Institute affiliated itself with universities. Comple incorporation in universities at that time was not yet possible, though now there are three or four universities in the country which have incorporated psychoanalytic institutes.

It could be done. In the first instance, I was opposed by Professor Tangl. This time I was opposed by my co-workers. I was the Director of the Institute. Whether the commitment comes from above or below makes no difference.

My third innovation was the idea that psychoanalysis is a kind of basic science—"psychodynamics"—which can be applied therapeutically in different ways, in different types of cases. The doctrine was that, in psychoanalysis, the patient comes five times a week to the doctor, lies down on the couch for an hour, and free-associates. This goes on for two, three, four, five, seven, or more years.

It occurred to me that maybe the same instrument—psychodynamic reasoning and understanding and knowing the language of the unconscious—can be applied more directly, at least to certain cases and maybe to all cases. Now that, of course, was sacrilegious in those days.

We finally sold the idea, but not fully successfully. I am not a good seller of ideas, in contrast to Mr. Ogilvy, but I sold it sufficiently so that at least a group of my collaborators undertook such treatments. It is still a controversial question, but today even orthodox psychoanalysts use psychodynamically oriented psychotherapy, and my prediction is that this is the music of the future.

Ogilvy

On the couch or not?

Alexander

Not necessarily.

Ogilvy

These quickies are not on the couch?

Alexander

Not necessarily. And they are not necessarily quickies either. They may last one or two years, but you do not see the patient every day. It is not monotonous. One adjusts the frequency to the needs of the patient, to the existing psychodynamic situation. You are not, so to speak, shackled by rules.

Ogilvy

I wish I had met you earlier.

Alexander

A further conviction that I came to was that all we know—all psychodynamic knowledge—comes from a highly private enterprise. The patient is closeted with the physician and the physician tells us what happens. He sees eight patients a day. How can he remember what happens? He selects material which caught his eye, which corresponded to his preconceived ideas, but he does not have the factual material of what is really going on when he wants to work up his cases. Moreover, the doctrine in those days was that the psychoanalyst is really a blank screen: The patient projects into him a father role, a mother role, or whatever it is, but he, his own personality, does not influence this process. He is a blank screen which has no design, and only the patient's own patterns are transferred to the screen; the nature of the screen makes no difference.

That was unrealistic. We can all see, with our students of psychoanalysis, that certain students cannot deal with women or with aggressive people, but can handle passive people very well. It is obvious that the analyst's personality counts. But how do you find it out? He cannot observe himself. So I proposed, and finally sold successfully, to Mr. Berelson—to Henry Ford through Mr. Berelson—that the psychoanalytic process should be observed by others, and the material should be recorded and saved, so it can be restudied like a microscopic slide. This is the method of every science. Your observations are put down so that others can repeat them. The process of treatment should be recorded and maybe even photographed.

Finally, I have become engaged in such a study. The material is overwhelming, but we can already see, for example, that the analyst as a person is a very important factor in the process. His personality is a variable which is extremely important.

Objections were made. Ordinarily, psychoanalysis is not observed by others. It is a private affair; it is a secret affair. If you observe it, if you record it, it is not the same. Well, as it turns out, it is practically the same. With certain patients, perhaps, the observation makes a difference.

My last venture was trying to study emotional stress—the physiological and psychological sequelae of the same emotional stress situations which we all encounter during our life. How can we study life? How can you bring life into the laboratory? For a long time, studies were done by artificial laboratory experiments. You would arouse the patient, make him angry, etc., but that is not the same complex situation which takes place in life.

These vicissitudes of life to which we are chronically exposed are supposed to cause certain chronic ailments of physical and psychological nature. Stomach ulcers were well known. To them, vicissitudes of life are important, but how can you experiment with life stress? How can you demonstrate, how can you see what the patient's stomach does when he is involved in a complex human situation?

It can be done by using modern methods of mass communication, particularly moving pictures. I can select any moving picture I want, pump into the patient an emotional, a complex, lifelike, emotional situation, by showing him the picture. He gets involved, he identifies himself with the hero, he gets angry, he is afraid, he falls in love, he feels pity, etc., and all these emotions can be very realistically reproduced and their effects studied.

In all these new ventures, commitment was the great enemy: You cannot do it, this cannot be done. My answer in every case was, let us try it. And even against this "Let us try it," you find a tremendous resistance because of previous commitments. Maybe the experiment will turn out positive: What then?

These examples were meant to show why I was challenged by the remarks made here about commitment. My observations were made in entirely different fields, not in business, but in scientific research.

Now I would like to add a few words. I should like to give you an idea of a creative organization in the field of education and research and see whether the same phenomena can be observed in this field as those we heard about in the field of business organizations.

I don't want to waste further time defining what is creative. I would say very briefly that creativity is an act which brings about something which did not exist before. (That does not mean that it is necessarily a good creation.) My contention is that creation is the result of playful intuitive experimentation with ideas and not of deductive reasoning alone. (I do not say that deductive reasoning does not play a role in creativeness, but it consists primarily in playful, intuitive experimentation with thoughts, with ideas.)

Freud defined thinking as experimenting in fantasy with acts: If I do this, then that will happen; then I will do this—without actually carrying out the imagined acts. You make these experimental small acts, as Freud expressed it, only in fantasy.

I should like to add one more important factor—that the new imaginative combination of ideas is governed mainly by intuitive hunches and guesses, until, through trial and error, a solution is found which satisfies the purpose of the originator. This applies to all fields, even to mathematics. We know very well that there are rules for solving differential equations. They are not the same for a complex integral. You must have a lucky idea; then you can test the correctness of your hunch by the opposite process. Division and multiplication have the same relationship to each other. Even in such a field as mathematics, solutions require intuitive hunches, guesses. Then you can test their validity.

It is suggested by different thinkers that the creative act is based not on conscious, verbal, mental activity but on preconscious, non-verbal, mental activity. Words represent generalizations. Using a word, one has already committed oneself to certain previously recognized and codified similarities between objects designated by the same word. Original thinking takes place mostly on a non-verbal level in which new combinations between objects can be made—new similarities are detected, which have not yet been recognized and codified by words. A good example of preverbal thinking is Kekule's discovery of the carbon ring. He saw suddenly in his dream, while dozing off, a snake rolling and biting his tail. He woke up and thought, "Eureka!" He discovered the carbon ring. This mental act is based on "dream thinking."

Many creative ideas occur in dreams or in relaxation. This is non-verbal thinking, in which one is not committed to previous knowledge. Words are very rigid designations based on generalizations to previous knowledge. Everything that looks like a cat is a cat. To discover that a lion also is a cat is possible before you have a word that generalizes and encompasses both cats—alley cats and lions. Such a word is created after the discovery has been made.

It is obvious that creative activity requires freedom from coercion, *every form* of coercion, no matter whether the coercion stems from other persons (authorities), from traditional beliefs, or from prevailing value systems.

Emergency situations represent a quite common form of coercion. They are just as unfavorable to real creative activity as dogma or the suppressive attitude of authority. Emergency situations require immediate reactions to a danger; there is no time for free experimentation, and only previously acquired knowledge can be used. Conditioned reflexes, for example, are the most rigid previously acquired mechanisms, most useful in emergency situations when there is no time for free experimentation. There is no time for toying with ideas. One must use what one already knows.

The creative process has its own natural history. It involves continuous tossing out of new ideas and gradual testing of their usefulness and applicability.

It was very well put before by Mr. Ogilvy that, during every creative act, many ideas are produced, but the mortality among these ideas is great. I like to compare this with biological mutation. Mutation is an experiment, the most creative act of nature, so to speak, but how many survive? Only those which, by accident, fit into the environmental conditions.

The same is true for creative ideas. Most of them are lousy; only one or two which satisfy the requirements are good. Emergency, therefore, is unfavorable for true creativity. It is true, and many people quote it, that the cold war, for example, stimulates certain technological inventions. However, of necessity they are of a highly circumscribed nature, because, first, the nature of the momentary need prescribes the nature of the innovation and, second, they are based on currently available knowledge and not on new principles. The theory of atomic structure, which is the basis of the construction of atomic weapons, is the result of long individual creative activities of scientists, which did not serve definite, practical, or immediate purposes. Niels Bohr did not think of an atomic bomb. These studies were pursued only for the sake of knowledge.

In true scientific creativity, the urge is knowledge for its own sake. It is not subordinated to practical goals. Atomic theory was the result of free, spontaneous interaction between the ideas of creative individuals. It was a collective achievement, it is true, but not by a strictly organized work plan. It did not follow a blueprint. It could be best compared with natural growth, in which different individual ideas and accomplishments influence each other in an entirely spontaneous manner. This is in striking contrast to the highly organized, blueprinted work in an industrial plant, in which already existing basic knowledge is planfully applied to bring about a product (a new product, maybe) designed for a specific practical purpose (such as the atomic bomb).

I have discussed this with a physicist, a Nobel Prize winner. I asked him whether basic research could be organized as a factory is organized. His answer was that it is preposterous even to ask such a question; the unknown cannot be blueprinted. Freedom from coercion by a highly circumscribed and preconceived plan, freedom from coercion dictated by compelling external circumstances such as prevail in emergencies, and (naturally) freedom from coercion emanating from autocratic leadership, are all necessary requirements for really creative mental activity.

I want to mention parenthetically here that I speak of basic creative acts, creative products of the mind in which new principles are involved. To apply creatively those things already known is another type of creativity.

Today, this is probably most important, because we have much basic knowledge which is not yet utilized fully for practical purposes. Atomic energy is one of them. This is not a value judgment; I only want to make clear that what I am speaking of now is the basic creative act which requires full freedom.

I will not discuss the development of creativity in a person, whether it is largely inherited or whether it is a result of later experiences. Very interesting attempts were made by Weisberg and Springer to establish the type of family constellation which favors the development of mental creativeness in children. The essence of this study is: A certain free atmosphere must prevail in the family from the beginning. The authors compared families from which creative children came with a control group.

I am concerned now with the question which interests us here: What type of an organizational system is favorable for stimulating the creative potentialities of its members? I agree with those who said that everyone has some degree of creativity. Everyone, perhaps, is an exaggeration, but the majority of people have some degree of potential creativity. It has often been stated that all children are creative, but gradually they lose their creativeness under the necessity to adapt and to conform. Latent creativity can be suppressed or activated by the spirit and the system prevailing in an organization.

The expression "creative organization" seems to imply a contradiction, particularly for those who were born in the last century. (I think I am the only one here.) One usually thought, during this period when I grew up, that creativity in an organization is an antithesis. In the nineteenth century, creation was considered a highly individualistic accomplishment; it was inseparable from the image of the original person who produces a new type of artistic representation, like Giotto; a new scientific principle, like Newton; new political or military strategy, like Clausewitz or Napoleon; or a new philosophy of industrial production, like Ford.

The prototype of the creator was the genius. He was contrasted to the faceless masses who have no initiative and who are incapable of innovations or original decisions. They follow their creative leaders. According to this tenet, only individuals are creative. Organizations consist of a collaborative system of individuals, each having a restricted and prescribed activity according to preconceived plan. Only the conceiver of the plan, the leader, can be creative. The other members of the organization have no choice but to carry out the creative ideas of the leader.

Accordingly, working in an organization would mean renouncing originality and following routine. Organized activity from this perspective appears as an antithesis of creative work, although the output of the organization as a whole might be creative. It implements the creative imagination of the leader. I want to show briefly that such an Aristotelian antithesis—organization versus creativity—leads to an "all-or-nothing" formulation which has little applicability to actual phenomena. There are creative organizations—we know it, it must be possible—so there is no such antithesis.

My experience has been with an educational and research organization, the Institute for Psychoanalysis in Chicago. For twenty-five years I served as its director, and I tried as consistently as possible to implement some of the principles I have described. This was a difficult undertaking, since the state of affairs in the field of psychoanalytic institutes at that time tended toward a highly centralized and rigid organizational philosophy.

Unfortunately, this trend has not abated. On the contrary, there is a growing trend toward standardization of theory and practice and in teaching these principles to the students. The basic orientation underlying this conservative trend is to try to preserve intact and pure the fundamental theories and therapeutic practices as they were conceived by the great innovator, Freud. This is a common fate of creative ideas which originally were bitterly opposed by contemporaries. The psychoanalytic pioneers grew up fighting a hostile world. They soon recognized that internal unity, a kind of conformism among themselves, was necessary to protect these new ideas from emotionally prejudiced and ignorant critics. How could they survive if they did not agree with one another?

This attitude of necessity led to a rigid organizational and hierarchical system within the so-called psychoanalytic movement. This system survived as an example of cultural lag, because it persisted even after the need for protection against external enemies no longer existed. In order to preserve these once new but now largely accepted achievements, the organization renounced further advancements and developed an ideological climate which did not tolerate internal disagreements and significant differences of opinion among its members. The need for internal solidarity required conformity, which is incompatible with the experimental spirit, which, as I have pointed out, is indispensable for creative activity. The spirit and the internal system of an organization depend upon the aims of the organization.

This was not sufficiently stressed to satisfy me. If the aim is to preserve achievements of the past and to produce fundamentally the same product with greater and greater precision, a rigid hierarchical organization may be most desirable. If you are satisfied with your product, then it is best to standardize it. If, however, the aim is to further new knowledge and to advance the field to which the organization is devoted, another kind of organization will be needed.

In 1932, when I organized the Institute, I was convinced that this field was in dire need of a freer type of organization which would stimulate creative activity among its members. It was clear that such an organization would have to emphasize research instead of merely teaching existing knowledge and that the teaching procedure must be progressive. (This was the first psychoanalytic institute in which collective, systematized research was carried out, and I think that during these last thirty-five years, only one or two other institutes have done research.)

Moreover, to foster an atmosphere of creativity instead of indoctrination, we must emphasize a self-critical evaluation of existing knowledge. Not only must members of the faculty have a great amount of individual freedom to communicate their different ideas, but the students must be encouraged to question the knowledge imparted. Emphasis in this type of institution will be on teaching the students how to think originally in their chosen field. A premium is to be placed on original ideas—not only those of the teachers, but also those of the students. It is obvious that the organizational structure of such an institution must fit this educational philosophy. It requires a democratic system.

The leader of the organization must refrain from imposing his own ideas and orientation rigidly upon the faculty. His leadership should consist only in jealously watching that the free academic spirit is maintained. The faculty should be chosen from independently thinking instructors. (How you find them, I don't know.) The institution should have two departments of equal importance: research and teaching facilities. Research should encourage the spontaneous interest and initiative of the research workers (research from the grass roots) instead of relying on highly organized and centralized research programs under the direction of one person. Leaders of research should not be formally appointed. (I know that the businessman will be aghast when he hears this, but his is a different kind of organization.) They should emerge by a process of natural selection.

The teaching curriculum should be flexible and somewhat experimental in nature. Teaching should be more present- and future-oriented than past-oriented. The history of existing knowledge should be taught in a critical fashion. Teachers of different orientations and persuasions should be encouraged to expose the students to their original ideas. (It is better to confuse them than to indoctrinate them, then they are challenged to think and to solve problems.) Stress should be placed upon exposing the students to those original observations on which theoretical generalizations of the past are based; in other words, on clinical teaching instead of theoretical indoctrination. (They should themselves go through the process with which the original formulations were made.)

The students should recapitulate during their learning process the same creative processes which led to the original formulations in the past. That is to say, the emphasis should be on teaching the students how to learn from their own experiences instead of imparting to them dogmatically already formalized knowledge. (I won't go into the difference between teaching and learning now—that is my hobby horse. They are very different. We use almost the same words for both processes.)

I mentioned before that, in the field of psychoanalysis, there were particular circumstances and difficulties which had to be faced in order to create this type of free academic institution. These difficulties only increased as time went on. The most important difficulty is a highly centralized system in the form of a national organization which prescribes minimal standards and enforces them in each member institute. This central organization of psychoanalytic institutes replaced the autonomy of the branch institutes, which they had had at least in a moderate form previously.

And now I come to Mr. Merton's topic: How important is the larger environment of the institutes? These rigid standards preclude the improvement of teaching procedures because individual experimentations in the branch institutes are no longer tolerated. Advanced fields can tolerate a great amount of standardization better than can young, immature fields. In a young field, such as psychoanalysis, this premature standardization of teaching is greatly detrimental to further development. It freezes knowledge and its teaching prematurely, when there is a dire need for further clarification and improvement of basic concepts and therapeutic practices. In general, institutionalization or organization by its very nature has a conservative tendency in every field.

Institutions try to conserve the achievements of the past. They standardize teaching and research procedures. They seldom favor dissidents and radical innovators. Institutions by their very nature move more slowly than individual knowledge does. Consequently, innovators and originators of new ideas have always had to face the inertia of institutions. The history of the church, the Catholic Church, shows that most beautifully (St. Francis of Assissi, etc.).

Nevertheless, institutions have their place. They preserve and refine previous knowledge and improve teaching practices. In well-established fields, their merits counterbalance their retarding effects. In younger fields, where basic knowledge still is vague and highly tentative, there is often great danger that the tentativeness of this knowledge is not sufficiently appreciated; hypotheses are treated as theories and theories as validated facts. This condition particularly applies today to the field of psychoanalytic treatment (not so much the theory), in which experimentation with new procedures is so cumbersome. Because the effectiveness of one procedure against another cannot be easily validated, there is a great danger that authority worship and tradition will preclude advancement.

My point is to emphasize that each discipline, according to the state of its development, requires different systems of organization and different educational philosophies. To organize psychoanalytic institutes after the model of an elementary grammar school is absurd. Neither can psychoanalysis be taught in the fashion that anatomy is taught in the first years of medical school.

The most difficult problem for institutional leaders is to find that amount of freedom which is optimal in their field. Complete lack of standards and too lax an organization favor chaos. Rigid standards, on the other hand, favor conformity and stagnation. To find the amount of flexibility and freedom and the permissible degree of individual difference which are appropriate to a specific field is the secret of creative academic organizations (and probably also business organizations). Depending upon the amount of this freedom, the creative activity of the individual members may be more or less encouraged.

For the whole of the organization to be creative, however, it is indispensable that it should retain a great deal of autonomy and the greatest possible independence from any central national organization of institutes. (There is no rigid organization of universities. Yale is different from Michigan; the University of California is quite different from New York University.) Only if institutions can develop their own peculiar features and can experiment with different types of educational procedures can a field advance.

Not only within the institution itself must academic freedom be guarded, but the institutions as a whole must retain their initiative. Only what is known can be organized. Consequently, a field in which knowledge is not yet far advanced requires organizational systems of greater flexibility, of more experimental spirit, and can suffer most from insistence upon rigid rules and regulations which stifle creativity.

These considerations motivated me during my association with the Chicago Institute for Psychoanalysis. The implementation of these guiding principles became more and more difficult as the trend towards organization, standardization, and conformity gained momentum, not only in our field but in all aspects of our society. We deal here with a universal cultural trend which does not favor originality and creativity. (It can't kill it, but it doesn't favor it.)

I could not predict when the pendulum of historical development will swing back again in the direction of more emphasis on the individual. The discussion of the type of cultural activities in which such a reversal of trend can be promoted lies outside the scope of my presentation. (And I am not even sure whether everybody would agree that such a swing is needed or desirable. Maybe we should go on, organize and organize, and eventually become a very effective ant community.)

16

The Center for Advanced Study in the Behavioral Sciences: an Experiment

RALPH W. TYLER

The Center for Advanced Study in the Behavioral Sciences provides a place where each year some fifty scholars and scientists who are judged by their peers to be outstanding students of human behavior spend the year in pursuing studies of their own choosing. The Center was established on the assumption that the behavioral sciences could be strengthened, and sound knowledge about human behavior could be obtained and organized more rapidly and effectively, if many of the abler persons working in these fields could for a time be freed from the responsibilities of teaching, of administration, and of conducting specific research projects to devote their full attention to studies they consider to be of greatest importance for the development of themselves and their fields. By bringing together fifty such people each year from various universities and research organizations in the United States and abroad, intellectual communication is facilitated and the scholars are able to learn from each other as well as to carry on individual work.

To understand the characteristics of the Center, it is necessary to note certain unique features. The research workers at the Center are normally there for only one year, on leave of absence from their usual places of employment. It is a place not for conducting long-range research projects but to review and reappraise their previous work, to obtain new ideas and to plan work for the future, which they will be carrying on when they return to their home institutions. Their stipends while at the Center are the same as they would have received had they stayed at home. Hence, at the Center, promotions and pay increases are not matters of concern to the scholars. The Center year must be viewed against the background of a longer research career. The Center provides special and unique opportunities which complement and supplement the opportunities available in universities and other research organizations, but the Center does not supplant them.

There are two bases for considering the Center a good environment for stimulating and facilitating creative work. One of these is the output of significant scholarly work which has been written in whole or in part at the Center. During the first seven years of its existence, that is, from September, 1954, to September, 1961, a total of 323 scholars have held Center fellowships. They have produced over 150 books and well over 1,000 published articles.

The publication of books and articles is not attempted by all Fellows, because each is free to do at the Center those things which he believes will contribute most to his development and to the building of a more adequate science of human behavior. Some Fellows devote a good deal of time to reading, to preparing memoranda to be criticized by others, to planning new research programs, to discussions with persons from other disciplines regarding research ideas, and to obtaining new views of the sciences and the disciplines on which they can productively draw for further developments of their work.

To get the reactions of the scholars and scientists to their Center experiences, each one is asked at the end of the year to write an evaluative essay which attempts to describe and assess his experiences and to indicate the things he found helpful and those he did not. These essays provide a second basis for believing that the Center is a good environment for stimulating and facilitating creative work. The following excerpts from six of these essays, chosen almost at random, will serve to illustrate the reactions of scholars and scientists to their period of residence at the Center.

A psychologist wrote:

This has been personally and professionally the most rewarding year of my life. I found the facilities here at the Center ideal for the kind of activities in which I was engaged—writing, planning research, reading, and discussing problems with others. The excellent library and secretarial facilities and the splendid physical plant, coupled with the diligent protection afforded by the staff against demands from the outer world, all combined to create a setting where any failure in writing or planning enterprise can be attributed only to oneself. Somewhat less apparent is the special nature of the interpersonal relations here. The almost total removal of all formal status and power distinctions, coupled with general abundance of free time for all, creates an atmosphere in which intellectual exchange can have a casual and even playful character, that is quite different from the typical structured, and necessarily functional, contacts that occur within the typical university setting. What I am implying is that, in a large university, everyone is sufficiently occupied with his own important activities so that it would be presumptuous to seek advice on a matter that was not manifestly important and well thought out in advance. I have no doubt that these conditions account for the fact that I have done more reading and exploration outside of my own discipline this year than at any time in my past.

A sociologist wrote:

Not only did I get much writing done, but on the less tangible side, I have done a great deal of reading and have had a number of discussions on several topics in which I have long had an interest but have not had time to pursue. As a direct result, I am planning a research program which will probably keep me busy for the next several years. I am convinced that the year at the Center will have a lasting effect on my activities at my own university. I had found that my time was so taken up with administrative matters that it was increasingly difficult to read in a wide variety of fields. My defense was to concentrate increasingly in a narrower field. For the first time in years, I have been free from administrative and committee responsibilities and have enjoyed my new-found freedom greatly. I am still at my office as early as ever, go home as late, and often work some at night and on week-ends, but I feel free not to and, best of all, do not have anything I must do on a particular day or hour. Consequently, I believe I have been more creative than usual.

A philosopher of science commented:

The year at the Center has been for me an unusually profitable one, and I found conditions just about ideal for doing the things I wanted to do. In particular, the freedom from unwelcome distractions which the Center provided, and the sense I soon acquired after my arrival that I was protected against enervating interruptions, enabled me to work with a concentration and for long hours each day that I did not think I could still sustain at my age.

Another psychologist, after mentioning that this had been by far his most productive year, said,

I suppose the Center's real virtue and source of impact is in the fact that it is a total environment, all of whose important parts are supportive of its major purposes of scholarly reflection, stimulation, and productivity. So there is a kind of massive influence that is constantly felt. Most any other scholarly environment, as in a university, provides important partial influence and support, but this is too often diluted or even counteracted by opposing pressures.

A political scientist summarized his experiences as follows:

Compared with other years, the year at the Center seems to me to have offered opportunities that one often dreams about but rarely hopes to realize. Not only was I freed from the numerous duties associated with membership on a university faculty, but I was able freely and without guilt to read, discuss, and think about numerous matters relating to social science that I would be reluctant, or unable, to take time for if I were at home. Although I have colleagues at home whom I occasionally consult about matters of importance to my work, I hesitate to trouble them and do so only in the most urgent instances. At the Center, on the other hand, I felt far more free to consult and to be consulted and, together with certain colleagues, to pursue at length questions of mutual interest to us.

Central to the value of the year was the unequaled opportunity to bring work to completion, to plan new research, and in these connections to read, think, and discuss. Inevitably, some people will find that their experience at the Center has turned them to new directions of thought and research, while others may gain greater command over familiar areas without undertaking entirely new directions of theory or research. In either case, a gain will be registered for social science.

A psychiatrist reported:

This was the most productive year for me in my writing. And I attribute much of the ease of writing to the freedom of the Center. Some of the Fellows developed anxiety in regard to their complete freedom, but on the other hand, we saw the most remarkable positive changes happen in some of the Fellows. And it was by no means only a psychiatrist who could see them. The entire lack of status problems, and the entire lack of the

question, "Will the head of the department love me?" and the lack of competition for purposes of being promoted, and so on, did something incred-
ible for many of the people, as did the free exchange with other scientists
not directed by any motives but those of really wanting to learn from each
other. We had people there who were really not the same as they were
when they came after their nine or twelve months at the Center. There
was one Fellow who was heard to say, "I have never been that happy
since I was 17 years old."

These excerpts from the reports of former Fellows indicate some of
the respects in which they felt themselves to have been creative while
at the Center, and they also suggest some of the features of the Center
to which they attributed their greater fluency and range of production.
The reactions of those who feel themselves influenced by an environment are significant, but it is also helpful in seeking to understand such
a phenomenon to get the comments of those who are observing the
influence rather than being affected by it. Hence, I shall try to analyze
the Center environment and its culture as I have perceived it over the
past seven years and five months.

In most universities and research centers, the daily life of the scientist
or scholar is largely shaped and supported by scheduled activities and
responsibilities, and by written or implicit rules, including the rules for
"getting ahead in one's profession." At the Center, an attempt is made
to shape daily activities through central values and expectations rather
than through any formal schedule or rules.

The chief values of the Center community are four:

1. *Intellectual Activity.* The primary work in which all Center
Fellows are engaged involves intellectual efforts, raising questions,
seeking to understand, investigating, explaining, studying, planning
research, and writing up investigations.

2. *Following One's Own Plans.* The Center year is a year free to
do the things which one has long wanted to do. If one is guided by
what others are doing, or seeks to please others, the unique freedom
of the Center is lost. The one who can drive ahead on his own plans,
following his own estimate of what is relevant and important, is the
one who makes best use of his fellowship.

3. *Concentrating One's Efforts on Those Things Which Are Difficult or Impossible to Do in One's Home Situation.* The freedom of
choice of activities at the Center can be most valuable when the time

is used for important activities which would be difficult or impossible to do at home. A Fellow who does at the Center what he could equally well do in his home institution is missing the unique opportunities the Center provides.

4. *Communicating with Other Scholars and Scientists on Matters of Possible Mutual Interest.* The two basic features of the Center are the freedom to pursue studies of one's own choosing and the availability of other highly competent scientists and scholars, many of whom are interested in similar problems. Great universities have a range of faculty members with a variety of interests and backgrounds, but each faculty member is busy with his own responsibilities and it is not easy to have extended communication with other faculty members on matters of mutual intellectual interests. Since all fifty Fellows at the Center are free from specific responsibilities, it is easy to establish continuing communication on matters of mutual interest and, each year, Fellows report that this opportunity for communication has been of very great significance. Hence, it is emphasized as one of the four chief values of the Center.

These four values are not only recognized by the administration of the Center but they are frequently expressed so as to keep them central in the "image" of the Center. In the first place, these values are stated and explained in the preliminary material sent to scholars who are being invited to the Center. An effort is made from the first letter of invitation to depict the Center as a place for intellectual work, where one is free to pursue studies of his own choosing, to do the things which he has long wanted to do but finds difficult or impossible to do in his home situation, and a place where he can learn from others who are interested in similar problems.

When the prospective Fellow accepts the invitation, correspondence with him relates to his own plans for work and the resources that he will need. He is also asked to name other scholars and scientists with whom he would like to work at the Center. This correspondence emphasizes the importance of his own plans and the way in which the Center can help him to do the things he wants to do that he cannot easily do in his normal situation.

When the Fellows assemble at the Center at the beginning of their period of residence, a general meeting is held to introduce each Fellow to the others and to make clear again that the Center is guided by efforts to attain these values rather than by a set of regulations.

Throughout the year, as individual problems arise and decisions need to be made which involve the Center administration, these values become the goals of the decision. For example, a Fellow may be asked by someone outside to engage in a seminar or lecture or consulting activity. Should he accept? In the discussion, I remind him that his time is his to use as he sees fit. The question becomes whether this activity will promote these values more than if he used the time in some other way. Or a Fellow may request funds to bring in a consultant, or to get more computer time, or to make a trip, or to employ another research assistant. Again, the discussion is an effort to analyze the situation, to judge whether this use of resources is more likely to attain these values than some alternative.

The establishment of daily routines and their modification are matters taken up each new year with Fellows, and settled in terms of the contribution of such routines to the chief values of the Center. All of these are efforts to make perfectly clear to Fellows that everything in the Center and its operations is available to promote its basic values. Hence, they, too, are free to shape their activities in the same way rather than being guided by external demands.

Closely related to the values of the Center environment are the "expectations" which Fellows perceive. Each Fellow comes with some notion of what will be expected of him while he is at the Center. These notions have developed from previous experiences and from hearsay about the Center. Some of these are distorted and conflict with, or at least are irrelevant to, the values of the Center. For example, one common notion is that everyone should participate in at least one group seminar.

Our experience has been that some Fellows communicate easily and gain a great deal from seminars, while others do not. Hence, we try to emphasize from the initial meeting with Fellows that there is no expectation on the part of the Center administration about how Fellows will pursue their studies. Each Fellow should make his own choices and learn as the year goes on how wise his choices have been in promoting his basic purposes.

Another false notion of Center expectations which some Fellows have when they arrive is that they are expected to write manuscripts and their productivity will be judged in terms of how many pages have been written at the Center. This idea is also mentioned at the initial meeting each year to emphasize the different expectation of the Center, which is that each scholar will do the things he considers most important for him, whether or not they involve writing.

The modification of false expectations is facilitated not only by comments at the initial meeting but also by informal conversations with Fellows as the year goes on, in which we ask about the progress of their work, what they hope to accomplish, and why and how the Center can help them further in accomplishing their purposes. Furthermore, as occasions arise in which decisions must be made about use of time, alternative uses of resources, and the like, the basic question always raised first is, "What are your own study plans and how will they be best facilitated?"

The conscious efforts to place these values and expectations in the foreground of the Center environment provide a major encouragement to pursue original work and to seek creative solutions to problems. The other kind of encouragement lies in the reward system of the Center community.

There is a good deal of informal conversation at the Center about the importance of the individual scholar's own satisfactions with achieving new understanding, working out new research attacks, and formulating new concepts. This helps to reinforce the internal rewards that come from intellectual achievements.

In addition, each Fellow usually seeks and obtains critical reactions from Center colleagues to his ideas. He may talk them over informally; he may write memoranda and ask for criticisms; he may present his material before a more formal seminar. The group concern with intellectual products and their appreciation of excellence in conception and formulation provide powerful incentives for creative work.

Finally, the fact that the Center administration offers assistance to each individual Fellow in facilitating his particular intellectual efforts reinforces his sense of the significance of his own individual work. Whenever the occasion arises, the point is made that the Center exists to facilitate the intellectual work of Fellows. Changes can always be made in the services, including the daily routines, whenever such changes help an individual carry on his own work more effectively.

We believe that this attitude in the Center community frees the individual from working out adjustments to irrelevant structures in the situation so that he can concentrate his efforts to deal with the relevant factors in the intellectual problems he is attacking. We believe that there is too much energy devoted in most organizations to surmounting obstacles and making adjustments which are internal to the organization, and consequently too much energy and intelligent effort lost to the real purpose and mission of the organization. The Center for Advanced Study in the Behavioral Sciences is an experiment in providing a different environment for scholars and scientists for one year.

In summary, it should be clear that the Center does not represent an ideal pattern which should or can be followed by all organizations which seek to stimulate and foster creativity. Several of its unique features have been mentioned. Perhaps the most important characteristic of the Center, the one which has most shaped its environment, is the fact that each Fellow invited to be in residence at the Center is judged by a panel of his peers to have demonstrated previously that he is intellectually productive, creative, and highly motivated to gain new knowledge and understanding. The Center environment aids such persons but it does not make creative scholars.

17

Concluding Remarks

(EDITED COMMENTS)

GARY A. STEINER

My subconscious hasn't had any time to work on this yet, Dr. Alexander, so I haven't been able to invoke the nonverbal symbols. But I will try to force myself to ask two general questions and give some simple-minded and pedestrian answers, as necessary.

What questions did we start with, and where do we stand now? It is clear that we started with one very general question: What are the factors that make some organizations something we call creative, whereas others do not turn out that way? We decided initially— and I still have seen no reason to change my thinking—that there are only three possible things: (1) the people in the organization; (2) how they are put together; and (3) how that organization relates to the outside world.

Now the data have dealt, in large measure, with the first question, with the people in the organization: How do we isolate creative people, if we can? And what kind of people are they?

We've also had a good bit to say directly on the second question: What are the characteristics—the internal characteristics—of an organization that is creative?

A great deal was said by implication, and to some extent explicitly, on the third one: How does it relate to its environment? What are the social conditions that produce a creative organization?

Let me try to go through these one by one and say what I think we've come to—not everything, certainly, and not necessarily in the words that were used—but the things on which there would be relatively little disagreement.

First of all, on the question of isolating and identifying the creative man, there is general agreement that tests can do something better than chance. There has been an apparent conflict between that position and the position that tests cannot do as well as an individual who knows and is in a position to judge, but it is only an apparent one. No one really said tests do *better* than a creative individual in a position to judge; and no one has said the tests do no better than chance.

That issue reduces pretty simply in terms of its organizational implications: If you are faced with the responsibility of selecting large numbers of people, and it is important that at least some of them turn out to be creative, then certainly tests should be of help. If, in addition, you have the opportunity to get to know these people very well, then obviously an intelligent rating along with that will increase their power. Typically, however, when you are recruiting large numbers of people, you are not in a position to know these people very well; and certainly not where people you think of as creative selectors get to know them very well. This would be the typical institutional situation—the university situation, the army situation, the large research laboratory situation.

On the other hand, at the top management level, you are selecting one or two people. You are not hiring by the hundred, and you do not have a pool of hundreds to select from. You *are* likely to have some detailed information from people you trust on the two or three candidates who might be available. So, clearly, the relative importance of tests decreases in that kind of situation.

There is a research approach suggested by our assumption that creative people will tend to select others with a higher rate. I think it might be a fairly simple matter to go into the history of corporate ratings, to see to what extent highly rated men turn out to be better, and whether men highly rated by more creative individuals turn out to be more creative later on. And the same thing could be done in science. You might make a very simple count of the number of "disciples" who have turned out to surpass, or at least equal, the master in some particular dimension. (It seems to me that there are two possibilities here: [1] More highly creative people ought to seek to work with other highly creative people, but [2] it is not as clear that a highly creative individual always will seek *subordinates* who are equally creative. Under certain personality assumptions, you might think of a highly creative individual shying away from subordinates who might be competitive.)

These are only questions that we raised and nothing that we have answered at this point.

With respect to the question describing the creative man, I think we have had pretty general agreement, from Moe Stein's study, from Frank Barron's study, and from most observations reported here, on several points.

First of all, everyone agrees that the more creative individual is different from other people and that he knows it. There is some element of self-concept, which means that he says to himself: I am not just one of the crowd. He sees himself in some important dimensions as different from others.

There is also good evidence that he is more independent than the average man; although that certainly is not sufficient. He is independent plus something else.

He is a hard worker; and there is a bit of disagreement in the conference, as I sense it, between what it is that makes him a hard worker. I have my own opinion, but the two points of view that I see are (1) he is a hard worker, because he has such a great interest in the problem itself that the *problem* drives him; he responds to the inner provocativeness of what he is working on, when he is working on problems that are truly interesting. The other point of view is (2) well, that may be true, but he does not always do that. Maybe he does not recognize the intrinsic attractiveness of the problem until someone else tells him, "You'd better do that, and you'd better do it within the next two weeks." Then suddenly it occurs to him how fascinating this problem always has been.

There may be some truth in both elements. For example, I think of something from my personal experience: I love to play chess, but I hate to start. Normally, I might be lazy, or want to do something else, but if someone talks me into a game, I will not leave it for anything. In other words, once you begin, you will be exposed to a series of stimuli and problems which you might otherwise not have seen; and perhaps external discipline can induce you to expose yourself to some of these stimuli. But it is not the external discipline that keeps you at the chessboard. So it may not be the external discipline that keeps the creative man at the task long enough to come up with the truly creative solution. This is in the realm of hypothesis, obviously.

The creative man is more likely to separate the source of a communication from the information itself, as Milton Rokeach pointed out; and by the same token, as Marvin Bower said, his basic criterion for the creative organization is that it is factual and objective in its approach. These two things seem to be very closely allied, and there is very little disagreement that they are good for creativity when in fact they occur.

Then, there is an interesting contradiction in the creative individual that we noted several times: At once, he is more impulse-ridden, more irrational in a sense, *and* he has superior controls. Frank Barron put it in terms of test scores: He has higher schizoid tendencies and more ego strength—which is a terribly rare combination. And it raises interesting hypotheses about what it is that is involved in the individual case and in organizations that provide fertile environment for such people.

Finally—this is the last point that I can see that we all agree on— he often appears wasteful to the outsider when he is working. This is an implication from several findings. For example, in Moe Stein's study, when he works the machine with the light, he does not start pushing buttons as soon as the less creative man. A less creative man begins his synthetic phase more quickly, while the creative man is more likely to expose himself to a wide range of stimuli first and then get to work on the problem once he has a total grasp of the situation. (Now, unfortunately, the man who never does anything also is a slow starter—and appears to be doing very little in the initial stages. He may spend his entire life exposing himself to stimuli. The important distinction is what is going on inside, but from an organizational point of view, watching from the outside, you might very well conclude: Here are six people who are not doing anything, and here are six people who are already busy pushing buttons.)

There are two levels on which you can proceed. First of all, you can do it simply by analogy. For example, let me just read the list again and see how each of these characteristics of creative individuals might make some sense, at least as a hypothesis, when applied directly to an organization:

The creative organization is different from others and it knows it. It is not an organization trying to be like others or one that conceives of itself as being another institution like so-and-so.

A creative organization is independent. (You can hardly argue that if it were not, it would more likely be creative.)

The creative organization is a hard worker—and largely out of its interest in what it is doing.

The creative organization separates source from information; that is, it has an objective, fact-founded approach, as Marvin Bower pointed out. It is able to draw on facts wherever it can find them and evaluate them in their own right, rather than depending blindly upon the authorities in the field.

The creative organization has more irrational impulses within it, and on the other hand, more effective controls for keeping these in the appropriate channels. Here you might conceive of a creative organization as having a wider range of people within it—some of whom are just terribly good idea generators and others who are just terribly good channelers—people who are able to take these ideas, see their implications, and put them into effect. These functions need not exist in the same individual in a specific organization.

Finally, the creative organization often appears to be wasteful. Here again, you may get into some argument when you talk specifically about profit-making organizations, because, if you appear to be wasteful for too long a time, you are obviously going to be out of business. You will never have a chance to get to the synthetic phase. Nevertheless, it is probably true that creative organizations will take more blind alleys, on the whole—recognizing them in time, of course—while less creative ones might tend to take the safe, tried-and-true way.

Now, the major implication of these personal characteristics, aside from such reasoning by analogy, is, of course, their direct application to the structure of the firm. If creative people are the way we have described them, and if we want creative people to work in the organization, then these characteristics obviously have direct implication for the kind of organization that will make an environment in which they can work.

Here, for example, we get into the issue of freedom versus structure, or firm goal-directed controls. This is an issue on which I sensed a real difference of opinion, between the positions represented by, on the one hand, David Ogilvy, and, on the other, Dr. Alexander.

One says, in effect, that what you need is to drive people to the task and tell them what to do, inspire them, and get them to do it. The other says that what you need is to allow people freedom to roam in their own ways.

I think that no one really disagrees that every individual should be entirely free to work toward *appropriate* goals; similarly, no one would disagree that every individual should be entirely under the constraints of his individual goals, if he is to be most *creative*. What this means, of course, is that every firm does not want every individual to maximize his creativity. There are many slots in industry where we cannot afford creativity at all. (If you are dictating an important memo, you cannot wait for the stenographer to develop a better system of shorthand.)

If you start from this model, I think you see that the crucial variable is the degree to which the organization's own goals coincide with the goals of intrinsic interests to those members within it who are supposed to create. Creators will be *less* creative, in terms of the general definition of creativity, if they are worried about other organizational goals than if they are worried about the problems. On the other hand, the creations will be of less use to the organization if they are not so constrained.

To illustrate, let me use this conference itself as a short-term creative organization. Milt Rokeach gave an example of a problem in psychology. His purpose in this problem was to demonstrate a psychological point. Dr. Shockley immediately seized on the problem but focused on it from the point of view of his own interests. In doing so, he was far more creative than he would have been had he followed the psychological connotations of the problem, but less creative from the point of view of the conference, except that he now demonstrates my point.

Now, at some points in industry, you get a happy marriage between individual interests and organizational objectives, and this is what I think happens in the Ogilvy case. The goals of the corporation are identical with interests of the people who will provide the creativity for it. The advertising agency thrives to the extent that it produces creative, outstanding advertising. Each individual in that firm personally thrives to the extent that he creates outstanding advertising. There is no clash; there is no problem. The reason you get away with regimentation in this case is that people are already preregimented in the same interest that you have.

The problem is: How do you accomplish this at top management levels? Here, I think, there is some inherent inconsistency in the notion that you want top management people whose professional skills and interests lie in developing management skills per se, but you also want dedication—substantial, long-range dedication—to the particular objectives of one firm.

This is a problem that requires sociological rather than conceptual resolution. Maybe it is a problem inherent in the system. Maybe, as some of you suggested, the breakup of firms is one way to handle this, so that, in any given corporate unit, the corporate goals and the interests of creators can be one and the same.

One final major issue that we have discussed in several forms is the concept of commitment. This was a key idea and, again, there is an apparent paradox. On the one hand, commitment to the wrong goal obviously is non-creative; but, by the same token, commitment to the right goal clearly is. If you let the good idea go too quickly, you are going to lose it; if you don't let the bad idea go, you are also going to be in trouble.

We pointed out that many factors can make for commitment to the wrong goals ("wrong," always in the sense of maximizing creativity as the criterion). Financial commitment was mentioned yesterday. A firm can be so heavily committed to a particular product line that it cannot afford to think of other products. The commitment is to a goal extrinsic to the problem for the creator; the commitment is to profit.

Commitment intrinsic to the problem is never bad, it seems to me, because it maximizes the likelihood of finding the right solution. Commitment to things extrinsic to the problem is likely to minimize the creative solution of that particular problem.

Personal, emotional commitment, as Dr. Alexander pointed out, is a horse of almost exactly the same color. It interferes only to the extent that the commitment is to things extrinsic to the problem: to status within the group; to looking good to colleagues; to maintaining the position one has adopted. If commitment is to the solution of the problem, these diverting results are not likely.

Finally, there is perceptual commitment, as Dr. Bruner's paper suggested. If you get a hypothesis, and you get it too early in the game, you may fix on it to the point that you can no longer back off. I think one general safeguard against various forms of undue commitment was suggested by Pete Peterson last night: limited-scale experimentation by those people who are in the greatest danger of forming the commitment. This does two things: It gets some information back, but, in addition, it puts the central people in a position of winning either way; they are committed to the experiment, but not to any particular outcome.

Finally, with respect to over-all environmental factors that influence the organization, we have found no definite answers but some fruitful issues have been raised with respect to the factors that produce a creative organization and the question of when you really want one.

The one overriding generalization, it seems to me, is that you never want creativity everywhere in your organization, and many times you don't want it anywhere. Sometimes you need it in order to succeed, and other times you will succeed more efficiently with it, but it certainly is not something like profits, that can be taken as a general corporate objective. There are isolated circumstances in which it is a necessity; there are others in which it is a help; and there are many others in which it clearly runs counter to the corporate goal.

We have had some hypotheses about the type of organization that is likely to exhibit and foster creativity. For example: Creativity is more likely to flourish in new firms than in old; in small firms than in big; in firms engaged in cutthroat competition rather than in firms that have the market all to themselves for a time; possibly in marginal firms, in the sense that they are staffed by people new to the particular industry and with different approaches; finally, in firms headed by people who are themselves creative.

I am getting dangerously near Dr. Bruner's point of premature, incorrigible hypothesizing. All these notions are still hazy and ambiguous (way back and out-of-focus in that "ambiguitor"), subject to reinterpretation. There is certainly no ambiguity, though, as to how worthwhile the seminar was for me, personally. I think there is very little ambiguity as to how productive it was for the field; and I hope that it has been productive to the participants.

Discussion

THE NEGLECT OF THE
SOCIOLOGICAL, ORGANIZATIONAL VARIABLES

Guetzkow

You have brought out something that Bob Merton and I have been feeling as we went along as, in a sense, the only two who are *really* interested in organizations and organizational environment: We could not generate the richness of hypothesis in this area, because so little work has been done in the area, as contrasted with individual creativity.

The one recommendation I would have for the McKinsey people, who are fundamentally interested in organization, is that we are not going to be able to do much creatively in conferences like this unless we have much more to feed in, in the sense of data, bodies of knowledge that have been generated. I get the feeling from your summary—and I would argue deeply—that your analogical cut is a very dangerous one. I would argue that unless you were immediately going to pit against that some non-individual–centered hypotheses, this could slow down the research that is done in this area.

Steiner

Do you think that the study of individual creativity is a rich source of hypothesis, regarding what organizational environments should foster creativity, in the sense that you say to yourself: If creative people are like this, what should the organization do, internally, in order to nurture this kind or response? I think this is the most powerful use of the individual data—not the analogy, by any means.

Merton

I should hope, Gary, that this tour de force of yours, of having pursued a half-dozen seeming analogies between the individual men who proves to be creative, and the organization, would disappear from view in the published proceedings. Otherwise, you might give a thoroughly misleading impression to readers who haven't had the benefit of the full flow of experience we've shared here.

I would agree that we can look at this two-day session as itself a case in point. The academic men in this group include seven people who are committed professionally to psychology and a lone deviant who is committed to sociology. This probably reflects the comparative amount of systematic work that has been done on the subject of originality and creativity; by far the greater amount of work has been done by the psychologists. But one byproduct of this disproportionate representation is that it would obviously have been absurd for any one man, even if he had the knowledge, to preempt seven times as much time as any other one man. And yet, even out of the depths of our ignorance, I could have reported aspects of organization which have not turned up in our transcript and that can be seen from your admirable summary.

For example, at no point do you refer to the norms and the rules that obtain in different kinds of organizations and their connection with the degree and character of creative work. Nor do you refer to the constellation of roles within an organization and their possible connections. In short, your summary refers to none of the primitive notions which sociologists believe are required even to describe organization, let alone understand them, since these notions didn't turn up in our conversation. Yet much of what you were implying by analogy has been independently worked out for organizations, partly in a speculative way and partly with empirical confirmation.

The point is that if, *faute de mieux,* you attempt to fill in the gaps left by your lone sociologist with analogies, it would leave an unfortunate impression with the reader of the proceedings. He could not know that we didn't pursue this line of organizational analysis.

Rokeach

I certainly agree with Merton that one should not do everything in this analogous kind of way. At the same time, I would like to side a little bit with Steiner in what he is trying to do. If this was another kind of a conference—say, a conference between psychology and sociology—one could ask whether it is conceivable on theoretical grounds that the variables sociologists talk about, and the properties they talk about, in attempting to describe social structure, could be represented in purely psychological terms like role, social structure, and role differentiation. I am of the opinion that this is at least theoretically possible, although we have not done this to date. I think this is the kind of thing that Talcott Parsons is trying to do; and while I do not necessarily believe that he has fully succeeded, he has made some important steps in this direction. The question whether the structural variables that operate out there can be represented, let us say in my terms, "cognitively," is an open one. But I want to consider the possibility and ultimately see if it is conceivable to have such an integration between psychology and sociology, and I *think* this is what Steiner was aiming at in his *tour de force*.

Merton

May I try to close the circle? I will agree with *you* now [Steiner] and disagree with part of what Milton has said. The importance of your swift summary for me was the following: Once you itemize what we take to be the characteristics of creative men, they become a useful guide to identifying the functional requirements of an organization that will evoke innovative behavior among such men.

Wallis

There has been awfully little said about the possibility of a creative organization that has few if any creative individuals. Does anybody know of any examples? Do you consider that a possibility?

Bruner

I don't mean to make a play on words, but I come back to the existence of an organization operating in a standby position—the military—providing the cadres for what you will go ahead and do, come another conflagration. Somebody once described the United States Navy as a system devised by geniuses for execution by idiots. This is not quite fair to the United States Navy, but there are organizations that are put together in a standby status to go on doing their work. What you want an organization to do is to fulfill the goals that you set for it. Not all those goals are quite as highfalutin as the word creativity would suggest. There are certain plain, bread-and-butter organizations, like Buildings and Grounds in Cambridge, Mass.— perhaps they can be a little bit more creative.

Ogilvy

The Roman Church.

Steiner

I think your question is a fundamental one, and belongs ultimately to Bob Merton. Conceptually, it seems obvious that you could have an organization that could be creative—by any criterion that you apply to the organization as a whole—without any given individual in the firm creating, by the same criterion. In some way, the organization can substitute for the individual components of creativity as they might exist in a particular creator. In the same sense, I suppose, you could look at the total culture as an organization whose creativity far transcends the creativity of any given individual, or that of any given organization within it.

Merton

Perhaps it would be possible to rephrase Allen's question and make it amenable to an answer, even if the answer will not be forthcoming. Rather than ask whether there can be a creative organization that does not have creative individuals in it, where I think we get hung up on *all* the connotations of the language employed in the question, we might put it this way: Are there certain characteristics of organizations which lead them to *evoke* more of the innovative potential of individuals in them than other organizations do? The evocative organization, in this sense, is what I would call the creative organization.

Steiner

But aren't there ways to maximize the creativity of an organization (and I should think this would be the position that you
would take, rather than I) *beyond* increasing individual creativity of members? Can some sort of different combination of what
people do make the net result far more creative—and perhaps
even require less creativity on the part of the individual?

Ogilvy

What I'm frightened of is when I hear, all the time in business,
a lot of stupid, dumb, dim, little people who can't do anything
by themselves saying, if they'd just get into a team . . .

Shockley

In which they're all protected; each is protected from his in-
security.

Wallis

That is a good definition of a conference: a group of people
who individually could accomplish nothing, getting together and
deciding that nothing can be accomplished. I hope this conference doesn't come under that heading.

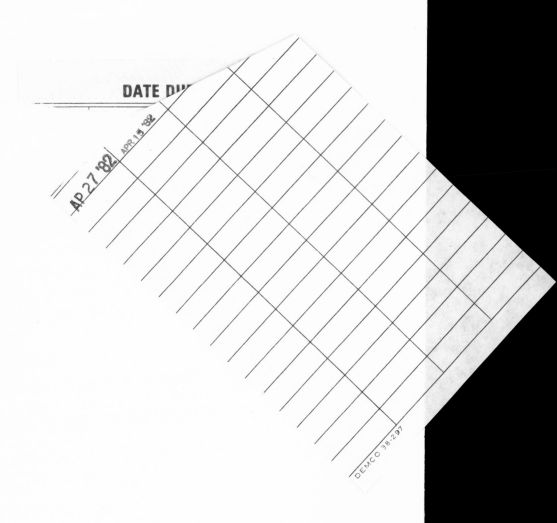